LEARNING RESOU

Y0-BRL-804

3 0147 1001 1947 1

NEW ENGLAND INSTITUTE
OF TECHNOLOGY
LEARNING RESOURCES CENTER

Portfolio

*Essays for Critical Thinking
and Writing*

PATRICK SCANLAN

NEW ENGLAND INSTITUTE
OF TECHNOLOGY
LEARNING RESOURCES CENTER
T. H. PEEK PUBLISHER

8-00

#44918445

Copyright 1998
T. H. Peek, Publisher

All rights reserved. No part of this publication may be reproduced or transmitted in any form or by any means, electronic or mechanical, including photocopy, recording, or any information storage and retrieval system, without permission in writing from the publisher. For information, address correspondence to T. H. Peek, Publisher, P.O. Box 50123, Palo Alto, CA 94303-0123.

ISBN: 0-917962-44-3

02 01 00 99 98
5 4 3 2 1

Manufactured in the United States of America

Contents

Acknowledgments

The publisher gratefully acknowledges the following authors and publishers for their kind permission to reprint the essays in this text. With the exception of "Of Time and the River," which, with permission, was condensed, all articles have been reproduced in their original text.

Addison Wesley Longman for "Spelunking," from *Sleeping at the Starlight Motel*, (pages 201–204). ©1995 Bailey White. Reprinted with permission of Addison Wesley Longman.

Arcade Publishing for "He and I," by Natalia Ginzburg from *Little Virtues*. Copyright © 1962 by Guilio Einaudi S.P.A. Turin. Translation copyright © 1985 by Dick Davis. First published in the United States by Seaver Books.

Beacon Press for the excerpt from *Notes of a Native Son*, by James Baldwin. © 1955, renewed 1983, by James Baldwin. Reprinted by permission of Beacon Press, Boston.

Deborah Blum for "The Subtler Side of Testosterone." This article first appeared in *The Washington Post*, October 19, 1997. Reprinted with permission from Deborah Blum.

Bebe Carmichael for "Morning, Noon, and Night." Originally appeared in *Survival*, copyright © 1989 by T. H. Peek, Publisher. All rights reserved.

Meg Cimino for "Vigilance." © 1997 Meg Cimino. Originally appeared in *The Atlantic Monthly*. Reprinted by permission.

Eve Clapham for "To Have and Have Not." Originally published in the *San Jose Mercury News*, January 29, 1998. © 1998 Eve Clapham, reprinted with permission.

Don Congdon Associates for "Have You Noticed?" by Russell Baker. Originally published in the *New York Times*. Copyright © 1985 by Russell Baker. Reprinted by permission of Don Congdon Associates, Inc.

Eugene J. Craig for "The Deal's Too Good for Big Tobacco." ©1997 Eugene J. Craig. Originally appeared in the *Seattle Times*, July 20, 1997. Reprinted by permission.

Latricia Dennis for "Once I Was a Hoosier; Now I Am a Texan." Originally appeared in the *Gulf Breeze*, spring 1994 issue. © 1994 Latricia Dennis.

Alan Dershowitz for "Shouting 'Fire!'" which originally appeared in *Best American Essays 1990*, published by Ticknor & Fields. © 1990 by Alan Dershowitz. Reprinted with permission.

Sandra Dijkstra Literary Agency for "In the Canon, for All the Wrong Reasons," by Amy Tan. Copyright © 1996 by Amy Tan. Reprinted by permission of Amy Tan and the Sandra Dijkstra Literary Agency.

Helga Erickson for "Fear of the Dark." Originally appeared in *Sequel,* copyright © 1989, 1991 by T. H. Peek, Publisher. All rights reserved.

Farrar, Straus & Giroux, Inc., for "Oh, Those Family Values" from *The Snarling Citizen: Essays* by Barbara Ehrenreich. Copyright © 1995 by Barbara Ehrenreich. Reprinted with permission of Farrar, Straus & Giroux.

Atty. General Christine Gregoire for "It's Not about Money, It's about Smoke." © 1997 Christine Gregoire. Originally appeared in the *Seattle Times,* July 20, 1997. Reprinted by permission.

HarperCollins Publishers, Inc., for "Fetal Alcohol Syndrome," from *Paper Trail,* by Michael Dorris. Copyright © 1994 by Michael Dorris. Reprinted by permission of HarperCollins Publishers, Inc.

HarperCollins Publishers, Inc. for "Mr. Ives' Christmas," by Oscar Hijuelos. Copyright © 1995 by Oscar Hijuelos. Reprinted by permission of Harper-Collins Publishers, Inc.

John Hawkins & Associates, Inc., for "Trespassing," by Joyce Carol Oates. Copyright © October 8, 1995, by the Ontario Review, Inc. Reprinted by permission of John Hawkins & Associates, Inc.

Hearst Newspapers for "The Roar of the Green," by Paul Zielbauer. © 1998 Albany Times Union.

Alfred A. Knopf, Inc., for "Computer Heaven," from *Odd Jobs,* by John Updike. © 1991 by John Updike. Reprinted by permission of Alfred A. Knopf, Inc.

Anne C. Lewis for "The Price of Poverty." © 1997 by Anne C. Lewis. Originally appeared in the February 1997 issue of *Phi Beta Kappan.* Reprinted with permission.

Vincent Lopez for "Schmooze." Originally published in the *San Jose Mercury News,* June 6, 1996. © 1996 by Vincent Lopez, reprinted with permission.

The *Los Angeles Times* for "Borderland," by Valerie Miner. © 1997 The Los Angeles Times Syndicate. Reprinted with permission.

Maclean's for "Breaking the Chains," by Brian D. Johnson. Originally appeared in *Maclean's,* December 15, 1997. Reprinted with permission.

MIT's Technology Review Magazine for "Electronically Implanted 'Values,'" by Langdon Winner. Reprinted with permission from *MIT's Technology Review Magazine,* copyright 1998.

Newsweek for "My Own Son Didn't Listen," by Carolyn Hanig. From *Newsweek,* Nov. 10, 1997. All rights reserved. Reprinted by permission.

The *New York Times* for "Border Crossings," by Jay Parini. Copyright © 1997 by The New York Times Co. Reprinted by permission.

The *New York Times* for "Boxed In," by Lise Funderberg. Copyright © 1996 by The New York Times Co. Reprinted by permission.

The *New York Times* for "Curfews Are for Parents To Set," by Geoffrey Canada. Copyright © 1996 by the New York Times Co. Reprinted by permission.

The *New York Times* for "The Good Guys," by Anna Quindlen. Copyright © 1993 by The New York Times Co. Reprinted by permission.

The *New York Times* for "The Numbers Racket," by Ann Finkbeiner. Copyright © 1998 by The New York Times Co. Reprinted by permission.

The *New York Times* for "School Uniforms, the $80 Million Boondoggle," by Micah C. Lasher. Copyright © 1998 by The New York Times Co. Reprinted by permission.

The *New York Times* for "What's Wrong with Standardized Tests," by Ted Sizer. Copyright © 1995 by the New York Times Co. Reprinted by permission.

The *New York Times Special Features* for "My Best Shot," by Mario Vargas Llosa © 1997, Prospect. Originally appeared in *Prospect,* May 1997.

The *New Yorker* for "Hock Tooey," by David Remnick. Reprinted by permission; © 1996 The New Yorker Magazine, Inc. All rights reserved.

Penguin Putnam, Inc., for "Bombay Theatre," from *India: A Million Mutinies Now,* by V. S. Naipaul. Copyright © 1990 by V. S. Naipaul. Used by permission of Viking Penguin, a division of Penguin Putnam, Inc.

Penguin Putnam, Inc., for "Chicago: The City that was. The City that is." from *It All Adds Up* by Saul Bellow. Copyright © 1994 by Saul Bellow. Used by permission of Viking Penguin, a division of Penguin, Putnam, Inc.

Penguin Putnam, Inc., for "Walking," from *The Journey Home,* by Edward Abbey. Copyright © 1977 by Edward Abbey. Used by permission of Dutton, a division of Penguin Putnam, Inc.

Aaron Priest Agency for "Confess, Early and Often," by Jane Smiley. Originally appeared in the *New York Times Magazine,* October 8, 1995. © 1995 by Jane Smiley. Reprinted with permission.

Gabriel Ramos for "My Girl," originally appeared in the *San Jose Mercury News* on July 8, 1996. © 1996 by Gabriel Ramos, reprinted with permission.

Random House, Inc., for an excerpt from "The Mute Sense," from *A Natural History of the Senses,* by Diane Ackerman. Copyright © 1990 by Diane Ackerman. Reprinted by permission of Random House, Inc.

The *San Jose Mercury News* for "Of Time and the River," by Esther Schrader. Originally appeared in the *San Jose Mercury News West* magazine, October 13, 1996. © Esther Schrader 1996. Reprinted with permission.

Emma Scanlan for "Which Side Am I On? Discrimination and Self-Discovery." © 1996 Emma Scanlan. Reprinted by permission.

Scribners, a Division of Simon & Schuster, for "A Clean, Well-Lighted Place," from *Winner Take Nothing* by Ernest Hemingway. Copyright 1933 by Charles Scribner's Sons. Copyright renewed © 1961 by Mary Hemingway. Reprinted with permission.

Simon & Schuster for "A Course Correction in the Capital of Liberalism," from *The Woven Fabric: Conservatism and America's Fabric* by George F. Will. Copyright © 1997 by George F. Will. Reprinted with the permission of Scribners, a Division of Simon & Schuster as originally published in *Newsweek* magazine, November 11, 1996 under the title, "Big Stick Conservatism".

Judith Stone for "Thumb and Thumber," © 1996 Judith Stone. Reprinted with permission of *Discover Magazine.*

Straight Arrow Publishers, L.P. for "Spiceworld," by David Wild, from *Rolling Stone,* December 11, 1997. All Rights Reserved. Reprinted by Permission.

Time Inc. for "Can Souls be Xeroxed," by Robert Wright. © 1997 Time Inc. Reprinted by permission.

The University of Chicago Press for the excerpt from *Young Men and Fire,* by Norman Maclean. © 1992 by the University of Chicago. All rights reserved.

Variety, Inc., for "The Comedy of Errors," by Dennis Harvey. © 1998 Variety, reprinted with permission.

Andrew Ward for "The Trouble with Architects." Copyright © 1980 by the *Atlantic.* Originally appeared in the May 1980 issue of the *Atlantic Monthly.* Reprinted by permission.

Introduction

What is good writing? The definition chapter in this book tells us that determining what something is can be a slippery business. Certainly "good writing" means different things to different people. The readings you will encounter in the following pages, however, will show common elements in effective writing. This book is about reading and writing essays, which boils down to shaping and developing your thoughts, ideas, and experiences into a variety of essay forms.

Most of us have tackled at some point the various forms of essay writing: argumentative, analytical, definition, and others. The composition texts that all students read usually stipulate basic rules and guidelines required in well-structured essays. Most of these guidelines address and elaborate upon the basic skeleton of introduction, body, and conclusion. This is not a composition book; the readings and discussions presented here generally will not deal with basic rules of grammar and organization.

What we will do is show how good writers formalize and organize methods of thinking that we all use. Everyone argues; tells stories; and uses comparisons, definitions, and examples. Essay writers organize their ideas and experiences around these modes of thinking. When we view writing in this way, some general guidelines do emerge: when arguing on paper we address and discuss opposing arguments; when comparing and contrasting in essay form there are certain ways of doing this coherently and effectively. The selections in this text reflect wide variation of style and structure, but reading through the more than forty essays, you will see writers shaping their thoughts and concerns within the outlines of the eight basic essay forms discussed.

Of course, no one thinks in tidy little categories, with imaginary cartoon balloons floating overhead labeled "argument" or "analysis." Thinking is a chaotic activity, with much cross-fertilization between different modes of thought. Something similar happens in essay writing. Argumentative essays often employ analytical techniques; description and example can be profitably used in definition writing. Most of the work discussed in this book uses other techniques to reinforce or enhance the ideas developed primarily through analysis, cause and effect, and so forth.

Lurking behind all the talk about how ideas are developed in essay form is the nagging question confronting all writers as they sit down facing that blank screen or paper, namely: what ideas? How do we know what to write about? Hopefully, the readings and the writing projects you are about to encounter will help you appreciate the dazzling variety of topic ideas available to all who get out of bed in the morning, live in a given place (see Saul Bellow, page 249), and smell the flowers or exhaust fumes on the way to work (see Diane Ackerman, page 32). The two authors noted are professional writers, but they write about experiences, ideas, and places common and accessible to us all.

As you become a good writer, you will also become a better reader. Writing and reading are closely linked; learning to read analytically sharpens the critical thinking skills needed to develop ideas in writing. Critical thinking enables us to probe why and how things happen to and around us, or to examine the meaning and style of what we read. The discussion questions following the readings will challenge you to think about what the essays are saying, how they are saying it, and how effectively. Many discussion questions in this text encourage you to approach the essays through an editor's eyes, considering how certain passages might be expressed differently or better. The kinds of questions we ask of these writers we should also ask of ourselves as we write and revise our own work.

The reading selections will also encourage you to tackle unfamiliar concepts and problems or familiar ones in a new light. For instance, Samuel Johnson exposes us to a forgotten problem in eighteenth-century England, arguing the injustice of debtor's prisons (page 210). In another vein, teenage father Gabriel Ramos (page 5) and novelist Amy Tan (page 99) challenge familiar attitudes about teen fathers and the supposed responsibilities of an American novelist of Chinese ancestry, respectively. Ramos uses the narrative essay form, depicting his struggle against the stereotype of the irresponsible teen father, and Tan employs analysis, rejecting the role of a standard-bearer of Chinese culture.

The goal of this book is to build on what you already know about essay writing and to help you experience the writing and reading process in new and exciting ways. Many people think of essay writing as boring or intimidating; it should be neither. Bringing your critical thinking skills to bear on reading and writing will be challenging, but the rewards will be evident in your academic coursework, on the job, and even when you go to the movies. Learning to read and write essays is not just about academic work, for you will develop skills to take out of the classroom door into the wider world.

1

Narrative and Descriptive Essays

Stories are built on a framework of narrative. Building stories means hammering together a series of events moving through time with a beginning, a middle, and an end. A narrative can be either real or imagined (fiction or nonfiction), but it is always ruled by the passage of time as the events of the story move toward a conclusion. A day, month, or year in our lives also flows by with a narrative force—today follows yesterday, tomorrow comes next, and the events of our lives fall in chronological order along that continuum.

Written narratives are also ultimately sequential, moving from beginning to end. Story time, however, is not necessarily governed by the chronological rule of the ticking clock in the real world. The narrative time of the story can be stretched and folded. The narrator can jump back to the past in a flashback, devote whole chapters to the events of a single day (or hour), or race ahead and touch down in the future. It all depends on where writers shed the light of their emphasis. Consider the almost surreal slowing of time in a harrowing scene from the novel *Mr. Ives' Christmas* by Oscar Hijuelos:

> On that lovely night, Ives and Annie and this other fellow, whose name was Carl, had crossed another street, when, as if to

accentuate the preacher's ongoing sermon, still echoing in the distance, "The door is constantly open for the salvation of the soul! But death will close it," they heard a tremendous commotion of shattering materials, glass and wood and metal, high above them, a large window on the twentieth floor bursting free of the corner building. Everyone on the street and sidewalk looked up and then ran in all directions, scattering in fear. Across the way, Ives calmly noticed what, at first glance, seemed like a falling comforter, a heavy coat, a laundry bag weighted down with clothes, all wavery and turning in circles. Then he thought that the form was a bundle of wildly agitated rags, and soon enough realized that he was watching a woman slipping down through the gusting, snow-dense winds.

They couldn't hear her screams.

As this passage opens, the narrative moves at a normal pace, describing ordinary things: strolling down the street, listening to a sermon. In the next few seconds, however, narrative time paradoxically slows and stretches as the action accelerates. The leisurely unfolding of descriptive details—"comforter," "coat," "laundry bag"—creates the impression that Ives is looking at a floating object, not a woman hurtling to her death. This is the point where narration and description meet; the almost dreamlike, slow-motion narrative momentum of the woman's fall is achieved by wrapping the terrible force of the incident in a wealth of descriptive detail.

Description forces us to pull up our socks and jump right into the physical world: description's territory is the five senses. Of course, description can stand alone without narration—you can describe a peach without telling a story about it. The peach can be described by sight, touch, and smell, as simply a fruit on a tree. If, however, you were to pick the peach and throw it at your best friend, you have started a story—a story that would probably include a narrative account of your motives for throwing the peach, the result of hostilities, and a description of the peach both on the tree and connecting with its target.

In addition to narrative time, the major components of narrative-descriptive writing are the design of narrative structure, the ordering of descriptive detail, and point of view. Following is a brief discussion of these three elements.

1. As the outline for the story of the peach indicates, many narratives begin with a problem or conflict, pushing it through some action to a climax. Sometimes, however, narratives do not follow such a straight line. For example, in the brief Joyce Carol Oates childhood memoir, "Trespassing" (page 13), there is really no narrative problem stated and no climax; the description of exuberant action consumes the story. Moreover, the narrative line from conflict through resolution can be affected by the length and complexity of a story. In most of the short sample writing in this chapter, however, the structure will be clear.

2. The arrangement of descriptive detail within a narrative is often of crucial importance—consider how Oscar Hijuelos quickly sketches in the first part of the passage, concentrating the description on the fall itself. If the fatal plunge had been described more simply, stripped of detail, the sense of narrative time and the tone of the passage would be radically different. The selective use of description is an important tool for writers to mold and push the narrative in the direction they wish it to go.

3. Narrative point of view is usually limited to first or third person. Generally speaking, use of the first-person point of view creates an impression of subjectivity and immediacy; the third-person perspective may be taken by a more detached observer, allowing for objectivity and distance. In the Hijuelos selection, consider what a dramatically different texture the episode would have assumed had it been a first-person narration ("I") by the falling woman. We can easily imagine the dreamlike flickering of images erased; the muted scream would fill the page.

Point of view, whether first or third person, most often remains consistent throughout the narrative. Sometimes point of view may change in longer fictional works. For instance, *Moby Dick* begins as a first-person narrative, switches to third person for the bulk of the story, and suddenly returns to first person at the very end as Ishmael announces his survival. Usually, however, writers avoid confusing their readers by maintaining a consistent point of view.

By now you should be prepared to think of narrative-descriptive writing as one term, as most writers do. Narration and description can stand separately, but they are most effective when joined, interlocking and shaping one another. The selections in this chapter will illustrate narration and description acting together, but there will be differences in emphasis. In some selections narration will be prominent, in others description, and in some they will be delicately balanced. The writing assignments will allow you to compose your narrations and descriptions, often based on your own personal experiences. Keep in mind that narrative-descriptive writing can be useful in reports, letters, memos, and essays—both in school and out.

GABRIEL RAMOS

How can you change your life? An unforeseen event in the life of Gabriel Ramos forced this question on him, and the answer drives this narrative. Ramos wrote this essay as a high school student enrolled in a summer journalism workshop at San Jose State University. The narrative covers events in the author's life over a two-year period. He uses a short narrative essay to compress a long period of personal growth and trauma into a story of failure, triumph, and struggle toward a "happy ending." This story graphically illustrates how personal problems and conflicts can be transformed into a powerful narrative. Watch how the writer deliberately uses this essay form to explain and dramatize a turbulent slice of his life.

My Girl

From the first day I saw her, I knew it was true love and we would never be separated. As a matter of fact, she recently moved in with me on a permanent basis, and I plan to spend the rest of my life with her.

My name is Gabriel Ramos, and I'm a teen dad.

This dream girl of mine is my very own 16-month-old daughter, Llesenia (yes-en-nia). She came into my life when I was only 15, and to be truthful, it couldn't have been a worse time for me. I was a sophomore at Gilroy High School and at the time I was heavy into gangs, drugs and alcohol.

My then-girlfriend broke the news to me on June 3, 1994, one week before my 16th birthday. I received the information over the phone and acted very nonchalant about it. I felt a "cyclone of emotion": I knew every emotion I was feeling, yet I could not fixate on any one of them. I gradually dealt with them one at a time, feeling mostly the anger of "why me?" Safe sex is supposed to be 99 percent foolproof, so why did I have to represent the other 1 percent? The following day at school, I didn't even acknowledge my girlfriend because I didn't know how to react to her.

I felt the only way to cope with the news was to stay involved in the drugs, gangs and alcohol, and support my partner while ignoring the problem. My mother met with her foster parents, who were intent on placing my girlfriend into a home for unwed mothers. After further discussions, they decided to let her stay and gave me a chance to be involved, which very few teen fathers get. It was the time to decide if taking responsibility for my actions was really worth it. This occurred when Daniel Castaneda, a Gilroy police officer, visited me at school as he commonly did to check up on me. After telling him my situation, he told me something that has always stuck with me.

He said "Gabe, do you want to be a father? Or do you want to be a statistic?"

He did not say deadbeat, or cop out, or deserter. He said *statistic.* That night, I literally quit drinking, smoking, and drugs, but was still affiliated with a gang. During the next six weeks, there was a rebuilding process between my mother and me, and a bond built between me and my sister, who is a teen mother herself. I began taking parenting classes with my girlfriend, got a job and stopped cutting school.

Now in any situation, it is very easy to quit under pressure. I chose to suffer through the storm when I saw the ultrasound picture of my unborn child. It was then that I completely committed myself to becoming part of the rarest of species: a teen dad who sticks around.

The next day, the gang I was in gave me the respect to leave them for my priorities, but refused to acknowledge me anytime thereafter. In all truth, I really did not care.

The irony of all this is that after all the trouble I went through to take responsibility, some people were even more annoyed that I had stuck around. They had already labeled me a "typical" teen father who would desert my family, and they hated the fact that they were wrong. It was the little things, like in Lamaze class, when they were doing introductions, they skipped my girlfriend and me. I began keeping a pocket calendar in which I wrote every single day's events until the day my beautiful daughter was born. You see, others may consider a baby as a piece of their life being taken away. I saw it as an opportunity to build on what was already lost, making up for the opportunities I had already blown.

Which leads us to the day Llesenia was born at Saint Louise Hospital in Morgan Hill. I had been awake for two whole days, timing my girlfriend's contractions and comforting her. I was the "typical" father, making phone calls at the hospital, pacing back and forth, being fanned by a nurse, and making sure I was involved in everything that happened. I held my girlfriend's hand and together we made it happen.

At 8:25 p.m. on Feb. 1, 1995, I held my daughter for the first time.

At that moment, we proved everyone that doubted us wrong, and it felt pretty damned good. Llesenia Anastasia Roselle Ramos was 201/2 inches long and weighed 7 pounds, 8 ounces.

From then on, things went great. It was awesome experiencing my daughter's development: those tiny hands held in my own, precious eyes so filled with hope. I switched to Mount Madonna High School, which has a nursery on campus, and was back on track in making up credits.

Stop yourself if you anticipate a happy ending. My girlfriend and I simply grew tired of trying to cope with each other every single day, and problems arose because of this. We made what we thought was the mature decision, and separated for the summer of '95. I'll never exactly know why, but things really went sour between us and a second chance was too far out of reach to see realistically.

It was like trying to hold on to an anchor attached to a thread. You just have to let go and move on sometimes.

In October 1995, Llesenia's mother told me she planned to move to Illinois with her brother and take the baby with her. This triggered my filing for custody of Llesenia, and my next teen father experience began. During that time, I saw very little of my daughter. I was dating someone new who had a little girl of her own and attended the same school. There were rumors that I had found a "substitute" for my baby in my new girlfriend's daughter. I had no choice but to separate with this girl and completely focus on fighting for my daughter, which was the best thing I felt I could do. It was.

Dec. 20, 1995, was our first court date, and they assigned us to mediation. Mediation was primarily to set up a visitation plan for me. We were supposed to resolve the matter May 21, but a huge change of events came May 10. Llesenia's mother called my house and simply said, "you win." She explained she had been kicked out of her house, lost her job, dropped out of school and she wanted Llesenia to live with me. When we went back to court, I explained the new situation, and she made a mediocre attempt to win back the baby. I was awarded full custody of Llesenia, then 15 months old.

I had roughed out the storm. When I got home at 4 p.m. on May 21, 1996, I held my daughter for the first time, again.

I do not consider myself a success story. At 18, I am simply making up for the mistakes I've made. I'm on pace to graduate from high school in 1997, and I plan to take a year off to work so I can save enough money for Llesenia and me to get a place of our own. Afterward, I would like to attend a junior college. I would like to study journalism and computer engineering.

As far as long-term plans, I have no idea where I'm headed. But I'm willing to take whatever steps are necessary to make sure Llesenia is well taken care of, happy and confident that I will always be there for her. It's an ongoing, uphill battle but I don't plan on giving it up.

People often ask if I regret having Llesenia because of the opportunities I have had to miss. But if it wasn't for her, I would have no opportunities at all. I would simply be a "statistic."

At 15, I couldn't picture myself with a child. Now, at 18, I can't picture myself without her.

DISCUSSION QUESTIONS

1. After reading the introductory paragraph, whom do you think the writer is speaking about? After reading the one-sentence second paragraph, how is your response to the opening paragraph changed?

2. If you were to read only the fourth paragraph, what would be your attitude to Ramos? How would the essay be changed if this paragraph were deleted?

3. Does the narrative provide enough detail about the people involved? If not, which people would you like to know more about, and why?

4. What are the incidents that motivate the author to take responsibility? Is he influenced by other people, by his own feelings, or both? What difference does his commitment make in his life?

5. Does the essay have a clear narrative structure? Describe the stages marking the progress of Ramos through these two years.

6. Does the conclusion support and reinforce the introduction? In what way?

7. How important is description to this essay? Do you think more descriptive detail would enhance the writing? Why or why not?

WRITING PROJECT

Write a narrative account of an important experience in your life or the life of a friend or family member. Try to choose an experience that changed your life in some significant way. One option for this project might be a short story, writing a fictional narrative of a character from your imagination.

In the two short autobiographical essays that follow, the well-known novelists Jane Smiley and Joyce Carol Oates recall incidents addressing the theme of childhood transgressions. The two essays are quite different in many ways. As you read these two pieces, think about the differences in tone, setting, and three-part narrative structure. Also, consider the relative importance given to narration and description in each selection. The discussion questions will ask you to consider what these essays accomplish, the differences between them, and the reasons for those differences.

JANE SMILEY

Confess, Early and Often

The term my grandmother used for my grandfather was "impatient." What I and the other grandchildren knew was that even though our grandfather indulged us with candy bars, teased us by grabbing our legs under the table and exclaiming, "Snakes! Snakes!" and taught us everything from diving to poker playing, he was quick to anger and a little unpredictable. It was therefore with horror that I watched my 9-year-old friend Susan Clayton rip one of the bridge cards while we were playing a forbidden game of slapjack. The point of the game was to slap one's hand down on the pile whenever a jack was turned over, and thereby claim the pile. The game was forbidden because we'd torn a card before. I had, in fact, climbed on a chair, and then the dining-room table, in order to get the cards down from the dish rail near the ceiling where my grandfather had put them. Now another card, from the deck bought to replace the damaged one, was torn. My grandfather believed in corporal punishment, and my grandmother, too. I was not too old to be switched, at 9. I had recently been switched for leaving my glasses in the mailbox, where they were broken by a heavy package. I gathered up the cards, including the torn one, and stuffed them back in their case beside the second, similar deck that was also ruined, then I climbed the chair and the table, and set them on the dish rail, exactly in the spot and the position where I'd found them. It was the middle of the afternoon, late summer. My friends and I went outside to find something else to do.

I entered upon a prolonged season of dread. I felt those cards above my head every time I walked through the dining room. The point, I well knew, was not the torn card but the defiance compounded by the secrecy. Secrecy, a form of lying, was a variety of interest that compounded daily. My grandfather hated secrets, hated dishonesty of any sort. His greatest compliment to my mother was that she was incapable of dishonesty. That meant his rearing of her had been a success. Clearly I now fell humiliatingly short of that standard. Humiliating for me, but also for him and for her.

The days clicked by, each given distinction by my fear that my grandfather would sit back one night at the dinner table and say, "How about a couple of rubbers of bridge?" The diabolical element of this scenario was that since my grandmother didn't play cards; the suggestion of bridge only arose if there happened to be company. For my grandfather to discover a torn card in his new deck, the card that would reveal everything about my personal corruption, in front of relatives, our only kind of company, would only be an added humiliation for him. When bridge players came to dinner, I could hardly keep myself from staring in blank dread at the glowing damaged cards above his head. Twice in the autumn when he suggested cards, I had to distract him without manifesting panic. I don't remember what I said or did. I only remember staring sincerely into his eyes with the intensity that comes from desperate lying. One morning toward Thanksgiving, when I was alone in the house, I climbed up and looked into the card case. The torn jack was still there, still torn.

My grandfather continued to express the friendliest and most affectionate interest in me. He drove me wherever I wanted to go. He told me jokes in the car. He said things like, "Keep your feet, you'll get a draw out of it" and "Longer than a Mormon clothesline," expressions that I didn't understand but represented some larger, more colorful way of looking at the world that I knew he exemplified. He sang "Streets of Laredo," "Lorena," "Oh, Shenandoah." He told his stories about the ranch and the tannery and his boyhood and my grandmother, about my mother and my aunts and uncles. I wondered how far he would withdraw once he knew; the torn card had disappeared, a tiny seed in a field of silent lies.

I took the coward's way out, and told my mother one night in the spring, after overhearing my family planning bridge that weekend with Uncle Berger and Aunt Elizabeth. She tried to be shocked and briskly disappointed, but she couldn't work up much outrage. She helped me buy another double deck of bridge cards at the drugstore. They cost 3 dollars and 75 cents and had pictures of Whirlaway and Determine[1] on their backs. I presented my grandfather with the new cards and the news of the torn jack at the same time, the next night at dinner. He couldn't work up much anger, either, not even for show. But then, he wasn't an authoritarian, only, as my grandmother said, "impatient."

I never again played slapjack. I learned to confess early and often, because the scariest thing after all was not what they might find out, but that they didn't know.

[1]Whirlaway and Determine were champion racehorses in the 1920s and 1930s.

DISCUSSION QUESTIONS

1. How does the long introductory paragraph establish the terms of narrative structure? What is the problem set up in this paragraph that must be addressed?

2. Is narration or description predominant in the Smiley story? Are the characters and settings in the story vividly described?

3. What importance does the three-part narrative structure—the statement of the problem, the action, and the resolution—play in the story?

4. What is the tone? Does the fact that Smiley is so worried about her secret add weight and importance to the development of the action and resolution?

JOYCE CAROL OATES

Trespassing

Childhood transgressions! If parents only knew.

Mine always involved forbidden places. Until the relatively mature age of 11, I did many absurd, pointless, dangerous things while "exploring" the countryside near my family's farm in upstate New York, and I marvel that I didn't seriously injure or kill myself. Abandoned buildings and sites seemed to draw me irresistibly. The sign "No Trespassing" exerted a strange fascination—even today it's a complex signifier that stirs ancient, atavistic memories. Yet more attractive was the sign "Warning—Bridge Out." I remember crawling on hands and knees across the skeletal, rusted girders of an old bridge above Tonawanda Creek, trying not to glance into the creek bed below, where jagged rocks and boulders poked above the water's surface, a possibly fatal place to fall. Yet the girders had to be crossed, recrossed. For years. Why do children perform such mad feats of daring, making of them secret rituals?

We tramped miles to explore "haunted" houses—abandoned farms in this region of northern Erie County. We prowled through deserted houses, barns, peered into wells and cavernous cisterns, climbed dangerously rotted staircases, even clambered on top of roofs. I seemed always to be the most reckless. Once, as other children looked on in amazement, and possibly in horror, I jumped from a farmhouse roof to hard-packed, grassless ground about 12 feet below. When I hit, I felt the force through the soles of my feet like a sledgehammer blow reverberating up through my spine, neck, head. My friends changed their minds about jumping and I was left with a dazed, headachy elation. *Who was so daring as Joyce?*

A quarter-mile from our farm was a boarded-up old cider mill on a sloping bank of Tonawanda Creek. Of all places this was forbidden: festooned with "No Trespassing" signs. Yet how many times, in stealth, I would push through a rear cellar window into the mill, frequently cutting myself on broken glass and exposed nails. Everywhere inside were cobwebs, grime, fantastical machines in various stages of rust and decrepitude. There were surely rats, and snakes. There were myriad buzzing flies and wasps drawn to the immense rotted-apple compost on the creek bank. Entire steps were missing from the sagging stairs to the first floor, and to the second, but that never deterred me. Upstairs, the floor swayed beneath my weight of perhaps 60 pounds. Sometimes it was so wobbly I had to crawl on my hands and knees, but I remember the thrill of getting to a window, jumping up to balance myself on my forearms, staring from this height at the creek below, or at the very house I lived in. Thinking with childish satisfaction, *So, this is how it is!*

DISCUSSION QUESTIONS

1. What is the problem set out in the opening two paragraphs? Does Oates seem to view this sort of transgression as action requiring repentance, as Smiley does?

2. What is the relative value given to descriptive detail in this piece, especially as applies to setting? How do the use and weight given to descriptive detail differ from the Smiley story?

3. Think again about Oates's attitude toward the "problem" posed by her actions? Is there a clear narrative movement toward resolution? Again, compare the narrative structure here to that in the Smiley story.

4. Is narration or description more important in this story? Why?

WRITING PROJECT

Write two short narrative-descriptive stories, based on personal experiences. In one story select an experience where setting and situation are important, as in the Oates story. Base the second story on an experience where you move urgently and quickly through a problem to a solution, as in the Smiley story. Do your two stories give varying weights to narration and description?

JAMES BALDWIN

James Baldwin was a preeminent novelist, playwright, and essayist who died in 1987. In this short autobiographical excerpt from *Notes of a Native Son,* Baldwin uses a powerful narrative-descriptive technique to recount a violent confrontation in the blatantly racially discriminatory world of Trenton, New Jersey, during World War II. In this excerpt, Baldwin employs an intensely subjective first-person point of view, describing his interior emotional landscape as he explodes against the relentless pressures of racism. The discussion questions will concentrate on point of view and how it drives the narration into the recesses of Baldwin's own embittered mind.

Notes of a Native Son

My last night in New Jersey, a white friend from New York took me to the nearest big town, Trenton, to go to the movies and have a few drinks. As it turned out, he also saved me from, at the very least, a violent whipping. Almost every detail of that night stands out very clearly in my memory. I even remember the name of the movie we saw because its title impressed me as being so patly ironical. It was a movie about the German occupation of France, starring Maureen O'Hara and Charles Laughton and called *This Land Is Mine.* I remember the name of the diner we walked into when the movie ended: it was the "American Diner." When we walked in the counterman asked what we wanted and I remember answering with the casual sharpness which had become my habit: "We want a hamburger and a cup of coffee, what do you think we want?" I do not know why, after a year of such rebuffs, I so completely failed to anticipate his answer, which was, of course, "we don't serve Negroes here." This reply failed to discompose me, at least for the moment. I made some sardonic comment about the name of the diner and we walked out into the streets.

This was the time of what was called the "brownout," when the lights in all American cities were very dim. When we reentered the streets something happened to me which had the force of an optical illusion, or a nightmare. The streets were very crowded and I was facing north. People were moving in every direction but it seemed to me, in that instant, that all of the people I could see, and many more than that, were moving toward me, against me, and that everyone was white. I remember how their faces gleamed. And I felt, like a physical sensation, a click at the nape of my neck as though some interior string connecting my head to my body had been cut. I began to walk. I heard my friend call after me, but I ignored him. Heaven only knows what was going on in his mind, but he had the good sense not to touch me—I don't know what would have happened if he had—and to keep me in sight. I don't know what was going on in my mind either; I certainly had no conscious plan. I wanted to do something to crush these white faces, which were crushing me. I walked for perhaps a block or two until I came to an enormous, glittering, and fashionable restaurant in which I knew not even the intercession of the Virgin would cause me to be served. I pushed through the doors and took the first vacant seat I saw, at a table for two, and waited.

I do not know how long I waited and I rather wonder, until today, what I could possibly have looked like. Whatever I looked like, I frightened the waitress who shortly appeared, and the moment she appeared all of my fury flowed toward her. I hated her for her white face, and for her great, astounded, frightened eyes. I felt that if she found a black man so frightening I would make her fright worthwhile.

She did not ask me what I wanted, but repeated, as though she had learned it somewhere, "We don't serve Negroes here." She did not say it with the blunt, derisive hostility to which I had grown so accustomed, but, rather, with a note of apology in her voice, and fear. This made me colder and more murderous than ever. I felt I had to do something with my hands. I wanted her to come close enough for me to get her neck between my hands.

So, I pretended not to have understood her, hoping to draw her closer. And she did step a very short step closer, with her pencil poised incongruously over her pad, and repeated the formula: ". . . don't serve Negroes here."

Somehow, with the repetition of that phrase, which was already ringing in my head like a thousand bells of a nightmare, I realized that she would never come any closer and that I would have to strike from a distance. There was nothing on the table but an ordinary watermug half full of water, and I picked this up and hurled it with all my strength at her. She ducked and it missed her and shattered against the mirror behind the bar. And, with that sound, my frozen blood abruptly thawed, I returned from wherever I had been, I *saw*, for the first time, the restaurant, the people with their mouths open, already, as it seemed to me, rising as one man, and I realized what I had done, and where I was, and I was frightened. I rose and began running for the door. A round, potbellied man grabbed me by the nape of the neck just as I reached the doors and began to beat me about the face. I kicked him and got loose and ran into the streets. My friend whispered, *"Run!"* and I ran.

My friend stayed outside the restaurant long enough to misdirect my pursuers and the police, who arrived, he told me, at once. I do not know what I said to him when he came to my room that night. I could not have said much. I felt, in the oddest, most awful way, that I had somehow betrayed him. I lived it over and over and over again, the way one relives an automobile accident after it has happened and one finds oneself alone and safe. I could not get over two facts, both equally difficult for the imagination to grasp, and one was that I could have been murdered. But the other was that I had been ready to commit murder. I saw nothing very clearly but I did see this: that my life, my *real* life, was in danger, and from anything other people might do but from the hatred I carried in my own heart.

DISCUSSION QUESTIONS

1. How does the introductory paragraph establish the sense of anger and bitterness that will drive Baldwin's emotions and actions in the body of the essay?

2. Identify the sentence that signals that the narrator has plunged into a dreamlike, turbulent state of mind. What are the emotions shaping his responses to the situation at this point?

3. How does Baldwin describe the other people he encounters, and why does he describe them as he does?

4. Baldwin's "nightmare" ends as abruptly as it begins, when he writes "I returned from wherever I had been. . . ." How do his perceptions and actions change when this occurs?

5. Discuss narrative time in this selection. How is narrative time affected as Baldwin descends into, and emerges from, his consuming anger?

6. What is the relative importance of narration and description in the essay?

7. Narrative time and tone are closely related in this excerpt. As Baldwin reflects upon his experience in the concluding paragraph, how does the tone shift as he ponders the combustible mix of racism and hate?

8. Where is the thesis located, and why is it placed there?

WRITING PROJECT

Using the first-person point of view, describe an episode that triggered a strong sense of anger, fear, or joy. Try to employ descriptive details, painting a vivid picture of your state of mind at the time.

EVE CLAPHAM

Unexpected experiences in unfamiliar places are often rich in narrative potential; they pull us out of our daily routine and force us to think about our actions and surroundings as part of a story, with an ending. When writer Eve Clapham's car broke down, it dropped her into an unsuspected world. This narrative is an account of her experiences in that world and the people she meets there. Clapham blends narration and description, creating a sense of a place completely separate from the freeway roaring just above. In the discussion questions, you will consider how she achieves that effect. (Clapham has since returned to visit the people described in this narrative.)

To Have and Have Not

The first sign of trouble was a loud popping noise, followed by a swerving of the station wagon, then smoke pouring out from the area of the front tire on the passenger side. I wrestled the vehicle to a stop in a narrow strip of freeway next to the metal guardrail. Four lanes of traffic raced past me at speeds in excess of 70 miles an hour. I swore inwardly. I sat for a while, then, fearing one of the speeding cars would crash into my disabled one, I struggled out, locked the door and appraised my situation.

The tire had apparently exploded. I was near the Army Street exit, on top of a steep, brush-covered hill. Far below, I could see the tops of seedy buildings that lined a section of old road. I stepped over the guardrail and began to make my way back down the freeway, pushing through rain-drenched bushes, stumbling over piles of trash and garbage.

There were signs in the undergrowth showing that, in drier times, people made nests to shelter them from the elements. The nests were empty. After what seemed an eternity, I slid and lurched in the thick mud down an embankment, beneath an underpass and toward a small corner market and a phone.

As my frozen fingers dialed three A's, hooded figures began to drift toward me. A quarter popped out of the phone slot and onto the wet pavement. Other frozen fingers picked it up and solemnly returned it to me. I thanked the man. The operator said to hold on. I waited.

On the wall, a poster with a handsome young individual advised, in Spanish, that anyone who thought he or she had AIDS to call for a confidential diagnosis. Someone had slashed out the eye of the person in the poster. A single-edged razor blade lay in the puddle at my feet.

The operator informed me a tow truck would be there as soon as possible—but that there was a tremendous call for services on such a stormy day. She inquired about my whereabouts. Frantically, I scanned the area for names of streets. I could see none.

A woman holding a small orange kitten detached herself from the circle of onlookers and quietly said Cortland and Bayshore. In front of the A&M Market, number 500. I repeated her directions to the operator. She repeated it would be a while. In the meantime, I should stay exactly where I was.

I thanked the woman with the cat and looked at her more closely. She was about 40. She wore a dirty knitted cap over her wet blond hair. She was shivering, but the cat in her arms was lovingly wrapped in a heavy jacket with a fur collar. Again, I thanked her and offered her a few dollars.

Indignation leaped into her eyes. She blazed that she hadn't helped me for money! Hastily, I replied I wasn't offering it to her—I wanted her cat to have some food. The woman suddenly smiled, took the money and disappeared.

More shadowy figures milled around me. We stood silent, glancing sidelong at each other, slowly turning to mush in the downpour. I could feel the water seeping through my coat, running down my legs in icy rivulets. Someone offered to share the doorway into the market. Eagerly, I accepted.

A voice asked me about my car, which was barely visible far above us, still perched on the edge of the freeway. I told him. Bummer, he muttered sympathetically. A man on my right shyly asked if I might have 40 cents. I handed him a dollar and he darted into the dark depths of the market.

Shortly after, he came out with something in a brown sack. He took a deep, long gulp, wiped his mouth, then silently handed it to the man next to him. This person drank, then lit a rumpled cigarette, took a puff and gave it to the man with the sack, who also took a puff, then offered it to me. I smiled, shook my head and explained I didn't smoke.

The woman with the cat returned. This time the animal sat in a wire grocery cat. It gobbled greedily at a can of freshly opened Friskies. The woman explained proudly that she took good care of the cat. It ate good! Inwardly, I wondered if the same could be said of her.

Quietly, she said her "old man" would change my tire for me. I said I appreciated his offer, but because of the dangerous location of the car, I wouldn't hear of him risking his life! Seemingly pleased, she smiled.

We began to talk—about cars, about cats, about friends and family, about what the new year would bring. And about home. The hooded shadows around us joined in. One man said he had almost bought a trailer once. The deal fell through. There was silence. The rain continued to fall. I described what I had almost forgotten. That, during the Depression, my father was crippled and we had lived first in our car and then in a chicken coop. Heads nodded in understanding.

Suddenly, after two hours of waiting, a cry went up from far down the street and streaked toward us with lightning speed. Lady, the truck! The tow truck is here! Electricity seemed to zap through all of us, as if something wonderful and magical had just happened.

Everybody stood around smiling and nodding and pointing to the big yellow vehicle. I shouted my thanks, and someone yelled to be careful crossing the road. As I climbed into the truck and we pulled away from the curb, I waved. One or two hands waved back.

Later, in my repaired and warm and dry station wagon, I again rushed to make my appointment. I thought of what had just occurred, what I had learned; or rather, re-learned. That the milk of human kindness still flowed in human veins, sometimes in the most unlikely places. And that the line between the haves and the have-nots in our society, between the relatively comfortable and the destitute, was thin. Very thin, indeed.

DISCUSSION QUESTIONS

1. What is the relative importance of narration and description in Calpham's essay?

2. When the narrative opens, events are moving very fast, literally at freeway speeds. What happens to the sense of passing time in the body of the essay? Near the end, the writer reveals that two hours have passed. Would it have seemed credible if she had said fifteen minutes? How are narrative and descriptive details employed to create a sense of passing time?

3. This is a first-person essay, but the focus is turned outward, toward the people Clapham meets and the street scene. Clapham reveals very little about herself, but she does establish a sympathetic connection with the apparently homeless people she encounters. How does she do this?

4. In her conclusion, the writer draws several lessons learned through her experience. Are her assertions supported by the essay? If you, as an editor, were to delete the concluding paragraph, would you be able to draw the same lessons from the essay? Why?

5. As is true of many narratives, there is no traditional thesis statement in the introductory paragraph. Let's put you in the role of editor again and add the following sentence to the first paragraph: "The milk of human kindness still flows in human veins, sometimes in the most unlikely places." If this statement had been included in the introductory paragraph, would it have changed your response to the essay? How?

6. In the preceding essay, James Baldwin also recounts a random encounter with strangers. Both Clapham and Baldwin employ first-person point of view, but the effects are radically different. In what ways does the first-person perspective in these two essays differ, and how are those differences achieved?

WRITING PROJECT

Imagine you are responsible for returning a lost child to its parents in a foreign city, where no one speaks your language. You have one hour to find the parents before catching a train, two miles away. Write a first-person narrative about your experiences in this imaginary hour. (If you wish, you may locate your essay in V. S. Naipaul's Bombay, page 27.) After writing your essay, compare the results with those of a classmate. Within the framework of the experience described, how have the results of the two essays differed, and how have you used narrative-descriptive detail and point of view to achieve those differences?

2

Example Essays

Anyone trying to understand an idea presented in class or to explain a principle to a friend needs to cite examples: specifics to illustrate or explain general categories or abstract ideas. Some essays amplify the meaning of the thesis statement through the use of examples, explaining a generalization in the thesis through specific illustrations. For instance, an essay exploring the meaning of moral courage might invoke the example of Rosa Parks sitting in the front of a city bus in the Mississippi of 1954; a meteorologist taking as his or her thesis the potential destructiveness of hurricanes will cite examples of similar storms in the past. Example essays are organized around the use of examples to illuminate the central idea. The need to explain our ideas and experiences through the use of illustrations is so vital to our thinking and writing, however, that the readings in this chapter serve as roadmaps to most of the other forms of essay writing discussed in this book.

Thinking in examples permeates much of what we say and write. Each time we begin a sentence with the introductory phrase "for instance" or "for example" we know illustrations follow, as they did in the introductory paragraph you just read. Examples perform many functions, defining or dramatizing, explaining or supporting, as appropriate.

Example essays can be purely informative, so the purpose of a survey of hurricane-inflicted damage in the past twenty years would be to inform and explain. However, if we proposed an argumentative thesis that lax building codes contributed to the damage wrought by Hurricane Andrew, we would still rely heavily on examples to support our argument. Similarly, literary analyses of theme in a Hemingway short story (see "Morning, Noon, and Night," page 93, and "Fear of the Dark, page 95) would employ examples to illustrate how theme is developed in the story. Examples saturate most of the selections in this text, from narrative to argumentative. To describe something, to argue, or to analyze without citing examples is like trying to eat soup with a fork: the texture and flavor of your arguments and ideas will slip away.

The selections in this chapter are organized around the use of examples to clarify or explain the central idea. Russell Baker illustrates his idea that "things are breaking down" by cataloging a list of frustrations and tribulations in the supposedly efficient systems of modern life. Diane Ackerman inquires into the nature of smell by illustrating the complex, intimate impact of odors on our lives.

The readings in this chapter are organized as example essays, but they also point us down the road toward other ways of thinking and writing. How much does Diane Ackerman rely on description? Do Russell Baker and Langdon Winner move toward argumentative assertions? How important is definition in Judith Stone's discussion of the "thumb's up" gesture? The example readings discussed here will get us thinking about the ways in which this form of essay intersects with the other forms of essay writing explored throughout this book.

As you read the following selections, think along two tracks: how the writing uses examples to clarify or reinforce the central idea, and the ways in which the readings employ or suggest other kinds of writing. The discussion questions will point you toward a consideration of work elsewhere in the book, enabling you to appreciate the usefulness of examples in virtually everything you write.

V. S. NAIPAUL

V. S. Naipaul is a novelist who has also written a number of travel books. Naipaul is of Indian ancestry, but he was raised in Trinidad and has spent much of his life in England and the United States. In this introductory section from *India: A Million Mutinies Now,* his first impressions of India coalesce around an episode illustrating the place of untouchables in Indian society. Indian culture is rigidly organized around the idea of caste, which traditionally divides Hindu Indian society into classes, or castes, of laborers, merchants, warriors, and priests, with many subcastes. Untouchables are the very lowest rung on the ladder, performing only the most menial tasks, with no hope of escaping their hereditary status. Although the caste system in India has broken down somewhat, the position of untouchables, and attitudes toward them, remains largely as it has always been.

Travel essays are particularly suited to the informative example mode; writers organize their impressions and experiences around illustrative examples of the places and cultures they encounter. In this excerpt, Naipaul vividly evokes a Bombay street scene to illustrate the place of untouchables in Indian society. Watch for how Naipaul weaves description, anecdote, and historical information into a brief portrait of untouchability in India.

Bombay Theatre

Bombay is a crowd. But I began to feel, when I was some way into the city from the airport that morning, that the crowd on the pavement and the road was very great, and that something unusual might be happening.

Traffic into the city moved slowly because of the crowd. When at certain intersections the traffic was halted, by lights or by policemen or by the two together, the pavements seethed the more, and such a torrent of people swept across the road, in such a bouncing froth of light-coloured lightweight clothes, it seemed that some kind of invisible sluice-gate had been opened, and that if it wasn't closed again the flow of road-crossers would spread everywhere, and the beaten-up red buses and yellow-and-black taxis would be quite becalmed, each at the center of a human eddy.

With me, in the taxi, were fumes and heat and din. The sun burned; there was little air; the grit from the bus exhausts began to stick to my skin. It would have been worse for the people on the road and the pavements. But many of them seemed freshly bathed, with fresh puja marks on their foreheads; many of them seemed to be in their best clothes: Bombay people celebrating an important new day, perhaps.

I asked the driver whether it was a public holiday. He didn't understand my question, and I let it be.

Bombay continued to define itself: Bombay flats on either side of the road now, concrete buildings mildewed at their upper levels by the Bombay weather, excessive sun, excessive rain, excessive heat; grimy at the lower levels, as if from the crowds at pavement level, and as if that human grime was working its way up, tide-mark by tide-mark, to meet the mildew.

The shops, even when small, even when dingy, had big, bright signboards, many-coloured, inventive, accomplished, the work of men with a feeling for both Roman and Sanskrit (or Devanagari) letters. Often, in front of these shops, and below those signboards, was just dirt; from time to time depressed-looking, dark people could be seen sitting down on this dirt and eating, indifferent to everything but their food.

There were big film poster on billboards, and smaller ones repeating on lamp-posts. It was hard, just at this moment of arrival, to relate the romance the posters promised to the people on the ground. And harder to place the English-language advertisements for banks and airlines and the *Times of India* Sesquicentennial ('Good Times, Sad Times, Changing Times'): to the stranger just arrived after a night flight, the city suggested by those advertisements was like an almost unimaginable distillation—a special, rich liquor—of the humanity that was on view.

The crowd continued. And then I saw that a good part of this crowd was a long queue or line of people, three or four or five deep, on the other pavement. The line was being added to all the time; and though for stretches it appeared to be standing still, it was moving very slowly. I realised I had been driving past the line for some time; perhaps, then, the line was already a mile long. The line was broken at road intersections: policemen in khaki uniforms were keeping the side roads clear.

What were these people waiting for? What was their chance of getting what they wanted? They seemed peaceable and content, even in the sun and the brown smoke of exhausts. They were in good clothes, simple, Indian-style clothes. People joining the line came almost at a trot; then they became patient; they seemed prepared to wait a long time. I had missed the beginning of the line. I didn't know what lay there. A circus? I believe there had been posters for a circus earlier on the road. An appearance by film stars? But the people in the line didn't show that kind of eagerness. They were small, dark, patient people, serious, and in their best clothes; and it came back to me that somewhere along the line earlier there had been flags and emblems of some sort.

I was told, when I got to the hotel in downtown Bombay, that there was no public holiday that day. And though the crowd had seemed to me great, and the line quite remarkable, something the newspapers might have mentioned, the hotel people I spoke to couldn't tell me what the line might have been for. What had been a big event for so many thousands in mid-town Bombay had sent no ripple here.

I telephoned an acquaintance, a writer. He knew as little as the hotel people. He said he hadn't been out that morning; he had been at home, writing an article for *Debonair*. Later, when he had finished his article, he telephoned me. He said he had two theories. The first theory was that the people I had seen might have been lining up for telephone directories. There had been trouble about the delivery of new directories—Bombay was Bombay. The second theory was something he had heard from his servant woman. She had come in after I had telephoned, and she had told him that that day was the birthday of Dr Ambedkar, and that there was a big celebration in the suburb I had passed on my way from the airport.

Dr Ambedkar had been the great leader of the people once known in India as the untouchables. He had been more important to them than

Mahatma Gandhi. In his time he had known honour and power; he had been law minister in the first government of independent India, and he had drafted the Indian constitution; but he had remained embittered to the end. It was Dr Ambedkar who had encouraged untouchables—the *harijans,* the children of God, as Gandhi called them, and now the Dalits, as they called themselves—to abandon Hinduism, which had enslaved them, and to turn to Buddhism.[2] Before his thought could change or develop, he died, in 1956.

No leader of comparable authority or esteem had risen among the castes for whom Dr Ambedkar spoke. He had remained their leader, the man they honoured above all others; he was almost their deity. In every Dalit house, I had been told, there was a photograph of Dr Ambedkar. It was a photograph I had seen many times, and it was strange that a better photograph hadn't been used. The Ambedkar icon was like a grey passport photograph reproduced in an old-fashioned newspaper process: the leader reduced to a composition of black and white dots, frozen in an image of the 1940s or 1950s, a plumpish man of unmemorable features, with the glasses of a student, and in the semi-colonial respectability of jacket and tie. Jacket and tie made for an unlikely holy image in India. But it was fitting, because it went against the homespun and loincloth of the mahatma.

The Dr Ambedkar idea seemed better than the idea about the telephone directories. There had, indeed, been a religious stillness about the people in the line. They had been like people gaining merit through doing the right thing. The Dr Ambedkar idea made sense of the flags and the emblems of which I had had a memory. The people I had seen were honouring their leader, their saint, their deity; and by this they were honouring themselves as well.

Later that day I talked to an official of the hotel. He asked for my impressions of Bombay. When I told him about the Ambedkar crowd, he was for a moment like a man taken aback. He was at a loss for words. Then, irritation and unhappiness breaking through his well-bred hotel manner, he said, 'This country's going from bad to worse.'

[2]The Buddhist religion does not recognize the caste system.

DISCUSSION QUESTIONS

1. Discuss the use of description in the essay. How does Naipaul use description to distinguish the line of untouchables from the uproar of the surrounding scene?

2. Naipaul attempts to get information about the crowd he had seen in passing from a variety of sources: newspapers, hotel clerks, an acquaintance "writing an article for *Debonair.*" What does the response of these sources suggest about their attitudes toward the Dalit?

3. Descriptions and discussions of poverty and the status of the Dalit in India often dwell on images of hopelessness and despair. Does Naipaul convey this impression of the Dalit? Discuss.

4. What purpose do the two paragraphs devoted to Dr. Ambedkar serve in the essay?

5. How does Naipaul use tone to suggest his response to the Bombay scene in general: the people, the heat, the shops, the billboards. Does his tone change in the essay? How and why?

6. There is no thesis statement in this excerpt. If there were, what would it be? Considering your suggested thesis statement, and the essay in general, comment on the concluding paragraph. What is Naipaul trying to convey here?

WRITING PROJECT

Most of us have visited an unfamiliar or even radically different place. Write an example essay that suggests your response to such a place you have known or visited. Description, comparison and contrast, or other essay techniques may be of use in writing for this project.

Diane Ackerman

Diane Ackerman is a poet and prose writer who has published several volumes of poetry and other works, including *A Natural History of the Senses,* from which this selection is taken. The book as a whole probes the five senses and how we experience the world through them. The following selection is the introductory section from the chapter on smell. This selection is a fine illustration of how an abstraction—the sense of smell—can be made tangible in a tapestry of sensual detail.

The Mute Sense

Nothing is more memorable than a smell. One scent can be unexpected, momentary, and fleeting, yet conjure up a childhood summer beside a lake in the Poconos, when wild blueberry bushes teemed with succulent fruit and the opposite sex was as mysterious as space travel; another, hours of passion on a moonlit beach in Florida, while the night-blooming cereus drenched the air with thick curds of perfume and huge sphinx moths visited the cereus in a loud purr of wings; a third, a family dinner of pot roast, noodle pudding, and sweet potatoes, during a myrtle-mad August in a midwestern town, when both of one's parents were alive. Smells detonate softly in our memory like poignant land mines, hidden under the weedy mass of many years and experiences. Hit a tripwire of smell, and memories explode all at once. A complex vision leaps out of the undergrowth.

People of all cultures have always been obsessed with smell, sometimes applying perfumes in Niagaras of extravagance. The Silk Road opened up the Orient to the western world, but the scent road opened up the heart of Nature. Our early ancestors strolled among the fruits of the earth with noses vigilant and precise, following the seasons smell by smell, at home in their brimming larder. We can detect over ten thousand different odors, so many, in fact, that our memories would fail us if we tried to jot down everything they represent. In "The Hound of the Baskervilles," Sherlock Holmes identifies a woman by the smell of her notepaper, pointing out that "There are seventy-five perfumes, which it is very necessary that a criminal expert should be able to distinguish from each other." A low number, surely. After all, anyone "with a nose for" crime should be able to sniff out culprits from their tweed, India ink, talcum powder, Italian leather shoes, and countless other scented paraphernalia. Not to mention the odors, radiant and nameless, which we decipher without even knowing it. The brain is a good stagehand. It gets on with its work while we're busy acting out our scenes. Though most people will swear they couldn't possibly do such a thing, studies show that both children and adults, just by smelling, are able to determine whether a piece of clothing was worn by a male or a female.

Our sense of smell can be extraordinarily precise, yet it's almost impossible to describe how something smells to someone who hasn't smelled it. The smell of the glossy pages of a new book, for example, or the first solvent-damp sheets from a mimeograph machine, or a dead body, or the subtle differences in odors given off by flowers like bee balm, dogwood, or lilac. Smell is the mute sense, the one without words. Lacking a vocabulary, we are left tongue-tied, groping for words in a sea of inarticulate pleasure and exaltation. We see only when there is light enough, taste only when we put things into out mouths, touch only when we make contact with someone or something, hear only sounds that are loud enough. But we smell always and with every breath. Cover your eyes and you will stop seeing, cover your ears and you will stop hearing, but if you cover your nose and try to stop smelling, you will die. Etymologically[3] speaking, a breath is not neutral or bland—it's *cooked air;* we live in a constant simmering. There is a furnace in our cells, and when we breathe we pass the world through our bodies, brew it lightly, and turn it loose again, gently altered for having known us.

[3]Etymology is the origin and historical development of a word.

DISCUSSION QUESTIONS

1. Ackerman evokes several kinds of examples to illustrate the impact smell has upon our lives. List and discuss the kinds of examples she employs.

2. "Smell is the mute sense, the one without words." If this is true, how does the author manage to write about smell?

3. "The brain is a good stagehand." What does Ackerman mean by this? How does it relate to her claim that most people can identify clothing by the sex of the wearer?

4. The writer contends that people are most intimately tied to their environment through the sense of smell. Do you agree or disagree with this statement? Why?

5. What is the tone of this selection, and how is it related to the images Ackerman evokes? If you wanted to change the tone of this reading, how would you do it?

6. Has the author successfully conjured up the sense of smell through her use of examples? Why or why not?

WRITING PROJECT

Write a short example essay on one of the five senses, concentrating on how smell, sight, touch, taste, or hearing has affected or influenced you at a given moment of your life. Remember that this is an example essay, but you will probably wish to employ other essay forms.

PAUL ZIELBAUER

Environmental problems can be successfully explored in the example mode; surveying what happens to the environment under given circumstances entails citing instances of natural or man-made actions or events. In this essay, author Paul Zielbauer, an environmental journalist and recipient of a Fulbright journalism scholarship, poses an implicit question: what happens to the environment when you pull the cord and start your lawn mower? The author uses examples to indict lawn care tools as pollution-spewing, ear-splitting machines. The discussion questions that follow will focus on how the writer paints his picture of lawn care machines run amok.

The Roar of the Green

Mowers, blowers, throwers and wackers—'90s men love their big lawn and garden tools. In suburban America, horsepower rules: The bigger the mower, the bigger the man riding it.

This year, Americans will purchase upward of 22 million gasoline-powered lawn and garden tools—a record number, according to the Environmental Protection Agency. And as sales of these tools grow, so too have the size of the engines powering them—and the egos of the men buying them.

"This is a very testosterone-driven business," conceded Bill Redmond, president and chief executive of Garden Way Inc., the Troy, N.Y., manufacturer of Troy-Bilt lawn mowers. Most buyers of lawn tools are men, he said, and most of them like to brag about the size and power of their lawn arsenals. "To some people," he said, "this is almost recreational and a toy."

A few years ago, the 4.5-horsepower Lawn Boy that you could hang on the garage wall after a day's work seemed good enough. No more. Nowadays, suburban lawn kings drool over souped-up muscle mowers with 8-horsepower engines and up to six gears (including reverse) that have reduced lawn mowing to a heart-thumping finger exercise.

Hearing Problems

Yet, for all this macho lawn technology, suburban yardmasters and their neighborhoods are paying a price. Namely, the ear-battering noise and noxious smog our gasoline-powered society generates.

From whining two-stroke leaf blowers to the $6,000, Buick-sized riding mowers, lawn tools have changed some suburbs into Dolby-style theaters of noise.

When it comes to backyard noise, leaf blowers rule. Blowers have become such a problem that several U.S. cities and towns ban them. In Los Angeles, where police receive 21 complaints each day, using one can cost a $271 fine.

Mow enough lawns without protecting your ears, and your hearing will suffer, said Dr. Donna Wayner, director of the Hearing Center at Albany Medical Center.

Painless Destruction

"Many times, people won't know that they're doing damage," she said. "Then all of a sudden they realize, 'Gee, I'm not hearing as well as I had been.' The tragic part is you can't undo it."

In her study of college students in Chicago six years ago, Wayner found that a full summer of lawn mowing noticeably damaged the students' high-frequency hearing.

Wayner said exposure to noise at or greater than 110 decibels—slightly louder than a 22 cc Weedwacker at full throttle—for more than one minute may cause hearing loss. Prolonged exposure to 90 decibels or higher—the average lawn mower hums at about 97—also can damage hearing.

Hearing loss aside, lawn tools are no friend to the environment. Because they often employ two-stroke engines that burn a noxious mixture of gasoline and oil, the small engines cause about a tenth of all airborne pollution.

Last year, America's lawn mowers, leaf blowers, hedge trimmers, weed cutters and chain saws spewed 492,811 tons of ozone-forming hydrocarbons and nitrogen oxides into the air.

That's about 10 percent of the nation's airborne pollution, EPA statistics show.

By contrast, the average passenger car, driven 14,000 miles a year, emits about 80 pounds of hydrocarbons a year.

Hydrocarbons create ozone, a principal ingredient in the lung-choking smog that accumulates in large urban areas.

Stricter Standards

To combat such pollution, the EPA last September began enforcing the nation's first limitations on emissions that it estimates will reduce small-engine hydrocarbon levels by 32 percent. Even stricter measures, cutting these emissions by another 30 percent, will begin in 2001.

Chain saws are the filthiest. Running a 4-horsepower chain saw for two hours produces the same amount of ozone-creating hydrocarbons as driving ten 1995 cars for 250 miles, according to the California Air Resources Board.

Dirty Devices

Lawn mowers aren't much better.

Today's average new mower will, after two years, produce 34 times as much hydrocarbons as an average passenger car, according to the EPA.

Instruction manuals for most of these new lawn tools even warn customers:

"Engine exhaust from this product contains chemicals known to the State of California to cause cancer, birth defects, or other reproductive harm."

None of these drawbacks, however, appears to be infringing on the American right of a lawn mower and a weedwacker in every garage.

While last year's federal emissions restrictions have made lawn mower engines $5 to $15 more expensive to make, Redmond said, the price of Troy-Bilt mowers has dropped.

"We're selling our lawn mowers for less than we did last year, as is Toro," he said. "We've had to do this to remain price-competitive." But, he predicted, as the trend toward reducing small-engine emissions continues, "this will end up costing the consumer more."

DISCUSSION QUESTIONS

1. According to the essay, who (primarily) buys and operates lawn care equipment? Give an example of a phrase illustrating the tone toward this group.

2. Cite one example each for the environmental/health impact of lawn mowers, leaf blowers, and chain saws.

3. "Yet, for all this macho lawn technology, suburban yardmasters and their neighbors are paying a price." What is the price? What type of sentence names the price?

4. There are several one-sentence paragraphs in this selection. Incorporate two such sentences into longer paragraphs in this essay.

5. Does this essay effectively cite sources for the various statistics presented?

6. What is the logical connection between the essay's introductory and concluding paragraphs? How could you rewrite these paragraphs to strengthen or change the connection?

WRITING PROJECT

Here are two options:

1. Survey some of your neighbors or nearby lawn care maintenance companies, determining their responses to the problems described in this essay. Write an example essay based on their responses to questions such as the following: Do they agree that there are environmental and health hazards entailed in the use of lawn care equipment? If so, would they consider changing their lawn care practices to help curtail such hazards? (Avoid a confrontational approach; your essay should explore only attitudes toward this issue and the reasons for those attitudes.)

2. Identify another environmental issue in your area, and write an example essay exploring that issue. Here are a few possibilities: How widely and effectively is recycling used in your town or neighborhood? Is there a local factory releasing pollutants into the air or water? If so, what are the consequences? Environmental questions are often broad

and complex; concentrate on local issues to help you narrow your thesis.

RUSSELL BAKER

Russell Baker is a Pulitzer Prize–winning author and syndicated columnist. Much of his writing looks at modern life from a humorous, sardonic point of view. This column, included in a collection of his work entitled *There's a Country in My Cellar,* dates from the mid-1980s, but its observations are still pertinent. Baker wields examples to dramatize his point, which marches in a constant refrain through the length of the essay. This selection calls for particular attention to structure and tone; think about how Baker organizes examples around his central idea.

Have You Noticed?

We stand at the outermost frontier. Human enlightenment is far advanced. We can now say "chairperson" without feeling absurd. Technological progress is miraculous. We have the digital wristwatch.

Yet things are breaking down.

Three weeks after I bought a roll of 22-cent stamps from the postal authorities, the stickum had dampened sufficiently to glue the entire roll tightly together. Stamps ripped apart in my hands when I struggled to salvage enough of one to pass the Postal Service's rigorous inspection. In a temper, I hurled them out the window.

"Things are breaking down," I shouted.

The splendor of our science tells us everything about breakdown. Old folks had to get by with only appendicitis, shingles and boils, but we have a stunning array of medical terrors. We have stress. We have Type A behavior. We have stroke induced by insertion of artificial hearts. Thanks to the electronic picture miracle, we have doctors available at breakfast to inform us about the newest bodily plagues.

Yet things are breaking down.

"Speaking of the Postal Service," said a woman who had seen me throw the useless stamps out the window, "what about the time the mailman threatened not to deliver any more mail unless you shoveled the snow off the steps?" Yes, I recalled that and recalled speaking to the mailman:

"Shame! Now as we stand at the outermost frontier, are we to have couriers whom snow can stay from the swift completion of their appointed rounds?" Too late, I realized he was drunk.

"Things are breaking down," I told him.

We have psychiatrists, and politicians to give comfort or warning. We have pills to distract one's mind from the breakdown. The young can be placed in front of miraculous boxes producing incredibly fast-changing pictures, which leave their minds too incapable of sustained thought to realize that things are breaking down. Persons unwilling to risk chemical or electronic help can be persuaded to think happier thoughts if cautioned that it is unpatriotic to notice that things are breaking down.

Yet things are breaking down.

Two months after ordering a washing machine for his new house, my friend Bob came by to weep. He had been to the huge national mail-order retail-house outlet that had taken his order. Why hadn't the machine been delivered? The human robot manning the inquiry booth checked his electronic miracle box and said, "Because you never ordered one." Bob said the miracle box was an imbecile. The robot said, "You can reorder with me now if you want, or buy one someplace else."

"Things are breaking down," Bob said.

Yet the machinery of efficiency has never been more complete. Police squads and ingenious barricades at transportation centers and public buildings, combined with seat belts and ingeniously designed highways, insure an all-time standard of safety. We have the most advanced weapons ever built. We have the car burglar alarm.

Yet things are breaking down.

A relative of mine, ticketed by highway police for driving ten miles an hour over the speed limit, recently had her insurance canceled, though she had fourteen years of driving experience without ever being previously ticketed for a moving violation. The police miracle box had reported her ticket to the insurance industry, which had not been

turning a profit in her part of the country. Because she shared ownership of the car with her husband, for good measure the insurance company canceled his insurance, too.

He phoned long distance, wanting me to tell him, "Things are
breaking down, boy, and the best thing for you to do is set your brain
down in front of that miracle box with the fast-changing pictures or
else take a pill."

He could not reach me. I had thrown the telephone out the window
in a fury at a mechanical voice that had been constantly telling me to
dial my miracle calling-card number again because the miracle number
I had just dialed was "not valid."

It had got so that I had to dial the "not valid" number three or four
times before the mechanical voice would say "thank you" and let the
call go through. So during a marathon session when the voice had told
me for the fifth time running that my perfectly valid card number was
"not valid," I told the voice, "Things are breaking down," and threw
the phone out the window.

That was childish, because we stand at the outermost frontier where
human enlightenment, far advanced, permits us to say "chairperson"
without feeling absurd. We have the digital wristwatch, we have
stress—not just boils and shingles—and we have the artificial heart that
can induce strokes. We have the car burglar alarm, the human robot,
the miracle box. We have couriers threatening to be stayed from the
swift completion of their appointed rounds by snow.

Yet things are breaking down.

DISCUSSION QUESTIONS

1. Discuss the tone of this essay. What is the tone and attitude Baker
displays toward his subject, and how does he convey it?

2. Imagine yourself as an editor deleting the continuing refrain of
"things are breaking down" and confining it to a thesis statement at the
beginning of the essay. Would the essay be improved? Why or why not?

3. How does the writer employ examples to illustrate the nature of breakdown? Are his examples effectively used?

4. Review your response to question 1. Would the tone have been changed if the author had included a specific reference to a friend dying as a result of an artificial heart–induced stroke? How?

5. The conclusion does not follow the usual essay form. Is it effective in this instance? Why or why not?

6. Look up the word *satire*. Does that term apply to this selection? Why or why not?

WRITING PROJECT

Think of a problem that bothers you, and construct an example essay explaining why your problem is a problem and how it affects you. The range of possible topics is broad: you can consider a general social problem, as Baker does, or a problem that affects you more personally, such as the behavior of fellow drivers or a school disciplinary policy.

LANGDON WINNER

Langdon Winner is the director of graduate studies in the Department of Science and Technology Studies at Rensselaer Polytechnic Institute. This essay discusses problems posed by the application of V-chip type technology to the Internet. The freedom of expression issues you will encounter in the essays by Will and Dershowitz from the chapters on cause and effect essays and combining techniques are tackled in a different way here, from a cyberspace context. For now, watch for how Winner uses examples to explain and illustrate the nature of the problem he poses.

Electronically Implanted "Values"

Laws, regulations, police, education, propaganda—these are among the means societies have traditionally employed to promote and defend the values they deem crucial. Yet these efforts are now challenged by the vast possibilities for misbehavior that arise in today's networks of electronic communications. People end up seeing pictures, reading words, and indulging in activities that sometimes depart from prevailing community standards. The growing response to these mischievous practices is to implant prohibitions within the electronic hardware and software itself.

One example is the V-chip, the device that television manufacturers must now build into every set sold in the United States. The V-chip will enable set owners to block programs with excessive violence or sex. Proponents of the V-chip, including President Clinton, hope it will allow parents to control the kinds of scenes their children see on television.

While giving families power of this kind is a positive development, the V-chip addresses only certain kinds of concerns. For example, many parents I know worry not only about the killing, brutality, and prurient sexuality that abounds on the tube but also the barrage of advertisements that push hollow consumerism as life's central goal. The same technology that spawned the V-chip could also enable a C-chip—a device giving parents the choice of deleting the commercials that bombard kids for 10 minutes out of every half hour. Why is no one promoting such an innovation? (Don't write me. I know the answer.)

Another domain in which the implanting of certain norms is becoming commonplace is the Internet. The Communications Decency Act, now before the Supreme Court for a ruling on its constitutionality,[4] makes it illegal to send indecent material over the Internet if children may see it. An alternative approach, one that many parents find appealing, involves the use of filtering software. A mini-industry has formed to sell products with names like Net Nanny, Safe Surf, and CyberPatrol. Parents can set these filters to block a computer user's access to Web sites that contain pictures of undraped bodies and the like.

It turns out, however, that the power of deeply embedded censorship can do more than weed out erotica. Recently it was revealed that one of the more popular smut blockers, Cybersitter, also makes it impossible for computers to access the home page of the National Organization for Women. Cybersitter was developed by SolidOak Software in close cooperation with Focus on the Family—a right-wing organization that has waged censorship campaigns seeking to remove books it finds objectionable from libraries and public schools. Thus, Cybersitter is actually an extension of Focus on Family's antifeminist, antigay, anti-abortion rights agenda.

The utility and seeming neutrality of the package has convinced companies that bundle software to include it in their packages. Do these companies and their customers know the political agenda that they are buying into? SolidOak doesn't conceal its connection to Focus on Family, but it doesn't advertise it either.

Other filters have also overstepped their advertised purpose. Animal rights and environmental groups complain that CyberPatrol, made by Microsystems Software, blocks their sites because the news and pictures they present are deemed "gross depictions." CyberPatrol also denies access to the League for Programming Freedom (an organization that opposes software patents) and to some 250 newsgroups, including the

[4]The Communications Decency Act has since been ruled unconstitutional.

distinctly nonpornographic offerings of alt.feminism and soc.support.fat-acceptance.

In addition to imposing a hidden political agenda, Cybersitter also encourages parents to spy on their children. As SolidOak's press release proclaims, Cybersitter can keep a "secret log" of Internet sites that a user visits, "making it easier for the parent to monitor their children's online habits." Other software filters offer similar recordkeeping features.

Products of this kind remind one of the totalitarian states earlier this century that tried to establish order by getting family members to spy on each other. Alas, the same practices could well greet parents when they go off to work. Employers can now deploy programs such as Web Track and Sequel Net Access Manager to monitor their workers' Internet activities and to block access to sites that might detract from productivity.

Both the V-chip and Internet filters reflect today's tendency to respond to legitimate worries with technical fixes. But citizens of cyberspace must learn to identify, criticize and, when necessary, resist the deeply embedded codes in these "protective" devices. Software purchasers should loudly denounce products that try to smuggle in repressive social agendas or limit free speech. Advocacy groups that find themselves blocked by the cyberfilters must similarly seize this issue as part of the causes they advance. We must not allow the new technology to become a covert carrier of highly dubious regimes of virtue.

DISCUSSION QUESTIONS

1. After reading the essay, reread the introductory paragraph. Is there a sentence that could serve as a thesis sentence? Does it adequately summarize the essay?

2. Do the examples used illustrate and explain the nature of the problem Winner proclaims?

3. Most of the examples are explanatory—but does something different occur in the third paragraph, when the author mentions the V-chip and

television? How does this paragraph differ from the explanatory intent of the bulk of the essay?

4. Most of the examples between the third paragraph and the conclusion are explanatory, but Winner's attitude toward filtering software is nevertheless clear. Why is this?

WRITING PROJECT

Most of use work with computers: at school, at work, or at home. Write an example essay discussing something you like—or do not like—about working with computers (including the Internet). If you are unfamiliar with computers, you may discuss some aspect of television or television programming.

JUDITH STONE

Judith Stone writes for *Discover* magazine. This essay surveys the meaning of body language in general, and the "thumbs-up" gesture in particular, across cultures. How are seemingly universal gestures interpreted in different societies? The examples Stone selects illustrate the role that cultural identity plays in determining how we respond to "thumbs-up" in ancient Rome, Brazil, or here. Pay particular attention to how the writer uses definition and examples to shed new light on the general concept of body language.

Thumb and Thumber

Nearly everything we think we know about the thumbs-up gesture is wrong. Do you want to tell Siskel and Ebert or shall I? Perhaps we should leave the task to linguistic anthropologist Joel Sherzer of the University of Texas, an expert on the thumbs-up sign, and especially its sociopolitical and psychological significance in Brazil. But before he offers a quick history lesson that may turn your world, or at least your thumb, upside down, let's define our terms: when Sherzer says thumbs-up, he means extending the arm with the hand clenched and the short first digit vertically erect. (When Lavinia Stratton [1841–1919] said "Thumb's up," she meant her husband had arisen; she was married to 40-inch-tall circus performer Charles Stratton, also known as General Tom Thumb.) Note, too, the single-digit inflation: we say thumbs-up, plural, but almost always only a single one is used.

Though the stout little appendage performs many other vital tasks— as Heloise might have hinted, "That thumb you use to pull out a plum is also dandy for sucking, pressing a remote control, pantomiming a phone receiver, or calling a runner out at third!"—Sherzer isn't as enchanted by them as by the familiar gesture we *think* we know.

"The popular notion," says Sherzer, "is that the use of the thumbs-up gesture to mean 'positive' or 'okay' originated in the gladiatorial combat of ancient Rome." You're sure you know the drill: the vanquishing warrior looms over the vanquishee and waits for crowd and emperor to turn their thumbs up and shout "Mitte!" ("Let him go free!"), or turn their thumbs down and shout "Iugula!" ("Kill him!" or, in an alternative translation, "Give him bitter lettuce!"). Well, you lose, Spartacus. That's not what happened.

The misunderstanding arose, according to anthropologist Desmond Morris in his book *Gestures,* from the faulty translation of the Latin phrase *pollice verso,* used by Juvenal in A.D. 2 to describe thumb mercy. Literally, it means "turned thumb"—an unspecified turn, neither up nor down. Early historians took it to mean turned up.

But according to Morris, the thumb gesture indicating that a gladiator should be offered mercy or a lucrative deal endorsing Roman Meal Bread was *pollice compresso,* "compressed thumb"—that is, covered up, or tucked out of sight. "What spectators in fact did was extend their thumbs for a kill and hide their thumbs for an acquittal," writes Morris. "This made sense in an arena as vast as the Colosseum, where the kill and no-kill signals would have to be strongly contrasting to be visible at all."

All very interesting, I hear you cry, but what's there to *study* about the thumbs-up gesture? Regardless of its origin, doesn't everyone understand the gesture to mean "okay"? Yes, said 738 of the 1,200 Europeans surveyed by Morris and colleagues in a landmark study. But 40 respondents said the thumb aimed heavenward indicated the number 1, another 36 considered it a sexual insult (up, you should pardon the expression, yours), and the rest mentioned hitchhiking. Recognition of the upturned thumb as an "okay" sign was weakest in Italy; Italians were surprised that other folks thought the gesture had Roman origins and considered it to be something imported by American GIs in World War II.

We aren't even going to discuss the 19 other gestures that Morris and company studied, including the fingertip kiss (denoting praise), the nose thumb (defiance), the cheek screw (she's beautiful, or, alternatively, you're crazy), the eyelid pull (I'm alert; be alert), the chin flick (aggressive disinterest), or the forearm jerk (a mock phallic thrusting indicating hostility). Morris barely touches on the finger jerk—rarely used in Europe but so very popular on the motorways of the U.S.A.— even though it's the oldest recorded obscene gesture. The Romans even had a name for it, the *digitus impudicus,* or "impudent finger." Zoologists report that apes may have obscene gestures, although no one has seen a chimp flip the bird.

Like Morris, Sherzer believes that the thumbs-up gesture (which he abbreviates as TUG in the interest of saving trees) predated gladiators, Roman *or* American. "The dichotomy of *up* meaning 'positive' and *down* meaning 'negative' pervades the language and gesture systems of Europe," he explains. "The thumbs-up gesture probably originates from this contrast."

The geographic range of the TUG, as well as its meanings, extends beyond the West, Sherzer points out. "In Bali, for example, the thumbs-up is part of a ritual way of showing respect to someone of a higher caste," he says. "It's done slowly and with deference, bending down."

Sherzer isn't all thumbs, of course; his field is the study of language and culture. (He teaches a class in language, culture, and society, including cross-cultural jokes. He told me some, but trust me, you had to be there. And you had to speak Navajo; many Native American jokes boil down to "What do you mean *we,* white man?") Sherzer became interested in gestures while studying the language of the Cuna Indians of San Blas, Panama. The Cuna perform a gesture they call *kaya sui sae:* making a long or pointed face. "They look in a direction, raise the head, open and close the lips in a quick pout, and lower the head," Sherzer says. Why the long face? For giving or asking directions, asking "What's up?," offering greetings, or gently mocking a friend. It was while lecturing on Cuna language and gesture as a visiting professor in São Paulo, Brazil, that Sherzer began to study the ubiquitous Brazilian TUG. He notes that anthropological observation suggests the TUG is used in Brazil with extraordinary frequency, perhaps more than anywhere else in the world.

"You learn a great deal about Brazil simply by looking at the thumbs-up gesture," he says. "The Brazilians want to be friendly, communicative, constantly in touch—but everyone knows how rough the streets can be. The TUG can not only reconcile the urge to connect with the self-preservation need for wariness but also defuse potentially explosive situations. "People use the thumbs-up in difficult moments— to stop traffic and be friendly about it, to say thank you, to answer a query, as a quick form of politesse on the run." And the way they wield a thumb, Sherzer says, reveals their social status: "I'm especially interested in the way physical restraint marks the stratification of classes. The higher the class, the more restrained the gesture."

This observation applies to another gesture in which Sherzer takes an interest. You might have seen the late French president François Mitterand do a mild, statesmanlike version in TV interviews: the barest lip-whirring expulsion of air accompanied by slightly raised eyebrows and the Gallic shrug that speaks volumes. (If you missed Mitterand, perhaps you'll recall the soigné cartoon skunk Pepe LePew executing the same move.) In France the gesture-plus-audio is called a *bof.* (Alternative spellings used by human ethologoists include *phew, pff,* and *pouah.*) The demographic group that Americans call baby boomers are known in France as the bof generation for the tendency to overuse this shtick to indicate *ennui, désillusionnement, cynisme,* and *mal de mer.*[6] Had another group of ethologists prevailed, this generation might have been called the Phew (the Proud, the Blasé).

Sherzer studied and cataloged naturally occurring examples of the bof. Here are variations on the theme:

Q.: "Don't you think you spent too much at the flea market?"
A.: [Bof, with strong bilabial onset—lip action—to indicate "What the heck!"]

Q.: What's your friend Gerard up to?
A.: [Bof, with long, slow exhale to indicate "Who knows?"]

---

[6] *ennui,* boredom; *désillusionnement,* disillusionment; *cynisme,* cynicism; *mal de mer,* queasiness, nausea

Interestingly, the bof can be created by either exhalation or inhalation, depending on the situation—"intake of air is more positive, expulsion more negative," Sherzer says. Tellingly, he can offer few examples involving intake.

"A gesture can capture the essence of a culture," Sherzer says. "The bof is the essence of Frenchness." Sure, there's a gradient from polite to vulgar; the further the *boffeur* is from upper-class norms, the more exuberant the bof: the more flatulent the lip noise and the more flamboyant the shrug and facial expression. And yet the gestural continuum, taken as a whole, Sherzer says, helps unify the French and strengthen their national identity. (Like it needed strengthening.)

In light of Sherzer's findings, and in the spirit of multiculturalism, perhaps Siskel and Ebert should consider expanding the gestural repertoire that's catapulted them to fame. Wouldn't filmmakers work a little harder to earn "shocking, irreverent, one of the year's ten best—two cheek screws!"? And though Siskel and Ebert's current gesture TUGs at the heartstrings, I think it might be more fun to hear "Gene, I have to disagree. You give *Tutu II* a fingertip kiss, but I say it's definitely a chin flick."

DISCUSSION QUESTIONS

1. The second sentence of this essay is "Do you want to tell Siskel and Ebert or shall I?" What does this tell you about the tone of the selection? Does the tone make the essay more or less effective?

2. What is the thesis of this essay? Can the thesis be found in any one sentence in the selection?

3. How effective are the examples in supporting the thesis?

4. What would you say is the author's attitude toward the other cultures discussed? (You may wish to consider your answer to question 1.)

5. If you were asked to edit this essay, is there anything you would delete or change? Why or why not?

6. Stone relies heavily on information from secondary sources: Joel Sherzer and Desmond Morris. In your opinion are these sources used effectively or overused? Discuss.

WRITING PROJECT

Write an example essay illustrating the ways in which one word, idea, or experience has different meanings to different people. For instance, you may follow up on a term from the Langdon Winner essay and explore what "gross depictions" might mean from different viewpoints. "Transgressions" meant one thing to Joyce Carol Oates in the first chapter, but what might be its significance from religious or other perspectives? There are many such terms with multiple meanings to build this essay around.

3

Comparison and Contrast Essays

As other chapters of this book have noted, many forms of essay writing used in English classes, and other courses, reflect and develop everyday ways of thinking. This is perhaps especially true of the comparison and contrast essay. Comparing and/or contrasting related parts of our experience seems nearly as natural as walking or breathing. We constantly compare and contrast ourselves to others, politicians to one another, foods we eat, films we see, and so on.

We usually think of compare and contrast as one term, but they are actually quite distinct activities. Comparisons reveal the similarities between related things. For instance, in the example chapter V. S. Naipaul observed a long line of people united by a common characteristic: they were all waiting patiently and quietly for an unknown reason. Contrasting, on the other hand, stresses the differences between related things. When reviewer David Wild considers the latest compact disc offering by the Spice Girls (page 133), he stresses the stylistic distinctions between songs, concluding "Variety is the spice of *Spiceworld.*" The same subject can also be treated as both comparison and contrast, seen from different perspectives. For example, the people pricking Naipaul's curiosity were especially striking because of their contrasting separateness from the surrounding scene: the noise, chaos, and poverty of

Bombay street life.

One important aspect of using a comparison and contrast strategy is to always be certain that the things compared and contrasted are logically related. It would make no sense, for instance, to contrast Spice Girls music to teenage curfews in Milwaukee. But, we could logically compare (and contrast) Franklin Roosevelt's New Deal with Lyndon Johnson's War on Poverty—they were both massive government programs designed to combat poverty in different historical epochs. However, were you to attempt a comparison between the New Deal and the economics of textbook publishing in the 1990s, your history instructor would demand to know the logical connection between these two things.

Most comparison and contrast essays follow one of two basic patterns: developing their topics point by point or subject by subject. The point-by-point strategy develops a compressed, rapid-fire series of comparisons—a written equivalent of watching a tennis ball batted rapidly back and forth across a net. With this strategy two subjects are compared point-by-point in consecutive paragraphs, sentences, or even within a sentence. For example, consider how the Italian essayist Natalia Ginzburg contrasts her interests with her husband's in her essay "He and I":

> He loves museums, and I will go if I am forced to but with an unpleasant sense of effort and duty. He loves libraries and I hate them. He loves traveling, unfamiliar foreign cities, restaurants. I would like to stay at home all the time and never move. All the same I follow him on his many journeys. I follow him to museums, churches, to the opera. I even follow him to concerts, where I fall asleep.

This is an excellent example of point by point contrast within single sentences: "He loves libraries and I hate them." This strategy is most effective when there are many detailed points of comparison or contrast as in the Ginzburg passage. The advantage of this strategy is a vivid, lively and precise arrangement of the points of comparison. The danger of this method, on the other hand, is that the reader may become lost in a maze of detail, or, to put it another way, the tennis ball will be volleyed so long that we lose track of the score of the match, or even who the players are.

Subject-by-subject comparison addresses subjects one at a time. The Ginzburg essay could be rearranged to employ this pattern; all of Ginzburg's likes, interests, and inclinations would be grouped together in a series of paragraphs, followed by the corresponding interests of her husband. In a longer essay, this strategy would force the reader to constantly refer back to compare details—Ginzburg's husband might be enjoying a concert on page one, but she would not be falling asleep at the same concert until page six. Obviously this arrangement would stretch the reader's memory and dilute the effectiveness of the essay.

Many writers use a mixture of point-by-point and subject-by-subject strategies within the same essay. This method of organization offers greater flexibility and may relieve the monotony readers may feel from marching along in lockstep with one strategy or the other through an entire essay. The pitfall of this method is potential disorganization; the two strategies must be kept within a recognizable pattern, not a scattershot jumble of point by point and subject by subject stirred together without rhyme or reason. One way of accomplishing this is to introduce and conclude the essay with a summarizing subject-by-subject comparison, reserving the body of the essay for a more detailed point-by-point approach.

As you probably noticed from the above references to the Wild critical review and the Naipaul example essay, the comparison and contrast method may be profitably employed in a variety of essay types. Examples of this method are sprinkled here and there throughout this book; an exercise following the selections in this chapter will ask you to spot them and determine how appropriately each is used.

Latricia Dennis

At the time this essay was written, Latricia Dennis was a student at Galveston College, in Galveston, Texas. The location is important because Dennis contrasts life in Galveston with her childhood home in rural Indiana. The compare and contrast technique is ideally suited to this essay: Indiana and Texas are described as dramatically different, but both have a strong influence on her self-image. As you read this essay, consider how Dennis uses the compare and contrast mode to develop a clear portrait of two very different places.

Once I Was a Hoosier; Now I Am a Texan

Once I was a Hoosier. I grew up a country girl in Northern Indiana, seven miles from the nearest town. The grocery store in that town included a horse hitch for the Amish buggies. The Amish came to town once a week to sell their eggs, fruits, and vegetables to the store owner. My family home sat on three acres that included apple trees, peach trees, raspberry bushes, and a chicken coop. Corn fields surrounded the country road; I still have memories of my mother telling me to run across the road to pick some corn for dinner.

Indiana has all the wonderful changes of seasons. In the fall, the leaves on the trees change to beautiful colors of red, amber, and gold before turning brown and falling to the ground. The branches, thereafter, become bare in preparation for winter. Winter included lots of sparkling white snow. There wasn't anything as beautiful as the snow covering the empty corn fields. Driving down the long country road, it was as if I were looking at a Hallmark greeting card. The snow plows made the rounds every morning ahead of the school bus so that the kids could get to school on time. Spring came every April followed by a summer which was never very hot. In-home air conditioning was considered only for the rich; there were many summer nights I fended mosquitoes from my face that had snuck in through the screens so I could go to sleep.

The schools, which consisted of one elementary, middle, and high school, were very family-oriented. The weekly basketball or football games were usually the times my parents visited with all the neighbors. I really enjoyed the smallness of the schools because I went from Kindergarten through the twelfth grade with just about all the same people. In high school I took classes that included home economics, small engines (in which I received an A), and FFA (Future Farmers of America). I graduated with honors, ranked number ten in my class. Of course there were only 126 graduating seniors.

Being a Hoosier, I grew up naive, sheltered from the real world. Our home was never locked. I did, however, grow up being a caring person, not afraid to trust anybody, and with a sense of security in myself. I wanted to conquer the world and was confident I would run out and do just that, not realizing what the real world really was. I was very surprised to find out that I didn't know as much as I thought I did. One thing I knew for sure was home was always available to run back to even if mom wasn't expecting me. Remember, the door was never locked. A Hoosier would say, "You guys (including girls) want a pop?" (which includes any kind of carbonated drink).

Now I am a Texan, a Galvestonian to be exact. Now I say, "Ya'll want a coke?" (which includes any carbonated drink). Becoming a Texan was a step into reality. At first I felt as if I had moved to another country, not speaking the same language or knowing the proper customs. I no longer drive down country roads and see corn fields for days. I drive down a sea wall surrounded by sand and the Gulf of Mexico. My husband says he will always have sand between his toes. I, on the other hand, he jokes, will always have corn between my teeth. There are no changes of season here in Galveston. The weather only seems to go from warm, to hot, to very hot.

I learned the first fall I was here, that the palm trees stayed green all year round. For the first time in my life I had a Christmas with no snow; in fact, it was so warm we had the air conditioning on. The schools are plentiful, but always seem to be overcrowded. The high school is so large it has two campuses. There is no FFA; instead, it has what's called ROTC. To this day I don't understand the purpose for it.

Crime slapped me squarely in the face the first week I lived here. My purse was stolen out of the back door of my father-in-law's office. I didn't know I was supposed to lock the door. I thought I was in a safe place but learned quickly that no place is really safe. To lock the door was good, and to deadbolt it was better. Public housing surrounds Galveston, and I have learned the realities of poverty. When money is short and I am feeling down, I need only drive a short distance to realize how good I truly have it. I now understand the importance of shelters and food banks. I try to donate regularly to the food bank because no matter how hard life gets, my children never go hungry.

When I return to visit Indiana, my family and friends tell me I have changed and that I no longer "act" like they do. To a certain extent, they are correct. I have changed. I am no longer naive. My outer shell has become tough in the eight years I have lived here. I feel I am still a caring and secure person, but now I am afraid for myself and my family—afraid to go into certain areas of town, afraid I can't protect my children 24 hours a day, afraid to trust even a nice looking stranger because, as everyone knows, child molesters and murderers look like next-door neighbors. These fears are not present in the family and friends that remain in Indiana. Fear has made me tough on the outside, but Indiana keeps me soft on the inside. Going back to Indiana now is like going back 20 years to another place and time. I remember the old expression, "It's a great place to visit, but I wouldn't want to live there." Although I don't wish to live back in my birthplace, it did, however, give me strong roots and a very good beginning. These roots formed the inside of who I am, but the branches that have grown from the roots came from the realities of becoming a Texan. Together with my roots and branches, I feel I have become a sturdy tree. The wind can blow me, but it takes lightning to pierce me.

Once I was a Hoosier; now I am a Texan. I am proof positive that you can take the girl out of the country, but you can't take the country out of the girl.

DISCUSSION QUESTIONS

1. Is the body of the essay written in a point-by-point mode, or subject by subject? Would the essay have been as effective had it been composed in the other mode? Why or why not?

2. Read the topic sentences in the introduction, the fifth paragraph, and the concluding paragraph. In what way are these sentences important to the structure and organization of the essay?

3. In the last two paragraphs Dennis switches to a different comparison and contrast mode. Why does she do this?

4. The writer views her two homes from a strictly contrasting perspective—there is no comparison of like with like. Why?

5. "Together with my roots and branches, I feel I have become a sturdy tree." What is the meaning of this metaphor?

6. What is the thesis statement? Where is it located in the essay? As an editor, would you relocate the thesis?

WRITING PROJECT

Write a comparison and contrast essay about two places you have lived in, worked at, or visited, concentrating on how they have affected you. You may focus on only one side of the equation, as Dennis has, or find both similarities and differences to write about. The possibilities are limitless: possible topics could include work at a homeless shelter, a visit to a foreign country, or a family move from Nome, Alaska, to Miami, Florida.

DAVID REMNICK

Pulitzer Prize–winning writer David Remnick is editor of the *New Yorker* magazine. In this essay, he employs comparison and contrast to discuss an infamous incident at the end of the 1996 baseball season, when the Baltimore Orioles' second baseman Roberto Alomar spit in the face of an umpire. Remnick uses the episode as a hinge for a discussion of spitting in a variety of contexts and as an examination of "thuggish" behavior in sports, past and present. Notice in this essay how the author weaves his way—by means of comparison and contrast—through his theme of thuggery versus civility back to the unfortunate Alomar incident.

Hock Tooey

Shakespeare's characters are awash in expectorate[7]—"If I tell thee a lie, spit in my face, call me horse," Falstaff cries; "Why dost thou spit at me?" the Duke of Gloucester, later Richard III, demands of his future wife, "If you had but look'd big, and spit at him, he'd have run," advises Clown in "The Winter's Tale"—but it is Shylock who is the most famous of the insulted and the injured. We feel Shylock's humiliation ("You . . . spit upon my Jewish gabardine")[8] whether his creator felt it or not. For there is no gesture more derisive than the propulsion of a great gob of saliva from a sneering mouth.

Umpires are accustomed to scorn, but seldom does the contumely to which they are routinely subjected reach Shylockian levels. Last week, however, as the baseball playoffs began, the executives of the American League dithered over what to do about Roberto Alomar, the brilliant second baseman of the Baltimore Orioles. In the final game of the regular season, Alomar had become aggrieved after an umpire named John

[7] spit
[8] a long cloak worn in the Middle Ages, especially by Jewish people

Hirschbeck called a close third strike against him. The call, Thomas Boswell wrote in the Washington *Post,* "was bad, but hardly the worst in history." After an exchange of what are traditionally known as "words,"

Hirschbeck ejected Alomar from the game. At that point, Alomar stopped shouting at Hirschbeck just long enough to let fly—copiously, with shocking force and directly into the unfortunate umpire's empurpled face—from about a foot away. "He spit all over my face—in my eyes, everywhere," Hirschbeck said later.

If Alomar had not already alienated everyone with his manners, he surely did so when he wondered aloud to reporters after the game whether Hirschbeck hadn't lost his keenness on the diamond after his seven-year-old son died, three years ago, from adrenoleukodystrophy, a rare genetic disorder that ruins the brain and the nervous system. "I think after he got problems with his family," Alomar said, in what was apparently a misguided attempt to express some sort of sympathy, "after his son died—that's real tough in life for any person—he changed. He got real bitter." Hirschbeck's surviving son, who is nine, also suffers from the disease. When Alomar was asked whether he regretted his actions, he said, "What's to regret? I don't regret nothing I did. It's one in a million. He caught me in a bad moment."

Three days later, finally sensing the threat to his image and his fortune, Alomar apologized, and donated fifty thousand dollars to medical research—but not before he had succeeded in branding himself a boor. Baltimore will forever have mixed feelings about Roberto Alomar.

Spitting, of course, is not unknown to baseball, or to popular culture in general. The chewing of tobacco is a habit that many baseball players are still enslaved to, and the field is their cuspidor. The deadliest pitch in baseball is the spitball, the spitter was long ago banned, and we still remember its most notorious practitioner, Gaylord Perry, as cloaked in darkness, like a warlock. The great Ted Williams further dampened his already soggy relations with the supporters of the Boston Red Sox when, in a moment of pique, he turned toward the stands and spat. It was a generalized sort of expectoration, and the Kid blamed fatigue, but the damage was done. The Fenway fans admired the Splendid Splinter, but they could never quite love him, especially after that phlegmatic gesture of moist disdain. Part of Reggie Jackson's ferocity at the plate came from his ability to spit through his teeth toward the mound, not once but twice, serially—two liquid tracer bullets of Yankee imperialism. As for popular culture, rock stars seem fond of spitting onstage, among them Johnny Rotten, Patti Smith, and, most recently, Liam Gallagher, of the British pop sensation Oasis. When it comes to actors, Al Pacino is the sultan of spit: whether as Scarface or as Richard III, he showers the boards in precious bodily fluids. The comedienne Roseanne, in her ill-starred attempt to parody baseball, grabbed her crotch while singing "The Star Spangled Banner"—and spat.

Alomar's offense, even in its particulars, was not unprecedented. In 1939, at the Polo Grounds, Billy Jurges, the Giants' shortstop, spat in an umpire's face. (Besides a fine and a suspension, Jurges got a punch in the jaw, delivered personally by the ump.) But Alomar's outburst seems indicative of a newly unhinged quality in sports and in public behavior. Contemporary players did not invent the art of dispute or the thuggish gesture. Ty Cobb was famous for his abuse; the Yank's Billy Martin had the worst case of short man's disease in baseball; Earl Weaver, of the Orioles, made an ass of himself every time he twisted the bill of his cap and kicked dirt all over an umpire's shoes—and that was rather often. But there is an obvious acceleration in expressed ill-temper—a change in degree—and it is a change now visible to even the youngest fan. New York and some other cities have been blessed recently with the advent of a new cable-television outlet, the Classic Sports Network. The network specializes in rebroadcasting old sporting events: there is a lot of filler junk—quiz shows, promotions for devices promising to harden the stomach—but more often one can watch the first of Jack Johnson, Joe Louis, and Muhammad Ali, or memorable World Series games, or classic N.B.A. playoffs, or ancient Wimbledon finals. Until now, for anyone under thirty, these events have had the quality of a legend; the network might as well be serving up videos of the Peloponnesian War.

Not long ago, the Classic Sports Network reran the event dearest to the heart of this city's basketball fans: the seventh, and decisive, game of the 1969-70 championship series between the Knicks and the Los Angeles Lakers. The beauty of the Knicks' victory is sublime, but only a sentimentalist would claim that the team of Willis Reed and Walt Frazier and Bill Bradley could beat the best of today, the Chicago Bulls of Michael Jordan. But what is most striking is the difference in the civility of the court. The Knicks and the Lakers never seemed to charge the referee or scream (as Alomar did repeatedly) a word that the *Times* would probably call a maternal-bedroom epithet. In our era, it is almost unthinkable for a referee's questionable call to be accepted with good grace; nowhere is what Robert Hughes calls "the culture of complaint" more in evidence than on the courts and the playing fields. Players seem duty-bound to whine, to stamp their feet, to rain down curses on authority. And it gets worse. On the baseball diamond today, it is almost unthinkable for a hitter not to charge the mound, bat in hand, after suffering a pitch he adjudges to have come too close to his person.

Professional sports are a multibillion-dollar industry and a year-round American obsession. No one has any illusions that the players of yesteryear were angels or models of deportment—not Ruth, not Mantle, not Jim Brown—but on the whole, even in ferocious competition, a certain decorousness, even civility, prevailed in their public performances. Roberto Alomar and his fellows in uncountable riches and unbridled complaint might reflect upon the advice one performer gives another in "As You Like It"—to "clap into't roundly, without hawking or spitting." Is that so hard?

DISCUSSION QUESTIONS

1. What is the purpose of the Shakespearian allusions in the introduction and conclusion?

2. What function do the second, third, and fourth paragraphs serve in the essay? What type of essay writing is reflected in these paragraphs?

3. Can the fifth paragraph properly be labeled comparison, contrast, or a combination of the two? How does the writer use this paragraph to

establish a difference between these various spitting celebrities and the more blatantly offensive Alomar incident?

4. In the middle of the essay, Remnick compares Alomar's act to a similar incident in the 1939 baseball season. He uses the topic sentence of the first of these two paragraphs as a jumping-off point for his central concern—the "acceleration of expressed ill-temper" in professional sports. Look at these two paragraphs as an editor would. Could you rewrite them to more succinctly state the contrast between athletes past and present? How?

5. The author concentrates on athletics, but he also discusses literary characters and other types of entertainers. Do you think he is attempting to suggest a larger point about the decline in "civility" in modern life generally? If so, how successful is the attempt?

6. Is this essay primarily point by point or subject by subject? Support your answer.

7. Does the sentence ending the introductory paragraph qualify as a thesis statement? If not, what do you think a one-sentence summary of the thesis should be? Can you find such a statement?

WRITING PROJECT

Think of an incident of rudeness or kindness that you have experienced (the seriousness and intensity is up to you) and build a comparison and contrast essay around it. Compare and contrast your incident with experiences of friends, family, or episodes in the society at large you have heard or read about. You may very well find yourself using narrative-descriptive or other essay types in your essay, and you may wish to make an argumentative point, as Remnick does.

DEBORAH BLUM

What are the basic differences between men and women? In this essay, science writer Deborah Blum offers a response to this question by using one side of the comparison and/or contrast equation to critique the other. Blum calls on recent studies of the hormone testosterone, suggesting that the supposedly dramatic contrasting biological differences between the sexes may be more accurately conceived in terms of a comparison of shared similarities. As you read this selection, consider how contrast can be used as a habit of mind to oversimplify or distort complex realities.

The Subtler Side of Testosterone

Can we put an end to the popular notion that men and women are from different planets? Yes, I'm talking about "Mars" and "Venus" here, and I'm not the only one losing patience with the sexes eyeing each other as distant alien creatures.

I'm in the middle of a tour promoting a book about the biology of gender, and I've been surprised by the questions about the Mars/Venus phenomenon and at their tone. People at bookstores ask me—with unexpected hope in their voices—if I'm against such divisions. Radio talk-show hosts ask me if I wrote the book to counter the notion that we are almost two species; I didn't. I respond that sex differences are fascinating, but nothing like the vast, cold distances implied by the interplanetary metaphor.

The biology that separates men and women is more subtle, more quirky, more deceptive and ultimately a lot more interesting. The approach cheats us—women and men alike—of full understanding. The sexes are stunningly alike in so many ways that an insistence on total sex differences blinds us to how much we share.

My favorite example of this is the testosterone myth—you know, all male, all macho, all mean. You can excuse the scientists who came up with the notion—the male biologists who injected pureed dog testes into their arms in a quest for virility—because they were products of the 19th century. Now we know that testosterone is nothing like an old-boys-only product. Yes, men make a lot more of it than women (estimates range between seven and 10 times as much) but both sexes produce it and both sexes respond to it. Think of body builders: it's not just men who bulk up in response to synthetic testosterone.

Far from being the all-defining fluid of maleness, testosterone may be a regulator or barometer of aspects of behavior generally, male and female. The best studies link the hormone in men and women less to aggression per se and more to an edginess, a competitive drive, an in your-face kind of attitude. This describes many people we all know, the high-intensity lawyer, for instance. One study by James Dabbs of Georgia State University found that lawyers overall had higher testosterone levels than ministers.

Women who pursue competitive and challenging careers tend to have higher levels of testosterone than those who choose to stay at home, according to research published in the Journal of Biosocial Science and in Social Biology. Did testosterone influence their choice? If so, was it that these women were born with above-average amounts of testosterone or did their levels rise as a result of the work they were doing? One on-going study led by Alan Booth of Penn State University is looking at adolescent girls, encouraged by their families to pursue more traditional male roles. The scientists are watching to see if their testosterone rises in response to competitive situations.

And the connection with competition reveals an equally remarkable ebb-and-flow relationship. It's not merely an issue of being born Mr. or Ms. Testosterone. Scientists have found that testosterone levels rise in anticipation of competition or confrontation, then stay revved until the outcome looms. In losers, the hormone tumbles. In winners, it stays high for a while. Physical aggression isn't necessary to trigger this pattern: Scientists have measured the same rise-and-fall in chess players and football players, basketball players and even those who don't play but just watch, like soccer spectators. It seems that one only has to be rooting for a favored team for the game to elevate testosterone levels.

And there's another facet that shows how closely—almost unnervingly so—the hormone reflects our status of the moment. Researchers have found that testosterone is higher when people believe they've won on merit. If they suspect that their victory was due to something else—the opponent was sick, took an unlucky fall, suffered from a visible hangover—they don't get the same sort of testosterone rush that comes with a win. Testosterone isn't easily fooled.

There are some logical evolutionary theories behind this pattern. As scientists point out, the last thing anyone needs is a hormone that won't let a loser retreat. If, indeed, testosterone helps sharpen a combatant before a fight, that's all well and good. But the loser needs to get out of there. The winner, on the other hand, may want to take on a few more challengers, unless he won by sheer luck. In that case, he may want to take a break. Either way, testosterone seems to be there to help regulate the behavior.

What makes testosterone so interesting and so tricky to understand is the way it responds on a far more ordinary level. There are studies that suggest testosterone soars in the stressful world of dating, settles down with a steady relationship and lifts off again if the relationship disintegrates. Some psychologists even speculate that monogamy developed partly as a way for females to moderate male testosterone levels, making their partners easier to live with.

Most of the studies have involved men. We're playing catchup in studying how testosterone works in women and whether it works differently. The early results suggest some marked differences. In women, for example, testosterone doesn't rise at the sight of an attractive, let's say, possibility. It does it men.

And what about aggression? Are higher-testosterone women more like men in terms of physical aggression? One woman found with super-high levels of testosterone (as part of a prison-based research project) had shot her husband through a locked door after deciding he was on the phone too long, and then smashed the gun to bits on the floor.

It's a provocative anecdote, but only an anecdote. Behavioral scientists admit that the connections between testosterone and aggression are poorly drawn. Female athletes in Europe, taking synthetic steroids, tended to be more irritable, more easily annoyed. But they didn't start shoving colleagues around on the track.

The point is that we can now ask the same questions for men and women about hormones, not only testosterone, but the many other hormones that both sexes share. We all produce estrogen, as well, and prolactin, oxytocin, cortisol—the list really does go on and on. So that Earth-borne species, like our own, have both the challenge and the inordinate fun of trying to figure out not only when we are different, but when we are not and whether the difference even matters.

It's not as easy, perhaps, as simply declaring ourselves in different orbits. But it holds a lot more promise, because the message is clear in the science of today that if we insist on compartmentalizing nature, it seems, we end up misunderstanding it entirely.

DISCUSSION QUESTIONS

1. What is the thesis of this essay? Where is it located?

2. How does the essay use research results to suggest the role of testosterone in motivation and response to specific situations?

3. Considering the middle part of the essay, how does Blum use an analysis of the workings of testosterone to build a comparison-based analysis for biological similarities between men and women?

4. What contrasting differences between the sexes does the author discuss? What effect do these differences have upon her thesis?

5. Is Blum's method of organization point by point, subject by subject, or a combination of the two?

6. Comment on Blum's conclusion. How does the conclusion work to reinforce the thesis?

WRITING PROJECT

All of us have opinions about gender differences. Write a comparison and contrast essay about gender: What are the differences as you see them, and what evidence can you offer in support of your conclusions? Most of your evidence may be anecdotal, but you could strengthen your work by including references to other literature or research on the subject.

ESTHER SCHRADER

In this article from the *San Jose Mercury News,* Esther Schrader makes effective use of various techniques to illuminate the sharply different experiences of Latinos in California and Texas. Discussing the differences between the two states, Schrader contrasts the tense, antagonistic relations cutting through the California/Mexico border with the fluid intermingling of Anglo and Latino cultures along the Texas border. Comparison and contrast are often employed in several ways in this newspaper essay; watch for the dramatic differences between the Texas and California borders and also for the rich synthesis of similarities and differences that has become Texan "borderland" culture.

Of Time and the River

At this quiet border town where ebony trees dip into the waters of the Rio Grande, a hand-drawn ferry moves people a hundred times a day from the United States to Mexico.

From morning to night, seven days a week, the ferry never stops—transporting people back and forth across the river and the border. On the U.S. side of the river an Immigration and Naturalization Service agent sips his morning coffee and chats with the river crossers, casually checking passports and calling out to ferry passengers he knows well. Ancient men in wide-brimmed straw hats collect 25 cents a crossing, tucking the money into creased change purses at their waists. Children skip mesquite beans on the river's quiet surface.

"The younger generation lives over here and the older folks live over on the Mexican side," says David Ramirez, 41, gazing across the river on a recent scorching day. "We share the river, we share the desert. You can't get much closer to Mexico than this."

While the Los Ebanos ferry calmly moves families across the Rio Grande and back again, a taut drama is playing out elsewhere on the border. It is the nightly game of hide-and-seek between Mexicans trying to slip into California and U.S. guards pledged to keep them out.

Unlike the people of Los Ebanos and Dia Ordaz, the Mexican town across the river, the two sides facing off on the shores of the Pacific have nothing in common. On one side are the Mexicans, determined to cross for hard, isolated lives in the ghettos of East Lost Angeles and East San Jose or the labor camps of California's fertile valleys. On the other side is the border patrol, out in force because the people of nearby towns and cities in California lobbied to keep the Mexicans away.

They are hunter and hunted, *los mexicanos* waiting for *la "migra"*—the border patrol agents—to take a coffee break and *la migra* waiting in their trucks. The foes stare at each other across the rusty iron wall and the hatred and resentment that divides them. The Mexicans wait for a chance to make a run for it. But *la migra,* one border patrol agent puffs, "never takes a break."

Accidents of History

How can the border be such a sharp divide across California and so soft and ephemeral along the shifting waters of the Rio Grande in Texas, three U.S. states away? The answer lies in accidents of history and geography that have molded the Texas borderlands for centuries into a place where being Mexican and being American is often the same thing.

Unlike California, where large-scale migration from Mexico is just half a century old, the people living within 100 miles or so of the Rio Grande trace their heritage to Mexicans who crossed the river long before map makers drew a line in the middle of it. Unlike California, where Mexican immigrants rapidly become faceless additions to Southern California's vast cities, in Texas Mexicans have made a place for themselves in small border towns separated from the heartlands of their country by vast deserts. With history and geography to unite them, dependent on their Mexican partner cities across the border for support and survival, the people of South Texas are a people unto themselves. The are of *la frontera:* the border.

On the surface, it seems California should have given birth to a border culture similar to that of Texas. Both states have a history of Mexican settlement predating their incorporation into the United States, and of illegal immigrants crossing into their territory ever since. Both have vast populations of Mexican-Americans and Mexican nationals. And both state economies rely on the labor of Mexicans in fields, factories, restaurants and homes.

And yet:

• Vigilante groups in San Diego fill the airwaves with anti-Mexican diatribes while Proposition 187, the law designed to deny government benefits to undocumented immigrants, earns millions of California fans. Meanwhile, along the Texas border, school boards don't think twice when Mexican children cross to the United States to go to school;

• A high wall lighted at night with searchlights and surrounded by movement sensors hidden in the ground separates San Ysidro, Calif., from Tijuana, while in Texas new bridges carry thousands of Mexicans across every day;

• At the Republican convention in San Diego, California's trepidation about Mexican immigrants once again drives the national agenda. In Texas, U.S. mayors eat lunch with their Mexican counterparts casually and lace their speeches even to Anglo audiences with Spanish phrases.

While Californians have built a border that reaches far from the physical frontier and into people's sense of themselves, in Texas that line is disappearing—if it ever really existed.

From the maquiladoras (factories) of Ciudad Juárez, Mexico, to the *tejano* dance joints of San Antonio to the Laredo country club where powerful Mexican-Americans are founding members, *la frontera* is a region where Hispanics, while living for the most part in intense poverty, are a majority and have begun to win corresponding political clout. Trade with Mexico is a cornerstone of local economies. Spiritual belief is a mix of the Indian Catholicism of Mexico and the Protestant ethic of European settlers. Music is a blend of German polka and plaintive Mexican folk melody. . . .

For the people of the border, being alive means there is music. And that music is *tejano*—Texan—love-driven songs to a polka beat that came to these parts with the Czech and German settlers of the 19th century, flourished in the cantinas of the Mexican working class and are now the hottest music in the region. Since the March 1995 murder of Selena, unofficial queen of *tejano*, it has also been one of the border's biggest exports. In San Diego, California's closest facsimile of a border city, you would be hardpressed to find 1,000 people who had heard of Selena before her death made headlines. In the borderlands, she had long been worshiped by millions.

"It's the national music of this region. It's the music that moves us," says Ramiro Burr, a native of *la frontera* and music critic for the San Antonio Express-News. "It's forged here on the border, and it has become successful. It means that Mexican-Americans are no longer ashamed of their culture." . . .

While borderlanders dance in public plazas Mexican-style, their spiritual side they keep very much to themselves. In the shantytown *colonias* (settlements) of "the Valley"—the stretch of land along the Rio Grande between McAllen and Brownsville—borderlanders who have lived in the United States for generations still frequent wrinkled *curanderos* (healers) instead of doctors. They revere local saints like *El Niño*, a faith healer who died in 1938 and has been canonized by acclamation, not by Rome. They set up shrines like the one to the sacred tortilla on which appeared an image of Christ's face.

"To the people of the border, you don't get sick like you do in America," says Americo Paredes, emeritus professor of anthropology of the University of Texas at Austin. "If you're sick, your spirit needs to be cured."

In a Mexican town near the border, a curious edifice stands as the most visible reminder of the borderlanders' faith: the Shrine to Our Lady of San Juan. The foundations of the San Juan shrine are dug deep into the shared culture of *la frontera*. They date back to 1623, when a child acrobat believed to be dying from a frightening fall came back to life at the touch of a statue of the Virgin Mary. From then on in Mexico, the statue was revered as a powerful healing force the faithful called the Virgin of San Juan.

Somewhere along the path of history, the cult to the Virgin jumped the border.

As reinterpreted by the people of *la frontera,* the shrine is a hulking modern building built in 1980, with a parking lot so immense its rows have street names. The shrine site has a nursing home, hotels, child care and community centers. Inside, priests are developing their own World Wide Web site. Under the statue of the Virgin mounted high on the wall, worshipers kneel in the heat of hundreds of candles wearing Dallas Cowboys jerseys and Houston Astros baseball caps.

"You gotta have faith, I couldn't face the day without it. And you have to renew it every so often," says Walter Watson, 51, born on the border to parents of European stock. Watson speaks fluent Spanish and is married to a woman of Mexican descent. He says his first loyalty is to the border. "I would say my culture is Hispanic, Mexican-American. I didn't find out I was an Anglo-American until I went away to college. I didn't like it, so I came back here. This is the best place in the world to raise kids. The don't grow up with lines separating people in their heads."

While California 200 years ago was settled only around its missions, beginning in 1748 the Mexican *rancheros* of the Tamaulipas region of Mexico were encouraged to settle along the Rio Grande to build a line of defense against the Indians. Once Mexico achieved independence a century later, the government parceled out most of the valley's land in the form of large grants to favorites of the new regime.

While Mexicans were pouring into the Rio Grande valley, California was being overrun by white settlers seeking gold. The gold rush—and, later, the coming of the railroads—opened up the state to Easterners who wiped out most vestiges of *mexicano* culture.

But it wasn't until the 1880s—some 30 years after railroads made their way to the Pacific—that the rush of settlers from the East penetrated what would become *la frontera.* Thus, Mexican influences in the region flourished, and border society, insulated by a wall of desert, remained isolated from the rest of the United States.

Today the long-ignored history of *la frontera* is beginning to be embraced. A burgeoning border literature has given rise to stars like Laura Esquivel, whose novel "Like Water for Chocolate" became a hit movie in Spanish and English, and Cormac McCarthy, whose novel "All the

Pretty Horses" romanticized the intertwined lives of Mexican *vaqueros* and U.S. cowboys.

"This has always been a Mexican place, a place where people can trace Texas and Mexican history through their fathers and their grandfathers," says Eugenia Calderon, who lives in Nuevo Laredo, Mexico, and works across the river in Laredo. Her ancestors came to the area two centuries ago. Like most of her friends, Calderon speaks fluent Spanish and English. She rarely pays mind to what language she is speaking at a particular moment, unconsciously switching back and forth mid-sentence.

"Borderlanders are isolated from everywhere else," Calderon says. "Borderlanders cling to each other. Our borders don't define our flags."

Sitting in the middle of the desert in far West Texas, El Paso would be an unlikely place for a booming city—but since the 1960s, when Mexican law created an industry of assembly plants known as *maquiladoras* along the border, that is what it has become.

El Paso is a suburban sprawl of 600,000 people, 72 percent Hispanic. It is a bedroom community to its twin, Ciudad Juárez, Mexico, three times as large. And it is growing 4 percent a year. Like half a dozen other cities along the Texas border, El Paso lives mainly off supplying materials and managers to Mexico's assembly plants, and off revenues from its international bridges spanning the Rio Grande. Thousands of U.S. citizens, including 10,000 plant managers, commute across El Paso's bridges to work in Juárez every day. Thousands of Mexicans commute the opposite way to restaurants and to jobs as gardeners and maids in El Paso homes.

This spring, El Paso and Cuidad Juárez agreed to monitor the air quality of the two cities together for the first time. Television weather reports in El Paso also give the weather in Juárez. As the *maquiladora* industry booms—85 plants have opened in Juárez since January 1995—those bi-city ties become even stronger.

El Paso is one of dozens of Texas towns capitalizing on a border synergy that California lacks. As the top U.S. exporter to Mexico—$19 billion annually, as compared with California's $6 billion—Texas ships as much merchandise across the border as the rest of the states combined. The Texas trade office in Mexico City is the biggest and oldest of any U.S. state.

Texas has 11 shared ports with Mexico and 26 international river crossings; California has two. At every crossing in Texas, thousands of Mexicans walk into U.S. territory unchallenged to shop or work, and Americans cross over to Mexico with barely a nod from Mexican immigration officials.

A 300-mile superhighway between San Antonio and the Mexican industrial powerhouse city of Monterrey is emblematic of this economic interdependency. Called the "NAFTA highway," after the free trade agreement, it is—like the Mississippi River of old—a grand north-south corridor for trade. All told, more than 36,000 trucks make the journey across the border every day. The Texas city of Laredo, with three bridges, hauls in more than $20 million every year in revenues from crossing fees.

"We know in Texas that tearing down the psychological border between Americans and Mexicans means a corresponding fall in the economic borders, and that is very much to our advantage," says Victoria Callaghan, president of the Border Trade Alliance, a bilateral trade group.

"The border is a major part of our economy, and a major part of our future."

Mrythala Alejo and Victor Padilla are at the altar, taking their wedding vows in a small Laredo church. The young couple join hands and smile, surrounded by the ranchers and bankers and entrepreneurs who are the elite of their world. As they are joined in matrimony, chimes fill the air and the valley's two most powerful clans are united.

The bride and groom and their families happen to be from opposite sides of the Rio Grande. But in Mrythala and Victor's world there are no borders. They attended the same school in Laredo, even though Victor's family lives 30 miles away in the Mexican desert. Their affluent parents move in the same circles. The priest marrying them has driven casually from his home across the border to perform the ceremony.

In the very seamlessness of the marriage, the line governments drew 148 years ago through the river is dissolved.

Laredo is a two-hour drive from San Antonio and right at the heart of *la frontera*. It was founded by descendants of Mexican adventurers given land grants a century ago. Today it is a society apart, a place where being Mexican-American often means being rich and powerful.

That Mexican-American elite has long controlled City Hall, banks and businesses in Laredo, as well as in other Texas border towns. As late as 1930, 60 percent of property owners in the border counties of Starr, Zapata and Cameron were descendants of the original Mexican grant-ees. Those families concerned themselves very little with what happened in the rest of the United States. When they traveled they went to Mexico; they sent their children to private schools in Mexico; they lived in Spanish-speaking communities with Spanish signs and store names.

In Laredo, the city's only country club has mostly Mexican-American members. The city philharmonic orchestra and chorus is a joint venture with Nuevo Laredo, across the river. On ranches outside town, powerful Mexican-Americans host governors and senators under portraits of their grandparents done in rich oils. The Fourth of July is celebrated with mariachi groups. Families pay ritual celebratory visits to cemeteries on the Mexican holiday Day of the Dead.

In Laredo, Mexican-Americans are the Establishment. Take Mercurio Martínez, county judge of Webb County and a borderlander through and through. With his Texas Stetson and his Mexican ponytail and a ranch to his name holding millions of dollars in natural gas deposits under its grazing meadows, he runs his world. Driving the wide highways of South Texas in his Chevy Suburban, cellular phone plastered to his cheek, the 58-year-old Martínez travels 90 miles an hour without fear. No one is going to give Mercurio Martínez a speeding ticket in Webb County.

"We have not lost our traditions, we have been able to become leaders here without losing our roots," Martínez says, showing a visitor around the ranch his father built in 1900, where he has entertained former Secretary of the Treasury Lloyd Bentsen and Secretary of Housing and Urban Development Henry Cisneros. "In politics down here, Mexican ethnicity means a built-in base." . . .

It wasn't always this way in Texas, and Hispanic leaders say that despite the progress on the border, their people are still politically underrepresented statewide. For hundreds of years, being a Mexican in Texas meant suffering levels of poverty and exploitation arguably higher than those borne by California Mexicans.

But "the fact that they had such a hard time of it [in Texas], that there was such a sense of anger, is what forged community institutions such as schools, churches, political organizations," says Peter Skerry, an expert on Mexican-American politics at the Brookings Institution.

"The community had boundaries around it, people couldn't move socially or economically very easily. [But] when political opportunities finally started to appear in Texas, those community organizations could take advantage of them. They had produced leaders who could provide a vehicle for the pent-up aspirations of the Mexican-Americans."

In California, Skerry argues, fewer opportunities exist for community-based politics. With the state so large and winning elections so dependent on raising huge sums of money for television advertising, Mexican community groups have never been able to launch their leaders to broader political office the same way they have in Texas. Neither have they been as successful in getting out the vote. Today, as Californians feel overwhelmed by more immigrants than their state's generous social service system can handle, immigration politicians are more vitriolic than ever.

Along the Rio Grande, Latinos have different concerns. Beginning in the 1960s, they fought hard for places on school boards and on city councils. In local high schools, they made their way onto student councils and cheerleading squads.

"We didn't just want a fair share of the pie, we wanted to help make the pie," says Lydia Camarillo, executive director of the San Antonio-based Southwest Voter Research Institute.

"Hispanics like me are demanding a voice," says Nestor Valencia, a banker and local political leader in El Paso. "We're educated. We go to the statehouse in three-piece suits, not like little Mexicans with *sombreros* in our hand. We've got doctorates, we've got law degrees, we've got votes."

Today, the turnout of Latino voters in Texas is nearly twice the turnout in California. As a result, no politician can win statewide office in Texas without substantial support from the Latino community. While California Gov. Pete Wilson proposes one anti-immigrant measure after another, Gov. George W. Bush of Texas, as dyed-in-the-wool a Republican as his father, shakes hands with Mexican President Ernesto Zedillo and weekly receives Mexican dignitaries in his office. In his 1994 campaign, Bush never mentioned the topic of immigration, and appealed for votes by making friendly relations with Mexico a campaign theme.

"In California," says Neil Foley, a professor of political science at the University of Texas at Austin, "Anglo politicians—[U.S. Sen. Barbara] Boxer and [U.S. Sen. Dianne] Feinstein—are reactionary when it comes to Mexican immigration."

"If they were to say that in Texas they wouldn't have a prayer of being re-elected."

It is the Fourth of July in McAllen, Texas, and in the staging area for the annual parade, Miss Border Fest is awaiting her moment.

April Barrera is queen of this year's fest; her reign more a celebration of *la frontera* than of U.S. nationhood. The truck bed she stands on has been made into a model of a bridge spanning the Rio Grande. On one side of a blue-painted river are the crepe-paper colors of the Mexican flag. On the other are the Stars and Stripes. Barrera was born on the border, as were her parents.

At 19, Barrera is oblivious to the irony of making U.S. Independence Day a celebration of cross-border cooperation. She is a child of the border, brought to womanhood in a world where many, often most, of her classmates have been Mexican nationals who live with relatives in the United States during the week and return to their homes across the river on weekends.

"At our school about 80 percent of the kids don't come from our side of the border," says William Jenson, the principal of an elementary school in Hidalgo, a Texas town between McAllen and Brownsville. "We don't stop them. Our philosophy is that we'd rather educate them."

An elementary school teacher agrees. "We're very much one culture," says Omelia Zapata Herrera, who teachers in the tiny town of Zapata on the banks of the Rio Grande. "We're not really Mexican Mexicans, and we're not really Anglos. We really have our own traditions. We are raised to think of ourselves as being very unique. We only look up to our grandparents, to our history. We belong here. We have our roots, we have our families, we have our land.

"We're from the border and that's it. That's our world."

Before a mariachi band leads off the Fourth of July parade, Barrera says, "I think we're the last frontier left, and I think in many ways the border is the future. It's a chaotic mess down here. It's a mixing of all the good and all the bad of two peoples into one. At first it's scary. But it's the future that most of the world is going to be facing. People just deal with it.

"Through art and spirituality and commerce, we just live—just live together."

DISCUSSION QUESTIONS

1. Let's describe the marriage of Mrythala Alejo and Victor Padilla as occurring in a comparison mode, and the Border Patrol in California as working in a philosophy of contrast. How is this so? What does it say about the use of comparison and contrast throughout the essay?

2. Latino influences in California and Texas are mostly viewed through contrast, but at one point the writer introduces apparent similarities between the two. Where does this occur, and what is its purpose in the essay?

3. What purpose does the discussion of historical developments—from the eighteenth century to modern times—serve in the reading?

4. Definitions are important to the comparison and contrast themes of the essay. Define the following terms, and discuss their importance to the thesis: *la frontera, borderlander, tejano, maquiladora.*

5. Is the selection written in a point-by-point, or subject-by-subject mode? What are the advantages of the method used?

6. Because this essay was written as a newspaper feature article, the introductory paragraphs only set the scene. Can you find a thesis sentence? What is it?

7. For Schrader, the Anglo-Latino experience along the California border is decidedly negative, while the experience along the Texas border is unequivocally positive. Are there any problems or weaknesses in this approach to the contrasting realities along the two borders?

WRITING PROJECT

Write a comparison and contrast essay discussing the similarities and differences between two people you know. If possible, consider how different historical or ethnic backgrounds may have shaped these similarities or differences. Be careful to avoid unsupportable generalities or stereotypes.

4

Critical Analysis Essays

Analysis provides a way of ordering what would otherwise be a chaotic jumble of impressions and experiences. Analyzers—all of us—examine and interpret by breaking a whole (idea, event, object, etc.) into its constituent parts and then illuminating those parts as a meaningful whole. We use analysis constantly in our everyday lives, and certainly in our everyday academic lives—analysis essays are a staple of literature, history, economics, and many other courses.

To appreciate the importance of analysis, imagine watching a basketball game without analyzing what you are seeing. There would be no teams, no referees, no court, no time clock; only a bewildering blur of bodies and motion. (For someone unfamiliar with the game, this is precisely what he or she does see.) However, for anyone with a basic knowledge of basketball, analysis is the tool used to make sense of what is happening: now we see two teams, each with five players on the floor, three referees, two coaches, and a time clock dividing the game into four quarters of equal length. So the game of basketball has been divided into categories of two teams (five members each), a time clock (four quarters), and so forth. We have employed analysis to impose order on a subject—the frenetic game of basketball.

In literature, we often analyze a short story or novel by dividing it into its common elements of theme, tone, setting, plot, character, and point of view. Depending upon the work discussed and our own preferences, we usually emphasize one or two of these elements—in *Moby Dick* we may concentrate on theme, but someone writing an essay on their favorite mystery author may focus on plot. In two paired readings in this chapter, students Bebe Carmichael and Helga Erickson have chosen to analyze Hemingway's story "A Clean Well-Lighted Place" by considering how character illuminates theme.

Analysis is also integral to many other types of essays; analysis is a fundamental operation enhancing our understanding of argument and comparison and contrast, for instance. In this chapter, John Updike analyzes the nature of computers, partially by gracefully swinging—in comparison and contrast mode—between a consideration of the differences and similarities between human and computer brains. In a later chapter, Lise Funderburg's argumentative essay "Boxed In" analyzes the relative merits of racial and ethnic categories on census forms.

If a subject of analysis is controversial, argumentative debating points will naturally arise, as they do in Lise Funderburg's essay (page 238) and also in Barbara Ehrenreich's "Oh, Those Family Values." When writers bring their own point of view to a subject—such as a poem, a political party, or a vaguely defined term like "family values"—the analysis is usually imbued with a persuasive charge. It is difficult to say something significant about a poem or novel, for example, without bringing your own interpretation to the work. In this sense, the critical analysis of a work of art or literature has much in common with the critical review, with this important difference: the overriding objective of analysis is to contribute to a fuller understanding of a work, whereas the purpose of a review is to evaluate or judge its effectiveness. Some kinds of analysis, however, are less controversial and more objective. An analysis of the components of a basketball game or the workings of an internal combustion engine focuses on agreed-upon rules or mechanical operations that leave little room for interpretation or debate.

Analytical essays illuminate a topic by examining its component parts and their relation to one another. As this introduction suggests, and as the following selections show, there are various ways of approaching this type of essay. There are, though, some general guidelines all successful analytical essays must meet. The details of a topic should all be clearly and fully explored; it is hard to spotlight a topic for analysis if the component parts are inadequately explained and their relation to one another unclear. This rule applies equally to interpretive and objective analysis. We cannot discuss the significance of the time clock to basketball without also dealing with the length of the quarters, the rules governing timeouts, and so forth. Similarly, we could not analyze the significance of setting in *Moby Dick* and omit the opening chapters set in Nantucket.

The flip side of good analytical writing is good analytical reading. As you read the selections in this chapter and elsewhere in this text, do not assume that the essays have been written in the best or only possible manner. If an argumentative point is made in an essay, is it supported by the analysis? Are the component parts of the topic clearly and fully stated? Asking these and other questions of ourselves as we read better prepares us to consider our own options before we start pounding those keys.

ERNEST HEMINGWAY

Some novelists are also particularly noted for their mastery of the short story form. Celebrated writer Ernest Hemingway (1898–1961)—author of such famous novels as *The Sun Also Rises* and short story collections such as *Winner Take Nothing*—uses the short story structure to telling effect in "A Clean, Well-Lighted Place." Following this selection, you will see how community college students Bebe Carmichael and Helga Erickson analyze the themes of this story, as expressed through Hemingway's three characters. After reading "A Clean, Well-Lighted Place" and the two student essays, the discussion questions and writing projects will return you to a reconsideration of this story.

A Clean, Well-Lighted Place

It was late and everyone had left the café except an old man who sat in the shadow the leaves of the tree made against the electric light. In the daytime the street was dusty, but at night the dew settled the dust and the old man liked to sit late because he was deaf and now at night it was quiet and he felt the difference. The two waiters inside the café knew that the old man was a little drunk, and while he was a good client they knew that if he became too drunk he would leave without paying, so they kept watch on him.

"Last week he tried to commit suicide," one waiter said.

"Why?"

"He was in despair."

"What about?"

"Nothing."

"How do you know it was nothing?"

"He has plenty of money."

They sat together at a table that was close against the wall near the door of the café and looked at the terrace where the tables were all empty except where the old man sat in the shadow of the leaves of the tree that moved slightly in the wind. A girl and a soldier went by in the street. The street light shone on the brass number on his collar. The girl wore no head covering and hurried beside him.

"The guard will pick him up," one waiter said.

"What does it matter if he gets what he's after?"

"He had better get off the street now. The guard will get him. They went by five minutes ago."

The old man sitting in the shadow rapped on his saucer with his glass. The younger waiter went over to him.

"What do you want?"

The old man looked at him. "Another brandy," he said.

"You'll be drunk," the waiter said. The old man looked at him. The waiter went away.

"He'll stay all night," he said to his colleague. "I'm sleepy now. I never get into bed before three o'clock. He should have killed himself last week."

The waiter took the brandy bottle and another saucer from the counter inside the café and marched out to the old man's table. He put down the saucer and poured a glass full of brandy.

"You should have killed yourself last week," he said to the deaf man. The old man motioned with his finger. "A little more," he said. The waiter poured on into the glass so that the brandy slopped over and ran down the stem into the top saucer of the pile. "Thank you," the old man said. The waiter took the bottle back inside the café. He sat down at the table with his colleague again.

"He's drunk now," he said.

"He's drunk every night."

"What did he want to kill himself for?"

"How should I know?"

"How did he do it?"

"He hung himself with a rope."

"Who cut him down?"

"His niece."

"Why did they do it?"

"Fear for his soul."

"How much money has he got?"

"He's got plenty."

"He must be eighty years old."

"Anyway I should say he was eighty."

"I wish he would go home. I never get to bed before three o'clock. What kind of hour is that to go to bed?"

"He stays up because he likes it."

"He's lonely. I'm not lonely. I have a wife waiting in bed for me."

"He had a wife once too."

"A wife would be no good to him now."

"You can't tell. He might be better with a wife."

"His niece looks after him."

"I know. You said she cut him down."

"I wouldn't want to be that old. An old man is a nasty thing."

"Not always. This old man is clean. He drinks without spilling. Even now, drunk. Look at him."

"I don't want to look at him. I wish he would go home. He has no regard for those who must work."

The old man looked from his glass across the square, then over at the waiters.

"Another brandy, he said, pointing to his glass. The waiter who was in a hurry came over.

"Finished," he said, speaking with that omission of syntax stupid people employ when talking to drunken people or foreigners. "No more tonight. Close now."

Another," said the old man.

"No. Finished." The waiter wiped the edge of the table with a towel and shook his head.

The old man stood up, slowly counted the saucers, took a leather coin purse from his pocket and paid for the drinks, leaving half a peseta tip.

The waiter watched him go down the street, a very old man walking unsteadily but with dignity.

"Why didn't you let him stay and drink?" the unhurried waiter asked. They were putting up the shutters. "It is not half-past two."

"I want to go home to bed."

"What is an hour?"

"More to me than to him."

"An hour is the same."

"You talk like an old man yourself. He can buy a bottle and drink at home."

"It's not the same."

"No, it is not," agreed the waiter with a wife. He did not wish to be unjust. He was only in a hurry.

"And you? You have no fear of going home before your usual hour?"

"Are you trying to insult me?"

"No, hombre, only to make a joke."

"No," the waiter who was in a hurry said, rising from pulling down the metal shutters. "I have confidence. I am all confidence."

"You have youth, confidence, and a job," the older waiter said. "You have everything."

"And what do you lack?"

"Everything but work."

"You have everything I have."

"No. I have never had confidence and I am not young."

"Come on. Stop talking nonsense and lock up."

"I am of those who like to stay late at the café," the older waiter said. "With all those who do not want to go to bed. With all those who need a light for the night."

"I want to go home and into bed."

We are of two different kinds," the older waiter said. He was now dressed to go home. "It is not only a question of youth and confidence although those things are very beautiful. Each night I am reluctant to close up because there may be some one who needs the café."

"Hombre, there are bodegas open all night long."

"You do not understand. This is a clean and pleasant café. It is well lighted. The light is very good and also, now, there are shadows of the leaves."

"Good night," said the younger waiter.

"Good night," the other said. Turning off the electric light he continued the conversation with himself. It is the light of course but it is necessary that the place be clean and pleasant. You do not want music. Certainly you do not want music. Nor can you stand before a bar with dignity although that is all that is provided for these hours. What did he fear? It was not fear or dread. It was nothing that he knew too well. It was all a nothing and a man was nothing too. It was only that and light was all it needed and a certain cleanness and order. Some lived in it and never felt it but he knew it all was nada y pues nada y nada y pues nada. Our nada who art in nada, nada be thy name thy kingdom nada thy will be nada in nada as it is in nada. Give us this nada our daily nada and nada us our nada as we nada our nadas and nada us not into nada but deliver us from nada; pues nada. Hail nothing full of nothing, nothing is with thee. He smiled and stood before a bar with a shining stream pressure coffee machine.

"What's yours?" asked the barman.

"Nada."

"Otro loco mas," said the barman and turned away.

"A little cup," said the waiter.

The barman poured it for him.

"The light is very bright and pleasant but the bar is unpolished," the waiter said.

The barman looked at him but did not answer. It was too late at night for conversation.

"You want another copita?" the barman asked.

"No, thank you," said the waiter and went out. He disliked bars and bodegas. A clean, well-lighted café was a very different thing. Now, without thinking further, he would go home to his room. He would lie in the bed and finally, with daylight, he would go to sleep. After all, he said to himself, it is probably only insomnia. Many must have it.

BEBE CARMICHAEL

Community college student Bebe Carmichael wrote this critical analysis of "A Clean, Well-Lighted Place," a well-known Ernest Hemingway short story (page 88). Carmichael focuses her analysis on one aspect of the story. This paper is a good example of how a short literary analysis can work, particularly on an aspect of a poem or short story. Watch for how Carmichael complements her analysis of theme with other essay techniques and with reference to other aspects of the Hemingway story.

Morning, Noon, and Night

"What creature," the Sphinx asked Oedipus as he ventured to enter Thebes, "walks on four feet in the morning, two at midday, and three in the evening?" The soon-to-be king established his wisdom with his reply: "Man, because he crawls upon all fours in the morning of life, walks upon two feet during midlife, and, aided by a staff, hobbles upon three feet in the evening of life." The ancient riddle that was so important to Greek literature comments upon a theme that remains relevant, the stages of human life in the passage of time. In his short story "A Clean, Well-Lighted Place," Ernest Hemingway uses an old man, a young waiter, and an older waiter to represent three of life's phases.

The old man represents loneliness and isolation. "It was late and everyone had left except an old man. . . . he was deaf and now at night it was quiet and he felt the difference." Sitting and quietly drinking in this bright cafe, he can pretend that he is more a part of the world than a rich old man whose only kin saves him from his suicide out of concern for his "soul" rather than for the quality of his life. The old man is closed off from hearing the conversations around him, but in this lighted cafe that does not matter. There are people here for him to enjoy vicariously. Deafness in his "golden" years allows the old man to ignore the unpleasant things said to him. Bright though the cafe is, he sits "in the shadow the leaves of the tree" cast.

The young waiter is filled with the impatience of youth. He is quick to ask questions and quicker to judge. "You should have killed yourself last week," he tells the old man who cannot hear him. In his frustration over the lateness of the hour and the stifling of his desire to be home with his wife, he overfills the brandy glass and the liquor slops into the saucer. The young waiter cares for nothing but his own comfort, "He's lonely. I'm not lonely." The young waiter's decision to close the cafe and send the isolated old man out into the darkness illustrates both his impatience and his lack of feeling for the old man.

The older waiter stands in the middle of life. He has the patience to keep answering the young waiter's questions. He has the wisdom to understand the needs of the old man. Yet he envies: "You have youth, confidence, and a job. . . . You have everything." Fatalistically, from the cynicism of his middle years, the older waiter sees the inevitability of his becoming as the old man. "Nada," he says. Everything really is nothing.

The enigmatic sphinx poses the universal riddle still; the writer responds. In youth, a man has vitality and companionship. In middle years, he steps away and examines his life. In old age, a man finds himself isolated and in limbo. At each stage, Hemingway demonstrates, a man needs a clean, well-lighted place to give him comfort and warmth.

DISCUSSION QUESTIONS

1. Does Carmichael's analogy from Oedipus contribute to the understanding of theme in the Hemingway story? Why or why not?

2. What other elements of the story are treated in the essay? How do they complement the discussion of theme?

3. What other essay techniques are employed in this analysis of theme?

4. Can you tell from the analysis whether the story was developed from a first- or third- person point of view? How would a consideration of point of view affect the analysis of theme?

5. Reread "A Clean, Well-Lighted Place" on page 88. Is Carmichael's analysis of theme is supported by evidence within the story? Why or why not?

6. If you were assigned the editorial task of placing the thesis statement at the end of the first paragraph and composing a conclusion to summarize the thesis, would you make any changes to the essay?

HELGA ERICKSON

There is no "correct" interpretation of a fictional work, and the following contrasting analysis of "A Clean, Well-Lighted Place" by community college student Helga Erickson illustrates how two careful, well-written interpretations of the same short story can arrive at different conclusions. BeBe Carmichael and Helga Erickson see some similarities in the Hemingway story, but their interpretations of theme and character diverge in important respects. (Although there is no correct interpretation of the story, one of the writing projects will give you the option of assessing the relative merits of the Carmichael and Erickson essays.)

Fear of the Dark

"A Clean, Well-Lighted Place" presents a view of an uneventful evening shared by three unnamed characters at an ordinary cafe. Two of the characters are waiters, who carry on a conversation inside the cafe, while the other character, an elderly deaf man, sits alone on a terrace drinking brandy. When the cafe is closed for the night, the old man and one waiter leave. The other waiter continues the discussion by himself for a time, then leaves the cafe and stops in at a bar before going home. "A Clean Well-Lighted Place" deals primarily with old age and its relationship to death, and symbolism is the most prominent literary device used by the author to illustrate this theme. While many aspects of the story can be interpreted symbolically, the weight of the theme falls upon the meanings of light and darkness as the author, Ernest Hemingway, uses them.

Light, as a major symbolic element in the story, is first introduced in the title and remains a key image throughout the text. Light represents youth and things which are associated with youth, such as security, confidence, companionship, and faith. One of the waiters is a young man who is anxious to close the cafe for the evening so that he can go home. The older waiter and the old deaf man are reluctant to leave the light of the cafe, but the young waiter is not afraid of the outside world at night because he has an "inner light," his youth, to protect him. The cafe, then, represents safety and comfort and protection from the darkness outside, which is only threatening to those who recognize it.

The significance of light to the theme of the story is accentuated by the presence of darkness, or nothingness, as a symbol. Darkness is suggestive of the unknown, and of the fears and doubts which come with age. The old man sitting on the terrace is continually in shadow, even though he is at a well-lighted cafe. He cannot escape the shadow because he is old and too near death, but he can surround himself with light and borrow some strength from it. The shadow has not yet enveloped either of the waiters, but the older one feels it approaching him and finds the thought disturbing. After the young waiter and the old man have gone, the remaining waiter recites to himself a version of "The Lord's Prayer," replacing all words of religious importance with the word "nada," or nothing. This is indicative of his growing doubt, as he moves closer to death, in things which the Church has taught him to take for granted. He wonders what will become of his soul when he dies, if indeed he has a soul at all, and he realizes that religion will not provide answers which he can trust to shelter him from the unknown.

The young waiter symbolizes the ignorance of youth. He does not understand why the older waiter and the old man wish to stay longer in the cafe; he is unaware of the nothingness outside. In the initial dialogue between the waiters, it is revealed that the old man has recently attempted suicide. When questioned about it by the older waiter, the young one does not know why the old man tried to kill himself except that he was in despair about nothing. The statements of the young waiter demonstrate, ironically, that although darkness, or old age, contains what is known, ignorance can be found even in the light. The old man tried to commit suicide because he felt the nothingness, or the shadow, which was all around him; when the young waiter says that the cause was despair and about nothing, he speaks the truth, but does not even realize it.

Each of the main characters in "A Clean, Well-Lighted Place" is in a different phase of life; one is old, one is young, and one is midway between the two. By comparing and contrasting these three men, the author makes a statement concerning the relationship of youth to age. The young man thinks that he has knowledge, when in reality he is ignorant; the old man knows that he does not have any answers. The difference in the way young people and old perceive the unknown is that the young are confident about the future but with age that confidence is replaced by increasing doubt. This perspective on youth and age is maintained throughout the story by the symbolic representations of light and darkness.

DISCUSSION QUESTIONS

1. Discuss Erickson's description of the structure of the story. How does her account of the structure compare to Carmichael's?

2. What does Erickson mean by the importance of symbolism in this story, and what impact does symbolism have on theme, character, and setting?

3. Is plot important to Erickson's interpretation? To Carmichael's? Why or why not?

4. "The young waiter symbolizes the ignorance of youth."

"The young waiter is filled with the impatience of youth."

How do Erickson and Carmichael arrive at these interpretations of the young waiter's character? After reading the story, do you think another interpretation could encompass both "ignorance" and "impatience"?

5. What does Erickson mean by "doubt" and "knowledge" in reference to the older waiter and the old man? What connection do these two terms have to the symbolism of the story, as seen by Erickson?

WRITING PROJECT

Here are two options:

1. Write another analytical essay of a different fictional work. This time, however, pair up with another class member, with both of you writing about the same work. After completing your essays, compare the two. What are their similarities and differences, and how do you account for them?

2. Compare and contrast the merits of the Carmichael and Erickson analyses. What are the relative strengths and weaknesses of the two essays? Based on your own reading of "A Clean, Well-Lighted Place," do you find one interpretation more compelling than the other?

AMY TAN

Novelist Amy Tan is well known as the author of *The Joy Luck Club, The Kitchen God's Wife,* and *The Hundred Secret Senses.* In this analytical essay she traces the patterns of what is fast becoming a part of college English courses; namely, interpreting the cultural significance of Amy Tan's fiction. Therefore, her rather unusual subject of analysis is her own work. After categorically arranging her interpreters, Tan offers her own views on her intentions as a novelist. The discussion questions will review this analysis of her fiction, according to and commented upon by Tan herself.

In the Canon, for All the Wrong Reasons

Several years ago I learned that I had passed a new literary milestone. I had made it to the Halls of Education under the rubric of "Multicultural Literature," also know in many schools as "Required Reading."

Thanks to this development, I now meet students who proudly tell me they're doing their essays, term papers, or master's theses on me. By that they mean that they are analyzing not just my books but me—my grade-school achievements, youthful indiscretions, marital status, as well as the movies I watched as a child, the slings and arrows I suffered as a minority, and so forth—all of which, with the hindsight of classroom literary investigation, prove to contain many Chinese omens that made it inevitable that I would become a writer.

Once I read a master's thesis on feminist writings, which included examples from *The Joy Luck Club.* The student noted that I had often used the number four, something on the order of thirty-two or thirty-six times—in any case, a number divisible by four. She pointed out that there were four mothers, four daughters, four sections of the book, four stories per section. Furthermore, there were four sides to a mah jong table, four directions of the wind, four players. More important, she postulated, my use of the number four was a symbol for the four stages of psychological development, which corresponded in uncanny ways to the four stages of some type of Buddhist philosophy I had never heard of before. The student recalled that the story contained a character called Fourth Wife, symbolizing death, and a four-year-old girl with a feisty spirit, symbolizing regeneration.

In short, her literary sleuthing went on to reveal a mystical and rather Byzantine puzzle, which, once explained, proved to be completely brilliant and precisely logical. She wrote me a letter and asked if her analysis had been correct. How I longed to say "absolutely."

The truth is, if there are symbols in my work they exist largely by accident or through someone else's interpretive design. If I wrote of "an orange moon rising on a dark night," I would more likely ask myself later if the image was a cliché, not whether it was a symbol for the feminine force rising in anger, as one master's thesis postulated. To plant symbols like that, you need a plan, good organizational skills, and a prescient understanding of the story you are about to write. Sadly, I lack those traits.

All this is by way of saying that I don't claim my use of the number four to be a brilliant symbolic device. In fact, now that it's been pointed out to me in rather astonishing ways, I consider my overuse of the number to be a flaw.

Reviewers and students have enlightened me about not only how I write but why I write. Apparently, I am driven to capture the immigrant experience, to demystify Chinese culture, to point out the differences between Chinese and American culture, even to pave the way for other Asian American writers.

If only I were that noble. Contrary to what is assumed by some students, reporters, and community organizations wishing to bestow honors on me, I am not an expert on China, Chinese culture, mah jong, the psychology of mothers and daughters, generation gaps, immigration, illegal aliens, assimilation, acculturation, racial tension, Tiananmen Square, the Most Favored Nation trade agreements, human rights, Pacific Rim economics, the purported one million missing baby girls of China, the future of Hong Kong after 1997, or, I am sorry to say, Chinese cooking. Certainly I have personal opinions on many of these topics, but by no means do my sentiments and my world of make-believe make me an expert.

So I am alarmed when reviewers and educators assume that my very personal, specific, and fictional stories are meant to be representative down to the nth detail not just of Chinese Americans but, sometimes, of all Asian culture. Is Jane Smiley's *A Thousand Acres* supposed to be taken as representative of all American culture? If so, in what ways? Are all American fathers tyrannical? Do all American sisters betray one another? Are all American conscientious objectors flaky in love relationships?

Over the years my editor has received hundreds of permissions requests from publishers of college textbooks and multicultural anthologies, all of them wishing to reprint my work for "educational purposes." One publisher wanted to include an excerpt from *The Joy Luck Club,* a scene in which a Chinese woman invites her non-Chinese boyfriend to her parents' house for dinner. The boyfriend brings a bottle of wine as a gift and commits a number of social gaffes at the dinner table. Students were supposed to read this excerpt, then answer the following question: "If you are invited to a Chinese family's house for dinner, should you bring a bottle of wine?"

In many respects, I am proud to be on the reading lists for courses such as Ethnic Studies, Asian American Studies, Asian American Literature, Asian American History, Women's Literature, Feminist Studies, Feminist Writers of Color, and so forth. What writer wouldn't want her work to be read? I also take a certain perverse glee in imagining countless students, sleepless at three in the morning, trying to read *The Joy Luck Club* for the next day's midterm. Yet I'm also not altogether comfortable about my book's status as required reading.

Let me relate a conversation I had with a professor at a school in southern California. He told me he uses my books in his literature class but he makes it a point to lambast those passages that depict China as backward or unattractive. He objects to any descriptions that have to do with spitting, filth, poverty, or superstitions. I asked him if China in the 1930s and 1940s was free of these elements. He said, No, such descriptions are true; but he still believes it is "the obligation of the writer of ethnic literature to create positive, progressive images."

I secretly shuddered and thought, Oh well, that's southern California for you. But then, a short time later, I met a student from UC Berkeley, a school that I myself attended. The student was standing in line at a book signing. When his turn came, he swaggered up to me, then took two steps back and said in a loud voice, "Don't you think you have a responsibility to write about Chinese men as positive role models?"

In the past, I've tried to ignore the potshots. A *Washington Post* reporter once asked me what I thought of another Asian American writer calling me something on the order of "a running dog whore sucking on the tit of the imperialist white pigs."

"Well," I said, "you can't please everyone, can you?" I pointed out that readers are free to interpret a book as they please, and that they are free to appreciate or not appreciate the result. Besides, reacting to your critics makes a writer look defensive, petulant, and like an all-around bad sport.

But lately I've started thinking it's wrong to take such a laissez-faire attitude. Lately I've come to think that I must say something, not so much to defend myself and my work but to express my hopes for American literature, for what it has the potential to become in the twenty-first century—that is, a truly American literature, democratic in the way it includes many colorful voices.

Until recently, I didn't think it was important for writers to express their private intentions in order for their work to be appreciated; I believed that any analysis of my intentions belonged behind the closed doors of literature classes. But I've come to realize that the study of literature does have its effect on how books are being read, and thus on what might be read, published, and written in the future. For that reason, I do believe writers today must talk about their intentions—if for no other reason than to serve as an antidote to what others say our intentions should be.

For the record, I don't write to dig a hole and fill it with symbols. I don't write stories as ethnic themes. I don't write to represent life in general. And I certainly don't write because I have answers. If I knew everything there is to know about mothers and daughters, Chinese and Americans, I wouldn't have any stories left to imagine. If I had to write about only positive role models, I wouldn't have enough imagination left to finish the first story. If I knew what to do about immigration, I would be a sociologist or a politician and not a long-winded storyteller.

So why do I write?

Because my childhood disturbed me, pained me, made me ask foolish questions. And the questions still echo. Why does my mother always talk about killing herself? Why did my father and brother have to die? If I die, can I reborn into a happy family? Those early obsessions led to a belief that writing could be my salvation, providing me with the sort of freedom and danger, satisfaction and discomfort, truth and contradiction I can't find in anything else in life.

I write to discover the past for myself. I don't write to change the future for others. And if others are moved by my work—if they love their mothers more, scold their daughters less, or divorce their husbands who were not positive role models—I'm often surprised, usually grateful to hear from kind readers. But I don't take either credit or blame for changing their lives for better or for worse.

Writing, for me, is an act of faith, a hope that I will discover what I mean by "truth." I also think of reading as an act of faith, a hope that I will discover something remarkable about ordinary life, about myself. And if the writer and the reader discover the same thing, if they have that connection, the act of faith has resulted in an act of magic. To me, that's the mystery and the wonder of both life and fiction—the connection between two individuals who discover in the end that they are more the same than they are different.

And if that doesn't happen, it's nobody's fault. There are still plenty of other books on the shelf. Choose what you like.

DISCUSSION QUESTIONS

1. Summarize the interpretations of her work that Tan discusses. What is her attitude to these interpretations, and why does she feel that way?

2. What does Tan say is the purpose or intent of her fiction? How does it differ from the various analyses of her work surveyed in this essay?

3. Is the author's critique of her interpreters an effective example of analytical method?

4. What is the tone of the essay? Does the tone shift? If so, how do you account for the shift?

5. Are there other essay techniques used here? What purpose is served by the use of other techniques?

6. What is the purpose of the comparison to Jane Smiley's work? Is this a valid comparison?

7. The conclusion introduces a new issue, the connection between writer and reader. How does this new idea relate to the essay as a whole? Are there any problems associated with introducing this idea at this point?

WRITING PROJECT

Read a short story of your choice, or one suggested by your instructor. Write an analytical essay about the story, focusing on one or two elements of the story (theme, plot, setting, character, or point of view). If possible, find an essay, interview, or article in which the author of the story you have read discusses his or her work, and include that discussion in your essay.

Mario Vargas Llosa

In this selection, Peruvian novelist and essayist Mario Vargas Llosa asks a basic question: Why do we read and write literature? Is it strictly for entertainment, or is it for something else? Llosa's analysis describes what literature can and should do by contrasting the possibilities of the printed word to the fleeting images of television and movie screens. Although this is a fairly short essay, it dwells on large themes of citizenship, democracy, and the role of the writer; watch for how Llosa condenses these sweeping concerns into a coherent analysis.

With Pens Drawn

My vocation as a writer grew out of the idea that literature does not exist in a closed artistic sphere but embraces a larger moral and civic universe. This is what has motivated everything I have written. It is also, alas, now turning me into a dinosaur in trousers, surrounded by computers.

Statistics tell us that never before have so many books been sold. The trouble is that hardly anybody I come across believes any longer that literature serves any great purpose beyond alleviating boredom on the bus or the underground, or has any higher ambition beyond being transformed into television or movie scripts. Literature has gone light. That's why critics such as George Steiner have come to believe literature is already dead, and why novelists such as V. S. Naipaul have come to proclaim that they will not write another novel because the genre now fills them with disgust.

But amid this pessimism about literature, we should remember that many people still fear the writer. Look at the criminal clique that governs Nigeria and executed Ogoni author and activist Ken Saro-Wiwa after a trumped-up murder charge; at the imams who declared a *fatwa*[9]

[9]an Islamic religious edict

on novelist Salman Rushdie for criticizing Islamic practices in *The Satanic Verses;* at the Muslim fundamentalists in Algeria who have cut the throats of dozens of journalists, writers, and thespians; and at all those regimes in North Korea, Cuba, China, Laos, Burma, and elsewhere where censorship prevails and prisons are full of writers.

So in countries that are supposed to be cultivated—and are the most free and democratic—literature is becoming a hobby without real value, while in countries where freedom is restricted, literature is considered dangerous, the vehicle of subversive ideas. Novelists and poets in free countries, who view their profession with disillusionment, should open their eyes to this vast part of the globe that is not yet free. It might give them courage.

I have an old-fashioned view: I believe that literature must address itself to the problems of its time. Authors must write with the conviction that what they are writing can help others become more free, more sensitive, more clear-sighted; yet without the self-righteous illusion of many intellectuals that their work helps contain violence, reduce injustice, or promote liberty. I have erred too often myself, and I have seen too many writers I admired err—even put their talents at the service of ideological lies and state crimes—to delude myself. But without ceasing to be entertaining, literature should immerse itself in the life of the streets, in the unraveling of history, as it did in the best of times. This is the only way in which writers can help their contemporaries and save literature from the flimsy state to which it sometimes seems condemned.

If the only point of literature is to entertain, then it cannot compete with the fictions pouring out of our screens, large or small. An illusion made of words requires the reader's active participation, an effort of the imagination and sometimes, in modern literature, complex feats of memory, association, and creativity. Television and cinema audiences are exempt from all this by virtue of the images. This makes them lazy and increasingly allergic to intellectually challenging entertainment.

Screen fiction is intense on account of its immediacy and ephemeral in terms of effect: It captivates us and then releases us almost instantly. Literary fiction holds us captive for life. To say that the works of authors such as Dostoyevsky, Tolstoy, and Proust are entertaining would be to insult them. For, while they are usually read in a state of high excitement, the most important effect of a good book is in the aftermath, its ability to fire memory over time. The afterglow is still alive within me because without the books I have read, I would not be who I am, for better or worse, nor would I believe what I believe, with all the doubts and certainties that keep me going. Those books shaped me, changed me, made me. And they continue changing me, in step with the life I measure them against. In those books I learned that the world is in bad shape and that it will always be so—which is no reason to refrain from doing whatever we can to keep it from getting worse. They taught me that in all our diversity of cultures, races, and beliefs, as fellow actors in the human comedy, we deserve equal respect. They also taught me why we so rarely get it. There is nothing like good literature to help us detect the roots of the cruelty human beings can unleash.

Without a committed literature it will become even more difficult to contain all those outbreaks of war, genocide, ethnic and religious strife, refugee displacement, and terrorist activity that threaten to multiply and that have already smashed the hopes raised by the collapse of the Berlin Wall. Removing blindfolds, expressing indignation in the face of injustice, and demonstrating that there is room for hope under the most trying circumstances are all things literature has been good at, even though it has occasionally been mistaken in its targets and defended the indefensible.

The written word has a special responsibility to do these things because it is better at telling the truth than audiovisual media, which are by their nature condemned to skate over the surface of things and are much more constrained in their freedom of expression. The phenomenal sophistication with which news bulletins can nowadays transport us to the epicenter of events on every continent has turned us all into voyeurs and the whole world into one vast theater, or more precisely into a movie. Audiovisual information—so transient, so striking, and so superficial—makes us see history as fiction, distancing us by concealing the causes and context behind the sequence of events that are so vividly portrayed. This condemns us to a state of passive acceptance, moral insensibility, and psychological inertia similar to that inspired by television fiction and other programs whose only purpose is to entertain.

We all like to escape from reality; indeed, that is one of the functions of literature. But making the present unreal, turning actual history into fiction, has the effect of demobilizing citizens, making them feel exempt from civic responsibility, encouraging the conviction that it is beyond anyone's reach to intervene in a history whose screenplay is already written. Along this path we may well slide into a world where there are no citizens, only spectators, a world where, although formal democracy may be preserved, we will be resigned to the kind of lethargy dictatorships aspire to establish.

DISCUSSION QUESTIONS

1. In one sentence, state why writers should write, according to Llosa.

2. Considering the thesis, what does Llosa mean when he distinguishes between "self-righteous illusion" (in the fifth paragraph) and a literature embracing a "larger moral and civic universe"? Does he draw the distinction clearly? Why or why not?

3. Why does the writer consider himself a "dinosaur in trousers"?

4. What does Llosa mean by the claim that audiovisual information "makes us see history as fiction"? Consider the following equation: television = entertainment = poor citizenship = weakened democracy. How—and how well—does Llosa's analysis support this equation?

5. How is comparison and contrast technique used in this essay? Does it help strengthen the analysis? Are all the points of contrast fully developed?

6. Llosa's analysis follows a path from personal experience and commitment to a general statement of belief. Comment on and describe how the writer does this.

WRITING PROJECT

Here are three possibilities:

1. Research biographical information on Llosa, and compose an analytical essay addressing how his life has shaped the analytical focus of "With Pens Drawn."

2. Consider the purposes of literature, and write an analysis of those purposes according to Amy Tan and Mario Vargas Llosa.

3. View the movie *Schindler's List.* The question for analysis is this: How does this film support—or undermine—Llosa's claim that "the written word . . . is better at telling the truth than audiovisual media." (It may help to know that the movie is based on a historical novel by the Australian writer Thomas Keneally. You may certainly include reference to the book in your essay, if you have read it.)

John Updike

John Updike is a well-known novelist who has also written several collections of essays and many reviews. In this essay, which was originally given as a speech at the Massachusetts Institute of Technology, he tackles a large subject—computers—and considers the different meanings computers hold for the scientist and the writer of fiction. As you read this essay, consider the ways in which Updike narrows this subject into a personal consideration and analysis of coming to grips with the meaning of the computer era.

Computer Heaven

When I recently visited the M.I.T. Laboratory for Computer Science, I felt much as when touring an old-fashioned factory: dazzled by the ingenuity of men, and somewhat dwarfed and dehumanized by men's works. But the old-fashioned mechanical factory at least produced a recognizable product, and the actions of its noisy machines were analogous to human actions and somewhat transparent to visual analysis. A computer center offers no such transparency to the layman: inscrutably the wheels spin, the screens flicker, the unseen electricity darts like lightning along is microscopic forked paths, and the product is labelled, again inscrutably, information.

A delicate opacity, as of a very finespun veil, is for the layman the computer's essence. When my word processor malfunctions, there is no part-by-part repair, no soldering or fine-fingered tinkering as with a machine of old, but, rather, the replacement of an entire sealed unit, in a few minutes of the repairperson's time, which is worth, a computerized bill later assures me, one hundred twenty dollars an hour. Today's high-school student, instead of laboriously performing a multiplication, extracting a square root, or resorting to a trigonometric table, presses a few keys of his hand calculator and copies down the answer that within nanoseconds is spelled out for him in numbers ingeniously formed of segments of a subdivided rectangle. The answer is achieved by methods radically different from the mathematics one is taught in elementary school—the little machine proceeds, in fact, in less time than we need to add six and seven, by a succession of narrowing approximations, as the algorithm submits numbers, broken into binary strings of zeroes and ones—offs and ons—to a loop again and again, until two results are identical to a specified number of decimals and thus the answer is reached.

The computer does not think as we do, though in its shining face and user-friendly dialogue it offers itself as anthropomorphic,[10] as a relatively efficient and emotionally undemanding colleague. Our brains, we are told, are made up of long strings of electrical connection, just like *its* brain, and the gap between our intelligence and its is bound to narrow to the point where, and not far in the future, any difference will be in the computer's favor. Already, computers outthink us in every realm that is purely logical; what remains ours is the animal confusion—the primordial mud, as it were—of feeling, intention, and common sense. Common sense is nothing, after all, but accumulated experience, and computers, let us hope, will always be spared the bloody, painful, and inconclusive mess of human experience. Let them be, like the spoiled children of men who have fought their way up from the bottom, exempted from any need for common sense, and let their first and only emotion be bliss, the bliss we glimpse in Bach fugues, in elegant mathematical proofs, and in certain immortal games of chess.

I am here at your celebration, I believe, as a token humanist—a laborer on the arts-and-humanities side of the gulf that, we were assured decades ago by C. P. Snow,[11] divides the realms of knowledge. The gulf is real. Just a few days ago, perhaps you saw, as I did, the item in the Boston *Globe* which revealed that twenty-one percent of adult Americans, according to a telephone poll, think the sun goes around the earth instead of the other way around, and seven more percent answered that they were undecided. Of the seventy-two percent who

[10] a nonhuman article or object assigned human characteristics

[11] C. P. Snow (1905–1980), an English novelist, was also a professional scientist early in his career.

answered that the earth *does* orbit the sun, seventeen percent said that it takes one day, two percent one month, and nine percent could not guess at any time span. Lest we laugh too hard at such ignorance, let me confess that, though I myself follow in the newspaper such dramatic scientific revelations as the existence of gigantic bubbles of vacuity in the universe and of intricate coupling attachments on the surface of the AIDS virus, I have no more first-hand evidence of such truths than medieval men did of the widely publicized details of Heaven and Hell. Most science is over our heads, and we take it on faith. We are no smarter than medieval men, and science tells us that our brains are no bigger than those of Cro-Magnon men and women, of cave people; the contemporary assertions that our world is round and not flat, that it is a planet among others, that our sun is a star among others, in a galaxy among billions of others, that the entire unthinkably vast universe was compressed fifteen billion or so years ago into a point smaller than a pinhead, that for aeons before men appeared on this planet mountains have been rising and sinking and oceans and continents shifting about and extraordinary animal species arising and going extinct, that intricate creatures exist too small for us to see, that lightning and thought are both forms of electricity, that life is combustion, that the heavy elements we are made of all came out of exploding stars, that atomic bombs release energy inherent in all matter—all these assertions we incorporate into our belief system as trustingly as Cro-Magnon man accepted, from his shamans and wizards, such facts as the deity of the moon, the efficacy of cannibalism, and the practical link between real animals and pictures of them painted on cave walls. Scientists are the shamans and wizards, the wonderworkers and myth-givers of today.

So, in the context of our ignorance and wonder, what do we humanists make of the computer? What is our mythic image of it? We feel that it is silent and quick, like a thief. It is not quite to be trusted, since computer error and computer viruses crop up. We notice that the computer plays games with children. Though not as thoroughly domesticated as the radio and telephone, it has undergone a disarming regression in size, having been cozily shrunk since the days of ENIAC from roomfuls of vacuum tubes and wires to models that sit in the lap and fit in the hand. Computers, we know, store information and make it retrievable: somewhere, somehow, they hold our bank balances and those of all the other depositors, right to the penny; they make it possible to check our credit rating in an electronic twinkling; they aid and abet the police in keeping track of traffic tickets and once-elusive scofflaws. Indeed, their capacity for the marshalling of data seriously threatens our privacy, and conjures up the possibility of an omniscient totalitarian state where every citizen is numbered and every hour of his or her activity is coded and filed. Some corporations, we read in the newspaper, oppressively clock their employees' every fingerstroke.

And yet totalitarianism is not really the computer's style. Freedom is the computer's style. In a recent novel from mainland China, written by a veteran of that country's prison camps, I read these sentences: "Technology did not stop at the borders of our guarded country. It broke relentlessly through the steel bars of ideology. It held the world together in its net with invisible electronic waves, looping back inside pieces that had been sundered from the rest." The author is speaking of radios, but the language seems flavored with computerese, and the message—technology overwhelms ideology—is the reverse of that of *Nineteen Eighty-four* and those other dystopian visions wherein information-processing reinforces tyranny. The electronic revolution seems to expand the scale of interrelations beyond the limits at which tyranny can be enforced.

In regard to the iron curtain that exists between the humanities and the sciences, the computer is a skillful double agent. The production and the analysis of texts have been greatly facilitated by the word processor: for instance, programs for the making of indices and concordances have taken much of the laboriousness out of these necessary scholarly tasks. In my own professional field, not only does word processing make the generation of perfectly typed pages almost too easy, but computer-setting has lightened the finicky labor of proofs. Where once the game was to avoid resetting too many lead lines on the Linotype machine, now the digitized text accepts alterations in an electronic shudder that miraculously travels, hyphenations and all, the length of a perfectly justified paragraph.

In sum, the computer makes things light; the lead and paper of my craft are dissolved into electronic weightlessness, ponderous catalogues are reduced to a single magnetized disc, and in computer graphics a visual simulacrum of the world can be conjured onto a screen and experimented upon. Our human lightening of the world is an ancient progressive tendency, with an element of loss. Man, beginning as an animal among animals, hunted and hunting, once shouldered the full dark fatality of nature. Taming other beasts to his use, taming wild plants to a settled agriculture, inventing devices to multiply his own strength and speed, he has gradually put an angelic distance between himself and matter. It is human to regret this leavetaking; our aesthetic sense has earthly roots. Computer-set type, for instance, is faintly ugly and soulless, compared with the minuscule irregularities and tiny sharp bite that metal pressed into the paper. In turn, manuscript inked onto parchment had an organic vitality and color that type only could weakly ape. But we cannot go back, though we can look back; we must swim, like angels, in our weightless element, and grow into the freedom that we have invented.

DISCUSSION QUESTIONS

1. Updike analyzes the computer by considering three basic aspects: how it "thinks," how it affects our daily lives, and its larger impact upon society. List and discuss examples of all three aspects.

2. How would you paraphrase the thesis? Keeping the thesis in mind, how would you characterize the tone?

3. The author devotes a long paragraph to a discussion of science-based facts that are poorly understood by most of us. What purpose does this paragraph serve? Is it relevant to the thesis of the essay?

4. Consider your answer to question 2, and think about the author's response to the computer's impact upon his life as a writer. Is there any ambivalence in this personal reaction to computers? What is the source of this ambivalence?

5. What other essay techniques are employed here?

6. Read again the concluding sentence. Why does Updike use this rather poetic image at the end of his essay, and what does he mean by it?

WRITING PROJECT

Write an essay analyzing the component parts of a tool or instrument you are familiar with. Include in your analysis, if possible, the impact of your chosen instrument upon your life and/or the lives of others.

Alternatively, return to "Electronically Implanted Values," page 44, and write an analysis using comparison and contrast methods to discuss the differing visions of the computer world expressed by Winner and Updike.

5

Critical Review Essays

Critical reviews discuss and evaluate the worth of an unfamiliar subject introduced by the reviewer to the reader. Most of us read critical reviews of movies, books, plays, or concerts in newspapers and magazines. All of us habitually have private reviews scrolling through our minds—we evaluate a teacher's lecture, a pitcher's curveball, the job performance of ourselves and coworkers, and a host of other things. To review is to rethink through an evaluative lens a given experience. We really cannot do otherwise; part of being human is to assign value to our experiences.

The primary difference between our private mental reviews and the kind put to paper in essay form is a matter of structure. We may think and talk casually about the latest John Travolta film or Toni Morrison novel, but putting our thoughts and opinions into essay form means describing and evaluating a work within certain conventions. Most critical reviews examine formal artistic works: books, movies, plays, concerts, art exhibits, and so on. Your opinion of an artistic work or event is only a starting point. Most successful reviews are composed within a general four-part framework—they describe the work, evaluate it, cite evidence, and strive for impartiality. Reviewers put different emphases on description and evaluation, depending upon the work discussed and the preferences of the reviewer. However, good reviewers justify their evaluations; if they do not, they have retreated from the rhetorical demands of the essay back to the starting point of private opinions. All reviews of merit must likewise strive for impartiality; the reviewer should bring an open mind to his or her experiencing of a work.

All reviews describe the subject of the review—the reviewer assumes the reader is unfamiliar with the work. Before tackling the description, however, the reviewer should identify and classify the work for the reader. To identify a novel, for example, cite author, title, publisher, and date of publication. A novel may be classified as a historical novel, mystery, science fiction, or some other form.

Descriptions are written in general terms but serve a specific purpose; your reader must have enough general knowledge of the novel, performance, or other work, to appreciate your evaluation and conclusions. It is important to remember, however, that a description of a novel or play should not be a detailed plot summary; be selective and brief enough to provide a sense of the work without overwhelming readers. For instance, Ann Finkbeiner's review of *The Universe and the Teacup,* on page 120, organizes the book's complex mathematical ideas into a few general themes.

Evaluation and fairness go hand in hand. The evaluation is your impression of how well a work succeeds. Evaluations are weakened if you prejudge a work based on the opinions of others or even your own familiarity with other work by the same author. To evaluate fairly means to bring an open mind to the work, withholding judgment until experiencing the work in its entirety. Sometimes, however, the line between prejudging and open-mindedness is not easy to determine. For example, is Dennis Harvey's response to a particular production of *The Comedy of Errors,* on page 140, overly influenced by his general opinion of Shakespeare's play? Reviewers may certainly use comparison and contrast to help judge a given work through reference to other work by the same person or by different people; the trick is not letting such comparisons blind you to the subject for review in front of your nose.

The reviews included in this chapter span a variety of works, from music to film to books of fiction and nonfiction. Despite the diversity of form and subject matter, you should think about the readings in this chapter in terms of the four-part framework discussed above. What weight is given to description and evaluation? Does the reviewer cite evidence effectively? Is the review fair and impartial, or do the biases of the reviewer adversely color his or her responses and weaken the review? By considering how—and how well—the professional reviews here meet the requirements of a good review, you will gain the knowledge necessary to transform your personal responses of the next film or concert you experience into an interesting, illuminating review of your own. The discussion questions following each reading will help you focus your response to the reviews.

ANN FINKBEINER

Ann Finkbeiner teaches science writing at Johns Hopkins University. This review discusses *The Universe and the Teacup,* a new book on mathematics by science writer K. C. Cole. The other reviews in this chapter cover various aspects of the arts: novels, films, plays, and music. Reviews of nonfiction works of science, history, or other subjects have much in common with arts reviews; science books are also described, evaluated, and approached with an open mind. In this review, notice how Finkbeiner balances description and evaluation in her assessment of *The Universe and the Teacup.*

The Numbers Racket

My innumeracy began early, when my father said that seven minus five is two. But when I imagined a line of numbers—say, 5, 6, 7—the difference between 5 and 7 could be one (6) or two (6 and 7) or three (5, 6 and 7). I never asked anyone about this problem, and I rest assured that I'm demonstrating fundamental ignorance about the concept of number. I have since learned that mathematics describes and connects most scientific truths and much beauty, and we innumerates will never understand the connections. So I should snap up a book subtitled "The Mathematics of Truth and Beauty," right?

The book is "The Universe and the Teacup," by K. C. Cole, a science writer for *The Los Angeles Times.* She explains the relation between mathematics and "the kinds of questions people really think and worry about." There are essays on how our neural wiring can interfere with understanding physical reality and how math helps that understanding; how reality is messy and how math helps us sort it out; the mathematical rules for fair, pleasant human interactions; and mathematical relationships between "causes and effects . . . evidence and proof, truth and beauty."

What the reader learns, in a disjointed way, is wonderful. One is the concept of exponential growth: if at 11 A.M. two bacteria settle in a Coke bottle and double their population every minute, and if at 11:58 the bottle is a quarter full, then at 11:59 it will be half full; and at noon, full. Message: the bacteria wouldn't suspect overpopulation until two minutes before disaster, at best.

Also, changes in quantity can become, at what is called the critical or tipping point, changes in quality. Water cools and cools a degree at a time until it turns into ice. Gravity would make a teacup the size of Jupiter change shape and compress itself into a sphere. Molecules make up proteins, proteins make up cells, and neurons make up brains, but the conglomerations can't be understood in terms of their constituents: a cat has 10^{26} atoms, but adding up the atoms won't tell you a thing about the cat.

The idea I liked best is that math can guide human interactions. To divide up pollution allowances, use the rule the Environmental Protection Agency calls "cap-and-trade": set a cap on the amount allotted and purchase any extra needed amount from those who haven't hit the cap. To divide up marital property, use a system called "adjusted winner": each partner gets 100 points and assigns each piece of property a number of points according to how he or she values it; then each is allotted property equaling 100 points. To set up fair elections, don't use a one-person-one-vote method, with the most votes winning, because that insures nonrepresentation. In a fairer system, voters would rank their first, second and third choices.

The idea Cole likes best is that of the mathematician Emmy Noether: to clear up an inconsistency in Einstein's theory of general relativity, she connected physicists' laws of conservation with the rules of symmetry. If conservation laws are truth, and symmetry is beauty, Coles writes, "truth and beauty are two side of a coin." In a book written for laymen in 1940, the British mathematician G. H. Hardy said, "The mathematician's patterns, like the painter's or poet's, must be beautiful."

Cole writes clearly, simply, and vividly; she so obviously likes mathematics, the reader can't help liking it too. But where Hardy walks readers through the math so we can see the truth and beauty, Cole tells us only the results of math, so we have to take her word for it. Nor is the relation between the math and its results always clear. In fact, much of what is presented as the results of math is actually physics. The mathematical idea that suffers most from these flaws is unfortunately Noether's: symmetry and conservation laws are explained by analogy, and their connection only asserted.

Maybe the math behind these wonderful ideas is so complex that showing it wouldn't help, but I wish Cole had tried. My father, as relaxation, worked out mathematical proofs, and while I had no hope of following them, I could see that their unfolding patterns were silent music. I'm still wishing I could hear it.

DISCUSSION QUESTIONS

1. What is the purpose of the introductory paragraph? What does the paragraph supposedly tell us about Finkbeiner's qualifications as a reviewer of this book? Does your opinion of Finkbeiner's qualifications change by the end of the review?

2. What is the overall topic of *The Universe and the Teacup* as described by Finkbeiner? Does her review effectively discuss and explain this topic?

3. Summarize what Finkbeiner likes about the book, what she doesn't like, and the tone of her general impressions. Is the book worth reading, according to the reviewer?

4. How does Finkbeiner support her evaluation? What reasons and evidence are given backing her judgments?

5. If you were asked to edit this essay, how would you tackle the first and second paragraphs? Would you make any changes? Why?

6. Consider the conclusion. What is the relevance of the conclusion to the body of the essay?

WRITING PROJECT

Write a critical review of a nonfiction book you have read. The book may be about anything from global warming to bicycle repair: the choice is yours. (If you wish, write a critical review of one of your textbooks.) Description and evaluation will be important, but obviously evaluating the artistic intentions in such matters as character development and cinematography will not be pertinent in reviewing a nonfiction work.

In the following two essays, Valerie Miner and Jay Parini take generally contrasting positions about *The Crystal Frontier,* by Mexican novelist Carlos Fuentes, beginning with a disagreement about defining the work as a novel at all. Reviewers of fiction consider theme, character, plot, setting, and structure as the elements that determine the quality and overall effectiveness of a story or novel. Miner and Parini—both novelists themselves—approach the work of Fuentes quite differently, leading them to generally positive (Miner) and negative (Parini) conclusions about the merits of *The Crystal Frontier.* Consider, as you read these reviews, how and why the authors have arrived at their contrasting conclusions.

VALERIE MINER

Borderland

"The Crystal Frontier," a novel in nine stories, explores the deceptively transparent border between Mexico and the United States. Carlos Fuentes' 19th book is amphibian fiction—a form hovering between long and short prose—an acute political novel and a cosmopolitan, intergenerational saga.

Fuentes crisscrosses the international threshold, driving air-conditioned limousines and wading through freezing river water, with members of the extended business and blood clan of Leonardo Barroso, a northern Mexican millionaire. At first the lyrical, suspenseful picaresque pieces seem oddly disparate. The nine stories concern Barroso's family, financial partners, friends of friends, even his almost anonymous factory workers. Their mutual bond on the illusory "Crystal Frontier" is revealed to be as inextricable as it is initially invisible.

Charged by a fierce current between intellect and art, Fuentes writes within a tradition of the novel of ideas. His book deals with Spain's genocide of native peoples, wars between Mexico and the U.S., the murky drug trade, PRI government policies and the shortsightedness of NAFTA and Proposition 187. Crucial to Fuentes' success is an active engagement of readers' imagination, intelligence and moral complicity.

"The Crystal Frontier" is a segmented novel about community and the individual within the community. A protagonist from one story appears in the wings of the next, then leaves for three chapters, only to be strangely pivotal in a later story. Fuentes' characters fade in and out of focus, provoking readers to see characters (and themselves) in complicated, shifting social contexts.

At the novel's center is the ruthless, extravagant life and the sudden, violent death of Barroso, who earns big profits from directing human traffic across the border. The charming, 50-year-old businessman has the ear of influential American tycoons and politicians (Robert Reich makes a cameo appearance as U.S. secretary of labor). While Barroso (whose surname means "muddy" in Spanish) is profligate in entertaining his daughter-in-law/lover, he is also cannily circumspect about public exposure. "Neither he nor the rich politicians ever appeared [in Fortune] . . . because none of their businesses had their names on them; they hid behind the seven veils of multiple partnerships, borrowed names and foundations. . . ."

Barroso controls the fate of strangers and people he hardly knows, like the young Juan Zamora, an employee's son, for whom he arranges a Cornell medical school scholarship. The bright, sensitive young man is confounded (and almost destroyed) by his encounter with American parochialism and entitlement. He is housed with a rich family whose privilege is constantly matched by their ignorance as they awkwardly treat the impoverished Juan as if he were a Spanish aristocrat. "Charlotte never called Juan Zamora Mexican. She was afraid of offending him."

Fuentes mingles generations, classes, geographies; sojourners move from Juarez, Mexico City, Tijuana, Juchitan, Compazas, Nogales and Mexicali to San Diego, El Paso, Los Angeles, Houston, Chicago and New York. They include Barroso's young lover who shops for designer clothes in Texas, a middle-aged housekeeper trying to buy her husband's release from an Illinois jail, a disgruntled taxi driver who harasses tourists, overworked mothers who slog in Barroso's profitable *maquilas,* or border factories.

The title story follows a 26-year-old Lisandro Chavez from Mexico City to New York as a "weekend contract" janitor. Barroso is the entrepreneur. Fly them in; fly them out and avoid American labor costs. Chavez's middle-class family has crashed on the Mexican economic roller coaster of the 1980s and '90s. ". . . I have to join the sacrifice of all, join the sacrificed nation, ill- governed, corrupt, uncaring. I have to forget my illusions, make money, help my parents, do what humiliates me least, an honest job. . . ."

As Chavez washes windows in the atrium of a 40-story Manhattan skyscraper, Audrey, an advertising executive, settles at her desk, hoping to catch up on her work on this quiet Saturday. "Lisandro had carefully cleaned the first window, that of Audrey's office, and as he removed the light film of dust and ash she had begun appearing, distant and misty at first, then gradually closer, approaching without moving, thanks to the increasing clearness of the glass." The two silently communicate with eye contact, gesture and the spelling of words (backward) on the transparent wall between them. "He placed his lips on the glass. She didn't hesitate to do the same. Their lips united through the glass. Both closed their eyes. She didn't open hers for several minutes. When she did, he was no longer there."

While the long narrative of "The Crystal Frontier" is cleverly structured, the stories vary in quality. Fuentes sometimes scrawls prosaically, forfeiting fresh, distilled language to a flat, cerebral statement. Description slips into cliché and stereotypes about Barroso who "girded his loins"; about the slick Chicago lawyer, who "nervously fingered the knot of his Brooks Brothers tie"; and about the WASP aristocrat reading "the number-one book on the New York Times bestseller list, a spy novel that happens to confirm his paranoia about the red menace."

"Rio Grande, Rio Bravo," the passionate final chapter, is a tour de force historical opera, staging Mexican history from early Indian settlement to the contemporary dramas of Barroso and company. One utopian vignette introduces Fuentes' alter ego, the long-haired José

Francisco, who is halted by Mexican and U.S. guards for transporting literature across the border. "The manuscripts began to fly, lifted by the night breeze like paper doves able to fly for themselves. They didn't fall into the river, José Francisco noted; they simply went flying from the bridge into the gringo sky, from the bridge to the Mexican sky, Rios' poem, Cisneros' story, Nericio's essay, Siller's pages, Cortazar's manuscript, Garay's notes, Aguillar Melantzon's diary, Gardea's deserts, Alurista's butterflies, Denis Chavez's thrushes and José Francisco gave a victory shout that forever broke the crystal of the frontier. . . ."

Throughout the novel, Fuentes plays with the tensions between durability and fragility, between exposure and protection, between visual transparency and physical barrier, as well as with other material and metaphorical properties of glass. In one story, Barroso's son imagines himself a Christ-like figure in a crystal coffin; in another, Barroso's politically progressive brother is portrayed as Cassandra screaming in a bell jar. Fuentes finds his crystal frontier in the infrared goggles of the U.S. Border Patrol, in the safety peepholes of urban apartment doors, in Manhattan's high-altitude windows and in the almost transparent body of a rich Chicago dowager. The border weather is always mercurial— baking heat, raging storms—but rarely does a rainbow get refracted on either side of the crystal frontier.

JAY PARINI

Border Crossings

The idea of Carlos Fuentes has always been more appealing than the writer's actual work. Literature needed a Mexican novelist of world-class stature, an articulate cosmopolitan with an insider's grasp of the United States and a profound empathy for his own rich, complex culture. Fuentes—who served as Mexico's Ambassador to France and has taught at numerous Ivy League colleges—was the obvious choice to play this role and, to a degree, he did not disappoint.

Over the past four decades, he has delivered if not the goods, then a lot of goods: more than a dozen novels and story collections, as well as play and countless essays. The range of his fiction is vast, from his first indictment of Mexico's moral decay in "Where the Air Is Clear" to his extraordinary portrait of a failed revolution in "The Death of Artemio Cruz"—his best novel by far—to his charming, best-selling novel about Ambrose Bierce in Mexico, "The Old Gringo." At the center of his corpus lies the massive "Terra Nostra," a verbal landslide that attempts to ground history in language itself, gathering into its swirl the future as well as the past.

"Terra Nostra," for good reasons, has been more admired than read, and this might be said of Fuentes's work in general. With a few notable exceptions, the fiction has often seemed ill formed, tending toward the heavily symbolic, the pretentiously experimental. Yet his work has often had polemical force; indeed, he has been very effective as a fierce spokesman for the oppressed and as a stern critic of the United States' foreign policy in its vexed relations with Mexico, regarding the border between these two countries as a wound that refuses to heal over.

This theme comes to the surface repeatedly in "The Crystal Frontier," a collection of related stories that do not, despite the claims of the subtitle, constitute a novel. What links those stories, however vaguely, is the figure of Don Leonardo Barroso, a Mexican version of Mario Puzo's Godfather. Don Leonardo is a familiar figure, "a powerful man here in the north as well as in the capital." In the movie version of "The Crystal Frontier," he would be played by Anthony Quinn (minus a decade or two). Don Leonardo loves life, especially his own, which is full of expensive houses, fancy cars, cellular phones, first-class airline flights and lots of submissive, adoring women.

One yearns for some revelation about this man that will rescue him, even briefly, from the Hollywood stereotype of a Mexican mogul, but it never happens. For the most part, one only hears people talking about him. They are usually afraid of him, but they envy him as well, and hope for a crumb from his large table.

Among the many who get something from the great man is the aristocratic but only modestly well-off Laborde family from the capital. Don Leonardo is the godfather, quite literally, of their beautiful daughter, Michelina, around whom the first story revolves. When she is ripe for the picking, he invites her to his compound on the northern border, where he plans to marry her off to his introverted son. Not surprisingly, he becomes Michelina's lover as well as her father-in-law, although one is never quite sure what her own motives might be.

The first story ("A Capital Girl") is easily the best, offering a sustained glimpse inside the Barroso family. In an entertaining scene in which Michelina is introduced to the gaggle of rich local women who surround Don Leonardo's wife, Fuentes's sense of satire blossoms:

"Michelina was the only one who didn't have a face lift. She sat down, smiling and amiable, among the 20 or so rich and perfumed women, all of them outfitted on the other side of the border, bejeweled, most with mahogany-tinted locks, some wearing Venetian fantasy glasses, others watery-eyed trying out their contact lenses, but all liberated. And if this girl from the capital wanted to join them, fine. . . . This was the girls' gang, and they drank supersweet liqueurs because they got you stoned faster and were tastier, as if life were an eternal dessert."

Fuentes has been criticized by feminists for his superficial treatment of women, and this problem persists in "The Crystal Frontier," from the subservient women who attend the Barroso family to Miss Amy Dunbar of "Las Amigas," a crotchety Chicago grande dame who, upon learning that her nephew has found her a Mexican maid, remarks, "Mexicans are supposed to be lazy." But the problem of stereotyping extends well beyond the women. Hardly a character in these stories rises above caricature.

There is also a problem with the dialogue, which is stilted and unreal. Perhaps the translator, Alfred MacAdam, is to blame? In "The Bet," for instance, a Spanish tourist unsheathes a quiverful of expletives worth deleting before concluding, "All you are is an insecure man in a macho suit." And in the title story, Don Leonardo meets the United States Secretary of Labor, Robert Reich, who declares, "I'm in favor of everything that contributes to the U.S. economy." Even stick figures have a right to believable dialogue.

On the other hand, there is acute observation in a few of those stories. In "Pain," one learns how a visiting Mexican medical student (whose homosexuality adds to his alienation) might feel in the context of a middle-class American family in upstate New York—although that family is horrendously caricatured. In "Malintzin of the Maquilas," Fuentes takes us, quite believably, inside the world of factory workers on the border, and for once his female characters—Marina, Dinorah, Candelaria and Rosa Lupe—are vivid and original.

Over all, though, "The Crystal Frontier" spins in circles around a woefully unimagined central character. Bits and pieces break off, shimmer, then fade. The author's well-meant political agenda—he condemns elites on both sides of the border who ignore the realities of ordinary lives and would trash what is valuable in Mexico's noble heritage—seems forced in the context of these oblique, uneven stories.

DISCUSSION QUESTIONS

Borderland

1. Does Miner consider the Fuentes work a novel? What evidence does she cite in support of her conclusion?

2. What is the thesis statement of the review and where is it located? Does the review effectively explain and develop the thesis?

3. What is the theme(s) of the novel, according to Miner? Where is theme discussed in the review?

4. Is Miner's discussion of plot and character sufficient enough to provide the reader with an appreciation of the book?

5. Consider the metaphorical concluding sentence. What is the meaning of this sentence? Does it effectively summarize Miner's impressions of *The Crystal Frontier*?

Border Crossings

(Note: As you consider the following questions, as well as the combined questions, keep in mind the differences between the two reviews.)

1. Consider the first three paragraphs of Parini's review. What do these paragraphs reveal about the author's attitude towards Fuentes' work? Has the attempt to put the work in context helped strengthen Parini's conclusions about this work?

2. What is the thesis of Parini's review? Where is it found?

3. What does Parini consider to be the theme of *The Crystal Frontier*? Does the writer think the theme is effectively developed in the book? What evidence does he cite for his opinions about the theme?

4. Parini does not consider *The Crystal Frontier* to be a novel. Why not? Does he support his conclusions about novelistic structure (or the lack thereof)?

5. What does the writer think about the development of character in the book? Why does he think some characters are strongly developed and others are not?

Combined Questions

1. Are Miner and Parini in agreement about any aspect of the book? What do they agree about and why?

2. Consider the quotations from *The Crystal Frontier* used by the reviewers. What do they indicate about what each writer considers most important and vivid about the book?

WRITING PROJECT

Here are some review ideas:

1. Read *The Crystal Frontier* and write your own review of the book.

2. Write a review of a novel or short story of your choice. Your review should evaluate the work and provide enough discussion of the fictional elements to support your opinions and give the reader an appreciation of the book.

DAVID WILD

Music reviews usually focus upon how well music and lyrics, vocals and instrumentals, and musical styles are integrated into a pleasing (or not) whole. *Rolling Stone* reviewer David Wild ponders how successfully the musical components mesh in the latest album by the Spice Girls, *Spiceworld.* In this essay, Wild's attitude and tone toward his subject lead him into a consideration of the whole Spice Girls experience and what it means to us as listeners and consumers.

Spiceworld

On *Spiceworld,* the Spice Girls take us deep into pop's heart of lightness, a happy place filled not with music of good taste but with music that tastes good—at least to a substantial portion of the planet. Listen closely to *Spiceworld* and hear the sparkling if scary sound of a universal pop phenomenon in full bloom. Like it or not, the Spice Girls are 1997's Fab Five, only this time there's nothing but cheeky Cute Ones. Time will tell whether their upcoming feature film will prove to be *A Hard Day's Spice* or a too-Vanilla *Cool as Spice,* but in the short run, it's foolish to bet against them.

To get to the toppermost of the poppermost, the Spice Girls have traded shamelessly—which is not to say shamefully—on their much-vaunted Girl Power, selling themselves as feminist cheesecake. On *Spiceworld,* they've added a sexy new curve to the mix—a learning curve. The act behind the smash "Wannabe" sounded like wanna-be's themselves on some of their hit-and-miss debut effort, *Spice,* an album that made Hanson's weightier *Middle of Nowhere* look like Robert Johnson's *King of the Delta Blues Singers. Spiceworld* is, relatively speaking, a masterful effort; at its best, it reaches creative heights that are downright Bananaramian.

Variety is the spice of *Spiceworld.* The LP seems less a song cycle than a series of aural production numbers. "Spice Up Your Life," the first single, is a global call to arms and legs with a distinct carnival-like flavor and a message of Up With Spice People positivity. "Stop" is a retro, Supremes-like confection that's as undeniable as it is unoriginal. The big finish, "The Lady Is a Vamp," is a vaudevillian track that name-checks Jackie O., Twiggy and Ziggy Marley among those who the Spice Girls apparently feel are "legends built to last."

The Spices and their producers borrow freely from legends of all stripes here. "Never Give Up" quotes Earth, Wind and Fire's "Let's Groove," and "Do It" recalls Madonna's "Express Yourself." The production throughout is a cunning rehash of hip-hop and pop clichés—"Denying," for instance, suggests Olivia Newton John produced by Dr. Dre. That's better certainly, than "Viva Forever," a big ballad that is about as convincing as the Spices' Spanish accents. Then there's the fizzy "Move Over," a nifty cross-promotion of a song that you might have heard first in the Spice Girls' Pepsi-Cola ads.

Of course, one could accuse the group of selling out, but what would they be selling? *Spiceworld* is not an artistic statement for critics to autopsy—it's well-made music to Stairmaster to, and by that standard the whole thing works rather well. One might have expected the Spices to call in hired guns like Babyface, Jimmy Jam and Terry Lewis, or David Foster to make the great pop leap forward, but almost movingly they've stayed with the guys who brought them to the pop prom: producers Richard Stannard, Matt Rowe and Absolute, all of whom collaborated with the Spices on their first album.

Now that they've achieved world domination, a change has come to the Spices. Now that the world is their spice rack, they're no longer the multiracial British girls next door but iconic commodities, mass-marketed objects of desire, and an adorable cottage industry. "Too Much" finds them dealing with the relative troubles of "too much of something" and "too much of nothing," and if we are to believe the lyrics on "Stop," they still need to kick back and have "a human touch" just like mere mortals. In the great pop tradition, their message is this: Have a good time, believe in yourself, and while you're at it, don't forget to buy a lot of Spice Girls merchandise.

Yes, they make Oasis look like visionaries, and, yes, their performance on *Saturday Night Live* was a fleshy train wreck, but nonetheless it's the Spice Girls' world now, and aren't the rest of us really, really lucky to live in it?

DISCUSSION QUESTIONS

1. How does Wild use comparison and contrast to critique the style and themes of the album?

2. What is the writer's tone toward the achievements of *Spiceworld*, and how does he develop that tone?

3. What is the thesis statement? Does the thesis effectively indicate Wild's opinion of the Spice Girls?

4. Does the review give us enough information about all the components of the album and how they are developed? Why or why not?

5. Here is a multiple choice quiz:

   (a) The Spice Girls make good, easily digestible pop music.

   (b) The Spice Girls make serious music.

   (c) The Spice Girls may appear soon as a series of action figures, sold at fast-food restaurants.

   (d) The Spice Girls make derivative music, inspired largely by other pop and rock artists.

Based on the information contained in this review, select any combination of the above, and defend your choice.

6. What does Wild mean by the rhetorical question concluding the review? In the context of this essay, is this an effective conclusion?

WRITING PROJECT

Review a CD or tape of your choice, attending to all of the elements covered in the Wild review. Your choice can be rock, jazz, blues, or some other genre. Musical tastes are very personal, so do not forget to cite evidence in support of your opinions and conclusions.

Brian D. Johnson

Reviewing movies is similar in many ways to reviewing fiction. Character, plot, setting, and theme are important, but in addition, the film reviewer addresses such elements as acting, direction, and cinematography. Steven Spielberg's *Amistad* is a much discussed film tackling the subject of slavery through the context of an actual historical incident. In this review, Brian D. Johnson, film critic for the Canadian magazine *Maclean's*, dissects theme, character, plot, setting, cinematography and the director's intentions in making a movie about such a crucial issue in American history. As you read the review, think about how effectively Johnson has balanced his consideration of the film's elements.

Breaking the Chains

It has been called *Schindler's List* on a slave ship, and although the analogy sounds cynical, there is some truth in it. With *Schindler's List,* director Steven Spielberg abandoned his Boy's Own world of action adventure to direct an Important Movie about the Nazi Holocaust. Now, after taking time out for a return joyride through *Jurassic Park,* the director peels back another painful layer of history to make an Important Movie about slavery, which some consider America's own Holocaust— the original sin that left an indelible stain on the country's democratic legacy. With *Amistad,* Spielberg tries to convey the horror and purge the trauma in one fell swoop. He depicts the atrocities of the infamous Middle Passage—the slaves' voyage from Africa to America—in excruciating detail. But this controversial film, which takes the form of a courtroom drama about white liberals rescuing Africans, also glorifies the redemptive power of American justice with a reverence verging on religious zeal.

There is much that seems admirable about *Amistad,* beginning with the mere existence of the movie, as a polished and prominent memorial to a little-known chapter in American history. One night in 1839, off the coast of Cuba, 53 Africans in the cargo hold of the Spanish slave ship *La Amistad* break free from their shackles, arm themselves and take over the vessel. Killing all but two of their captors, they order the survivors to steer the ship back to Africa. But the Spaniards trick them and plot a meandering course up the eastern seaboard, where the ship is captured by an American naval vessel near Connecticut. The Africans are jailed and, facing Spanish murder charges, become defendants in an extradition hearing.

Abolitionist Theodore Joadson (Morgan Freeman) champions their case, along with a shady young real estate lawyer named Roger Baldwin (Matthew McConaughey) who volunteers to get them acquitted on the grounds that the Africans are "stolen goods." Baldwin sets out to prove that they were not already plantation slaves—and the property of Spain—but had been illegally snatched from an African village. With Baldwin serving as the butt of lawyer jokes, *Amistad* at times takes on a weirdly contemporary ring—asked by an abolitionist if Christ would have hired a lawyer to get him off on technicalities, Baldwin replies: "But Christ lost." The story acquires weight, however, as U.S. President Martin Van Buren (Nigel Hawthorne) intervenes against the Africans to appease the pro-slavery South. The case goes all the way to the Supreme Court. An ex-president John Quincy Adams (Anthony Hopkins), an august eccentric devoted to potted plants, is coaxed out of retirement to deliver an impassioned plea for justice.

Already controversial, *Amistad* has generated a court case of its own. Author Barbara Chase-Riboud has launched a $14-million lawsuit charging that Spielberg's studio, Dreamworks SKG, stole from her 1989 novel, *Echo of Lions* (the studio in turn claims that she stole from the film's official source, the 1953 history *Black Mutiny*). Meanwhile, some members of the black community have expressed dismay that the story was being told by a white film-maker, and from the viewpoint of white characters.

But *Amistad*'s problems are as much dramatic as political. Spielberg deserves credit for casting real West Africans and having them speak authentic tribal languages—this movie is closer to *Dances with Wolves* than *Schindler's List*—but their characters remain undeveloped. Despite a powerful and dignified performance by Djimon Hounsou, the African leader, Cinque, is never allowed to be much more than a presence. It is partly a language problem—the Africans' sparse dialogue is conveyed through subtitles until finally, after an hour, an ex-slave steps forward to translate. But it is also that Spielberg never gets under the skin of his African characters. They remain at a remove, nobly iconic, but inscrutable. Cinque is another incarnation of Spielberg's E.T., an imprisoned alien who just wants to go home.

At one point, Adams asks of the Africans, "What's their story?" explaining that "in the courtroom whoever tells the best story wins." The movie never tells it. Instead, we get harrowing flashbacks to their shipboard ordeal—scenes of the prisoners being whipped, beaten, shot and flung overboard. Even then, even in horrifying tableaus of slaves stacked on top of each other in the ship's hold, naked and starving, Spielberg is much too enamored with the play of light on buffed, glistening bodies.

The whole film, meanwhile, is suffused with a luminous religiosity, from the choir music that floods the sound track to a scene of an ex-slave enlightening an African prisoner about the story of Jesus. In forcing a cozy symmetry between white Christian liberalism and African culture, *Amistad* also makes some wild leaps of faith—as when Adams equates the African invocation of ancestral spirits to America's veneration of presidents such as Washington and Jefferson. But *Amistad*'s main failing is Spielberg's distance from his subject. Trying to dramatize the issue of slavery with appropriate decorum, he offers a history lesson that is absorbing, often shocking, yet emotionally uninvolving.

DISCUSSION QUESTIONS

1. Briefly summarize Johnson's evaluation. Can you find a statement in the review matching your summary?

2. The writer finds the characterizations disappointing, particularly because "Spielberg never gets under the skin of his African characters." Reread the James Baldwin essay in the first chapter. Does the Baldwin selection shed any light on what Johnson means by this statement?

3. Consider the following assertion: The cinematography of the movie sometimes compounds the problem of Spielberg's detached treatment of the African characters. What evidence from Johnson's review would support this assertion and why?

4. How does Johnson use a discussion of plot to further his thesis? Is the plot element sufficiently described and considered? Are the acting performances well enough discussed?

5. Historical films (or novels) should be considered in the context of the events that inspired them. Does the reviewer do an adequate job of filling in the actual historical context?

6. It may sometimes be difficult for reviewers to keep an open mind when evaluating a movie that is by a celebrated director, or is a major media event. Does this review demonstrate open-mindedness? How does or does not it do so?

WRITING PROJECT

See a movie of your choice and write a review. One possibility for this project would be to compare and contrast two films of the same genre, such as two comedies, dramas, or action movies.

DENNIS HARVEY

Theater reviews share some common elements with film reviews: acting, direction, and visual impact are important in both mediums. There are also important differences. A play as presented on stage is most often a direct, word-for-word enactment of a written text, whereas movies usually are not. Directors and actors can bring their own interpretations to the lines of the play, however. In this review of a stage version of William Shakespeare's *The Comedy of Errors,* watch for how reviewer Dennis Harvey responds to what he sees as the interpretation shaping this particular staging of the play.

The Comedy of Errors

There's a muted tenor to Tim Supple's Royal Shakespeare Company production of "The Comedy of Errors." While it displays the proficiency of the R S C's younger, less laureled thesps to good effect, this uncommonly leisurely, often serious-minded version meets some resistance in trying to pull a semi-dark and bilious evening from one of Shakespeare's lightest efforts.

A simple, sunbaked set of slanted planes and manor frontage sets the scene for this mistaken-identity farce. Separated from each other and their parents by shipwrecked circumstance, the two Antipholuses are fated to meet again in Ephesus; little do they suspect their aged father, Aegeon (Christopher Saul), has landed there as well, and faces beheading as an enemy if heavy bail isn't posted.

The traveling-through bachelor Antipholus of Syracuse (Robert Bowman) soon finds himself bewildering Adriana (Sarah C. Cameron), whose husband Antipholus (Simon Coates) has lately exasperated her patience. The latter, meanwhile, is incensed by the behavior of both wife and two merchants (Andy Williams, Gary Oliver) to whom he's indebted as words, actions and payments get confused between the look-alike sibs. Long-parted twin servants Dromios (Dan Milne, Eric

Mallett) get caught in the middle, and become the frequent brunt of everyone's frustration.

These last bits are neatly worked out in Supple's clever blocking.[12] But this "Comedy" is less interested in slapstick than in the work's undertow of spousal rage, offended reputation and legal peril. It's a stretch, since such elements remain rather silly despite best-shot efforts at ominous weight.

Supple alternates antic, brisk scenes with ones whose rhythm slows to a mannered attenuation. It's an interesting approach that may ultimately be wasted on a play so determinedly, joyfully frivolous. Typical is the long coda in which the Abbess Emilia (vinegary Ursula Jones) welcomes nearly every character into her sanctuary, one by one. The shocked tentativeness they exhibit toward reconciliation is touching but eats up more stage time than Shakespeare can possibly have had in mind.

The result is a show more admirable than funny or engrossing. It's kept afloat by nicely honed lead performances: Bowman gets both melancholic and comic mileage from his Antipholous (despite an over-indulged gurgling laugh), balanced by Coates' more hotheaded sib; the two Dromios are well matched in skinhead cheekiness. Cameron's wife starts out too harpyish, then gains strength as her anger turns to desperation. Thusita Jayasundera makes a smart, modern impression as Luciana.

Subsidiary roles are generally well turned. Three live musicians stay within view stage-right, playing the exotic instruments required by Adrian Lee's Middle-Eastern inflected score.

This modest RSC roadshow is technically sleek within its chosen, rather visually unexciting limits. But "Comedy" seems more burdened than freshened by Supple's dogged search for Meaning.

[12] the positioning of actors on the stage

DISCUSSION QUESTIONS

1. What problems does Harvey see with this interpretation of the play? What evidence does he cite in support of his criticisms?

2. How does Harvey's own interpretation of *The Comedy of Errors* influence his opinion of this production? Has he prejudged the production and therefore failed to approach the play with an open mind?

3. Does the reviewer give the reader enough information about the acting and characters, the visual effect, and the plot?

4. What purpose do the introductory paragraph and the conclusion serve in the structure of this review?

5. Theater reviewers should be aware of how the staging of a play—when and how the actors physically interact with one another—enhances or detracts from the action. Comment on how this review takes staging into consideration.

6. Many reviews use comparison and contrast to help evaluate a work by considering other work by the same or different artists, authors, actors, or directors. Does Harvey do this? Would more or better use of comparison and contrast strengthen this review?

WRITING PROJECT

See a play of your choice and write a review. The play you select could be anything from a school play to a professional production by a theater group in your city. If possible, read the play first and use your response to the author's work in your review.

6

Definition Essays

> Alice felt dreadfully puzzled. The Hatter's remark seemed to her to have no sort of meaning in it, and yet it was certainly English.

This passage from Lewis Carroll's *Alice's Adventures in Wonderland* illustrates a key feature in Alice's predicament: even if she carried a bagful of dictionaries down the rabbit hole, she would still have trouble making sense of Wonderland, where things often mean something quite different to the supposedly English-speaking inhabitants. The adventures of Alice dramatize how dependent we all are on definitions to bestow the meanings of words, to provide the verbal keys that allow us to think, feel, and act upon our shared language.

Dictionary definitions usefully tell us the standard, commonly agreed upon basic meaning of a word. In essay writing, though, we will be dealing with extended definitions, which discuss the fuller meaning of an idea, an emotion, a value, or a place by drawing boundaries around the term and discussing what it is and also what it is not. For instance, in Anna Quindlen's "The Good Guys" (page 154), she defines the "good guys" of the title primarily by the outrageous behavior of some young men decidedly unqualified for that nod of approval. The challenge for the writer of extended definitions is to draw clear, specific boundaries around vague, complex, or disputed terms. Quindlen's essay should give you an appreciation for the difficulties involved in squeezing large ideas in small boxes. The rewards are worth it, however; writing successful extended definitions is a good way to bring your ideas to life.

Distinguishing between what something is and is not is one part of drawing boundary lines, but there are other challenges involved. Many terms have multiple meanings or meanings that evolve from a commonly agreed upon base to encompass the personal point of view of the writer. Extended definitions may tackle an idea that means different things to different people, such as socialism or courage. Extended definitions may also describe words with highly charged personal meanings for the writer, for example, Chicago. Personal definitions are vital to Saul Bellow's combined techniques essay (page 249). Bellow's "Chicago" mixes the present with private and public history to arrive at a personal, idiosyncratic portrait beyond the scope of any dictionary.

Bellow's essay, the essays in this chapter, and the extended definition essays you will write employ other essay techniques to enhance and complement their definitions. Don't be surprised to find comparison and contrast, narrative and descriptive, critical analysis, or other essay techniques appearing in extended definition writing. In fact, as the readings in this chapter will show, employing other essay techniques is vital to fleshing out an extended definition. Conversely, you will find definitions, implicit or explicit, occurring in readings throughout this text. For example, in Jane Smiley's story "Confess, Early and Often" (page 10), the meaning and consequences of confession loom over her childhood memories like an impending avalanche. For a look at how you have already written an essay strongly influenced by definition writing, review the writing project after "Thumb and Thumber," on page 53.

The choice of what other techniques to use will be influenced by the kind of definition essay you are writing. If Smiley's primary concern had been to define the meaning of confession to her, she could have shaped her definition by narrating the same childhood incident. If writing an extended definition of your hometown—as Bellow does—you would probably rely largely on description and comparison and contrast. Similarly, if attempting a definition of capitalism, you would contrast it to socialism or communism. An argumentative essay proposing the superior merits of capitalism would, of course, also need to carefully define the competing systems.

Most of us tend to think of finding and using definitions as a rather dry business; looking a word up in the dictionary seems about as exciting as finding the number of a plumber in the phone book. However, what if you discover that the term "plumbers" was the name given to government employees busily burglarizing various offices in the Nixon administration? As the readings in this chapter will suggest, composing extended definition essays embroils us in controversies, adventures, and challenging points of view. The discussion questions following the readings will examine what marks these widely varying pieces as extended definition essays, and how they integrate definition with other essay strategies.

Vince Lopez

Definition essays can address slang terms, such as "schmooze." What is schmooze? In this selection, Generation X representative Vince Lopez elaborates upon dictionary definition of this term, which is displayed up front in the title of the essay. Lopez builds his definition around a proposed lifestyle for his generation. Does the author really mean to suggest how to live well? As you read this selection and consider this question, think about how this particular slang term shapes and colors tone.

Schmooze

n. 1) idle talk, chat. 2) a lifestyle for twentysomethings

As a culture, we've been through free love, be love, be-ins, sit-ins, situation comedies, comedic presidencies, bad television, good television, punk, rock, grunge, grunge punk rock, and now here were are, thrust halfway through the 1990s, the age where nothing really happens, really.

The 0's are coming up in only four years, and what do we have to show for it? Informercials (albeit a fantastic tradition to leave for our children) and yet another decade of nasty golfing outfits. And I've found that a lot of Gen X is pretty tired of the whole "X" scene altogether. The slacker angle has been overworked, the angst thing is very draining on the karmic energy and the slobbering hordes of product marketers are beginning to ignore us. X is dead. Long live X.

Still, the other options seem so daunting. Real jobs, real careers? Yeah, right. Who wants a career if he can live like a rock star/celebrity/tortured artist? Seem impossible? Well, welcome to the schmooze lifestyle. In a survey of kids ages 12-26, 99 percent said "what was the question again?" and the other 1 percent found that living schmooze was the career of choice.

But how does one live schmooze? And what the hell is schmooze, anyway?

Martinis and Sunglasses

Remember seething anger? Remember self-loathing and resentment, the bitter "beer and pretzels" mystique that used to fill your every day with (relative) joy? Well ditch it all, baby. Welcome to martinis, sunglasses, Monte Cristo sandwiches and arrogant sarcasm. Living schmooze is like being in a Fellini film, driving in a Bing Crosby and Bob Hope road movie and drinking a smooth glass of Ovaltine rolled into one.

The Schmooze Philosophy

Well, technically, it's not a philosophy—denoting something as a "philosophy" somehow infers there's been some heavy thought put into it. We know what a drag that can be. No, schmooze is just a rebellion against rebellion, the acceptance of one's current self as a crashing bore and the struggle to restructure one's life to imitate the twisted values of literature, television, movies, art and other expendable media.

What *about* it? The best part of schmooze is that it embraces both ends of the spectrum. Deep and lengthy discussions of literature and style do take up large amounts of time, so freeing oneself from the heavy burden of having to exchange physical and/or mental labor for paper currency can help release quite a bit of stress. But, suppose you do need some sort of reliable income to pay for clothing, trips to the Bahamas, or even food and shelter? Possible solutions? Join a band. No, really. Become an artist. Or best of all, become a critic (in the media of your choice). But if it is your proclivity, go ahead and work for that back-fracturing conglomerate—the coffee's much better than anything you could whip up at home. And free doughnuts on Wednesdays!! There is no selling out in schmooze, unless of course you stop dressing well or start missing the major golf tournaments.

Second-Hand Shopping

If you don't have a job, you won't have the money to buy new clothes, and of course utilizing the five-finger discount at your parent's house only lasts for the back half of the closet where all the choice smoking jackets, penny loafers, Izod polos and Chanel party dresses are hidden. This means you have no other option but to shop second-hand. But sisters and brothers, throw away the baggy corduroys, thrust the baby doll dresses from your sight—for we have seen the future, and it is . . . surprisingly tidy! Checked shirts? Fantastic. A nice pair of slacks? A staple. Once you start to schmooze, you'll be drawn to the right clothing items just like dysfunctional families to a King's Table.

Sports? Yes, Sports

Football and basketball are definitely not schmooze, but baseball seems like it might fit right in. Baseball has a cool, mellow pace, and it's perfect for those days when you want to bring out the cigars and martinis and just relax. Plus, you can get a damn fine Caesar salad at Johnny Love's in Candlestick, and the frozen espressos aren't half bad, either. But still, as an actual game it doesn't precisely fit the bill (too much running, hitting, pitching, activity, blah blah blah). Golf, however, has everything in a neat package—atrocious (but slightly schmoozy) outfits, pomposity, loads of moola and almost no physical exertion whatsoever. You cannot, however, get a damn fine Caesar from Johnny Love's at a golf tournament.

This is a tough one. Coffee workers have the pious and acidic behavior embraced by schmooze, but yet the atmosphere is so, so "disgruntled miscreants/yuppie royalty"-ish. How to solve the situation? Well, go to the coffeehouses, but put yourself apart from the crowd by A) Actually avoiding eye contact. Once you get rid of the whole "see/be seen/cruise" atmosphere involved with the coffee thing, you'll notice that you can actually use coffee establishments for studying, reading or writing out endless streams of song titles to songs you'll never write (a favorite hobby of mine). B) Take in cereal and milk (I prefer corn flakes, but any of the Cap N' Crunch flavorites will do fine). I mean, why go for good coffee if you can't enjoy it with a complete and balanced breakfast? Take the paper, some slippers and the fox terrier and you're set!

The Transportation Issue

Obviously the bus (aka the "shame train," or during the winter, the "plague bus") isn't going to cut it in a world of schmooze. Of course, not having a job begs the question "how can I afford a car?" The solution is simple—why have a crappy new car when you can get a crappy, but much nicer looking, old car? So maybe they don't run so good. But there's a bright side: "Hey, can you drive to the city?" "Nope, my car won't make it there." See? No more having to chauffeur your friends around. And with gas prices skyrocketing, who needs a car that actually moves, anyway?

One final note: I am not schmooze. I'm punk/grunge/angst with a tasty slice of sellout. Thank you for your time.

DISCUSSION QUESTIONS

1. In his introductory paragraph, Lopez calls the 1990s "the age where nothing really happens, really." What does he mean by this? Who is the intended audience?

2. Where is the thesis statement? Does the thesis statement provide a clear idea of the nature of schmooze?

3. The writer fleshes out his definition through prescriptive anecdote: what to eat, wear, and write at the coffee shop. Does this strategy build sufficiently upon the definition of schmooze in the thesis to give us a fuller understanding of the term?

4. "There is no selling out in schmooze, unless of course you stop dressing well or start missing the major golf tournaments." What is the tone here? How does the tone affect your reaction to Lopez's definition and suggested way of life?

5. Consider the conclusion. Most conclusions reinforce and summarize the body of the essay. How is this one different? Does the conclusion work well in the context of this essay?

6. Reread Russell Baker's "Have You Noticed?" on page 40. Does this essay resemble Baker's in any way?

WRITING PROJECT

Build a definition essay around a slang or unusual term. Your essay may be satirical or more serious, depending on the term you select. For example, a definition of a relatively new term such as *ethnic cleansing* should suggest a dramatically different approach than Lopez chooses for schmooze.

CHARLES DICKENS

Charles Dickens (1812–1870) was a major nineteenth-century English novelist. In 1842 he visited the United States, compiling his impressions of the young country in *American Notes*. Throughout his life Dickens was concerned with questions of social justice and political virtue, and in this excerpt from *American Notes* he turns his sense of moral outrage to the task of defining the American congressman. Tone and attitude are crucial to shaping this exercise in extended definition; as you read this short essay, consider how Dickens effectively wields attitude to carve a definition of political character.

Congressmen

Did I see in this public body an assemblage of men, bound together in the sacred names of Liberty, and Freedom, and so asserting the chaste dignity of those twin goddesses, in all their discussions, as to exalt at once the Eternal Principles to which their names are given, and their own character and the character of their countrymen, in the admiring eyes of the whole world?

I saw in them, the wheels that move the meanest perversion of virtuous Political Machinery that the worst tools ever wrought. Despicable trickery at elections; under-handed tamperings with public officers; cowardly attacks upon opponents, with scurrilous newspapers for shields, and hired pens for daggers; shameful trucklings to mercenary knaves, whose claim to be considered, is, that every day and week they sow new crops of ruin with their venal types, which are the dragon's teeth of yore, in everything but sharpness; aidings and abettings of every bad inclination in the popular mind, and artful suppressions of all its good influences: such things as these, and in a word, Dishonest Faction in its most depraved and most unblushing form, stared out from every corner of the crowded hall.

Did I see among them, the intelligence and refinement: the true, honest, patriotic heart of America? Here and there, were drops of its blood and life, but they scarcely coloured the stream of desperate adventurers which sets that way for profit and for pay. It is the game of these men, and of their profligate organs, to make the strife of politics so fierce and brutal, and so destructive of all self-respect in worthy men, that sensitive and delicate-minded persons shall be kept aloof, and they, and such as they, be left to battle out their selfish views unchecked. And thus this lowest of all scrambling fights goes on, and they who in other countries would, from their intelligence and station, most aspire to make the laws, do here recoil the farthest from that degradation.

That there are, among the representatives of the people in both Houses, and among all parties, some men of high character and great abilities, I need not say. The foremost among these politicians who are known in Europe, have been already described, and I see no reason to depart from the rule I have laid down for my guidance, of abstaining from all mention of individuals. It will be sufficient to add, that to the most favourable accounts that have been written of them, I more than fully and most heartily subscribe; and that personal intercourse and free communication have bred within me, not the result predicted in the very doubtful proverb, but increased admiration and respect. They are striking men to look at, hard to deceive, prompt to act, lions in energy, Crichtons[13] in varied accomplishments, Indians in fire of eye and gesture, Americans in strong and generous impulse; and they as well represent the honour and wisdom of their country at home, as the distinguished gentleman who is now its Minister at the British Court sustains its highest character abroad.

[13] refers to James Crichton (1560–1582), a Scottish scholar and adventurer called "The Admirable Crichton"

DISCUSSION QUESTIONS

1. Nineteenth-century syntax was often more convoluted than is usual in modern usage. Acting as an editor, rephrase the rhetorical question

comprised by the opening paragraph, making it more easily understandable to a modern reader.

2. Look up definitions for the following words: *yore, faction, station,* and *profligate.* After you have rendered these terms into modern usage, consider their meaning. Might any of these ideas be considered of lesser importance or different meaning today?

3. Discuss the negative characteristics Dickens lists in his definition of the U.S. Congress. Why is he so critical of this institution?

4. In the concluding paragraph, Dickens abruptly changes course, celebrating men of "high character and great abilities." Why does he do this? What effect does this sudden celebration of political virtue in (some) representatives have upon his harsh criticisms in the preceding paragraphs?

5. What is Dickens's definitional portrait of a U.S. Congressman? Is there anything confusing or uncertain about this definition?

6. Does this brief portrait of American politicians lack some common elements of essay writing that would make it more persuasive? If so, what?

WRITING PROJECT

Most people have ideas about politics and politicians. Write a definition essay about the ideal politician, contrasting this definition, if possible, with the strengths and shortcomings of a real political figure.

ANNA QUINDLEN

At the time this essay was written, Anna Quindlen was a newspaper columnist; she is currently a novelist. In this short essay she uses two notorious incidents of a few years ago as examples of predatory young male conduct. Quindlen scrutinizes conflicting social attitudes and expectations as a means of thinking about, and defining, "good guys" and "bad guys." In the discussion questions, you will be asked to analyze Quindlen's approach to defining a certain group of people through their actions.

The Good Guys

Before another television talk show hands out money to chat with the members of the Spur Posse, the low-life band of high school jocks who measured their own self-worth in terms of how many meaningless sexual encounters they'd had, the people who produce and host the shows should acknowledge something about their guests.

And that is that as surely as if they were paying white supremacists to come on and spew garbage about black people, they are enriching those who happily present the worst and most distorted view of an entire class of human beings. And I don't mean women, although most teenaged members of this sexual street gang treated girls like garbage while they were passing them around and trashing them afterwards.

The Posse members reflect a demeaning and insulting view of men, and the good guys, wherever they are, should rise up and say that that view stinks.

The ethos of this bunch of boys from a California suburb is part of a continuum that has played itself out over the last few months. Their cousins, metaphorically speaking, were the jocks of Glen Ridge, N.J., who were accused of using, among other things, a baseball bat on a retarded neighbor in a group sexual assault in the basement of a tidy family home.

Three of these guys were convicted, but not before a theme emerged clearly in their defense: "boys will be boys," according to one attorney. It is the same tone that suffuses the Lakewood story, and it is this: that young men are incapable of bringing either responsibility or humanity to their sexual activity.

Part of the defense in the Glen Ridge case, and part of the discussion of the Spur Posse, is that the sexual revolution made a lot of this happen, aided and abetted by MTV and Hollywood violence. And probably the culture has made it more open, more egregious.

But at base it all feels like something at least as old as I am. The girls get called sluts. And the boys get flown first class to some big city to brag on national television, the electronic-age version of standing around in the locker room talking about what a pig she was. People always blame the girl; she could have said no. A monosyllable, but conventional wisdom has always said that boys can't manage it.

Interestingly enough, the "boys will be boys" ethos has also been a big part of the debate over gay people in the military. Although women are several times more likely to be discharged from the service because of sexual orientation, there has been nary a word about barracks full of women soldiers terrified of lesbian sneak attacks.

Virtually all the fear fantasies have focused on gay men who will not be able to keep their hands off straight ones, despite the fact that gay men have usually done just that. That's because straight men have been projecting onto gay ones a stereotype that is demeaning to both: that male sexuality is by nature predatory.

But don't ever forget that in the Glen Ridge case, there were boys who walked away from that basement because they thought what was happening was wrong. Don't forget that what happened in Lakewood, the conspicuous consumption of other people, was less a matter of sex than a cross between a track meet and a slave auction.

Some of the mothers of Spur Posse members, who used their evanescent high school jock popularity to entice and then discard girls, were crushed to hear that their sons had been so cold in their attitude toward women. And no wonder. Sex aside, this was basically a question of whether your kids had grown up to be cruel or kind.

But one blowhard father bragged, "Nothing my boy did was anything that any red-blooded American boy wouldn't do at this age." That, thankfully, is not true. Boys may have sex earlier now, with more impunity, with a more casual commitment, in a cultural environment saturated with soft porn and cinematic violence.

But that doesn't mean that all of them, or even most of them, use sexual encounters, as the boys in Lakewood and Glen Ridge did, for cruelty and intentional degradation. The good guys should stand up and say that. The talk shows should put them on and stop handing out payoffs to a bunch of losers who give all men a bad name. Testosterone does not have to be toxic.

DISCUSSION QUESTIONS

1. What is the author's definition of "bad guys," and what is the nature of the evidence used for this definition?

2. What is the definition of "good guys"? Do you think they are adequately defined? Why or why not?

3. Are there analytical components to this essay? What are they?

4. Could this essay be written as a comparison and contrast study? How would you go about doing that?

5. Why has Quindlen entitled her essay "The Good Guys" when the focus is mostly on their opposite numbers?

6. What is the tone in the essay? What effect does it have on the author's position?

7. Review Deborah Blum's compare and contrast essay on page 67. What would Blum say about Quindlen's concluding sentence?

WRITING PROJECT

Think about opposites. Write an extended definition that defines through considering the differences that are ordinarily thought of as antonyms: love and hate, idealism and cynicism, and so forth. Use specific examples and also employ comparison and contrast or other essay strategies that seem appropriate.

BAILEY WHITE

Georgia native Bailey White is an essayist who explores a variety of places, emotions, and ideas through her own experience and history. In this essay, she delves into the world of spelunkers, who squeeze and shimmy through pitch-black, coffin-sized tunnels deep underground, for fun. This essay paints a vital extended definition portrait of spelunking. The discussion questions will consider how White draws her definitional picture.

Spelunking in Middle Age

There I went, crawling on my hands and knees, the light strapped to my forehead illuminating the rump of the spelunker in front of me. At times the tunnel walls were so tight we had to turn sideways and shove ourselves through by paddling against the ground with our feet. At other times the ceiling was so low we had to lie flat on our bellies and scoot along, our chins rooting up the damp sand. The stale air shifted from one underground room to another through this tunnel, creating a cool, fetid wind that smelled like damp rocks and bat guano.

I got into this cave by spiraling my way down a rocky natural chimney, my back braced against one side, my feet scrambling to find little niches on the opposite side, my hands grappling against the rough rocks. The chimney ended in the domed ceiling of the first room, and when there was nothing but open air below me, I just turned loose and dropped the five feet to the floor of the cave.

Now, on this hour's crawl through a tunnel to another room where I was told we would see "formations," I kept telling myself how to breathe: in and out, in and out. I kept smelling the bat guano and wondering two things: How am I going to get out of this cave? and Why did I come in? Could it be the same impulse that made me, last month, ride a mule to the bottom of the Grand Canyon, and yesterday send off an order form requesting more information on rafting down the Colorado? Could it be a middle-aged urge to overcome lifelong fears and dreads while we still have the strength? Could it be a desire to check out many ways of dying so that when the time finally comes we can say, "Oh yes, I remember this one," and enjoy the meager comfort of familiarity?

We stopped. There was some muffled conversation up ahead of me. The tunnel had become so constricted that the first man could not get through. He began to dig out the sand with his hands. I squirmed into a sitting position, my shoulders hunched over, the back of my head pressed against the tope of the tunnel. I pulled my handkerchief over my nose to filter the bat smell, and imagined the death I might have had in the Grand Canyon. The fatal slip, maybe just a moment of scrambling and heaving as my white mule tried to regain her foothold, and then the free fall through the clear air, the sky domed above us with the sun at its peak, the smell of sage and fresh air, and then instant death on the most beautiful rocks in the world. Here, underground, death would be gray and damp, without air or light, slow and strangling, with the little malevolent faces of the bats looking on and the smell of their excrement in my last gasp.

I heard the steady *scritch scritch* of digging, then some scraping sounds and grunts and groans. Finally the word was passed down: the space was too tight. We had to turn around. Scooching and slithering, we dragged ourselves back through the tunnel, back through the big room where the bats were hibernating, back down a hallway, to the room with the chimney. I stood underneath it and peered up. But there was a rocky outcropping over the cave entrance, so I couldn't see the sky.

One spelunker after another climbed up the chimney and out. Then it was my turn. Telling myself how to breath—in and out—I hauled myself into the chimney. One foot found a step, and I shoved up, then one hand found a higher grip, and I dragged myself up a little farther. As slow and steady as a snake swallowing a rat, I rose up the chimney and out into the late afternoon of a drizzly fall day. I stood for a minute on the slope of the sinkhole and looked around at the dripping trees, their leaves just beginning to turn, and the dazzling green of the ferns and moss. I hardly knew the three spelunkers who brought me here, but looking at their muddy faces now as they gathered up their gear and pulled of their helmets, I felt like they were my oldest and dearest friends.

We walked through the woods to our cars, and I loved every step I took. I loved the tree limbs fallen across the road. I loved the red clay. I loved the little white farmhouse in the distance. I loved the chickens on their roost. I loved the row of collard greens straggling across the garden. I loved the teenaged boys who stopped their pickup truck and asked, "Did y'all go down in that cave?"

"Yes," I told them, "and we came out."

We stood around saying good-bye for a while before we got into our cars. One of the spelunkers began talking about another cave in another county. There is a tight crawl through a tunnel, he said, but then a room with beautiful formations, the most amazing boulders, and transparent stalactites.

An old man came out of the little white farmhouse across the road, sat down in a chair on the porch, folded his hands over his belly, and looked out at the rain. He began to rock. I loved that old man.

"Can I come too?" I asked.

DISCUSSION QUESTIONS

1. Discuss the series of questions in the third paragraph, in which White speculates on her motivations. Does the tone she uses in the fourth paragraph to imagine death by falling differ from her imagined death by spelunking?

2. How would you characterize the descriptive imagery of the spelunking passages? Considering the tone of these passages, what would you say is White's apparent attitude toward this activity through the first page of the essay?

3. There is a sharp shift in tone on the final page. How do you account for this? Does it suggest any other motivations for spelunking than those listed earlier in the essay?

4. Do you have a fuller appreciation of what spelunking is after reading this piece? Why or why not?

5. What other essay techniques does the author employ in this essay? Are they effective?

6. Look up the definition for spelunking in a dictionary. Extended definition essays elaborate and embroider upon strict dictionary definitions in various ways. With this in mind, what is the significance of White's title?

WRITING PROJECT

Write an extended definition of an activity. It may be a hobby, sport, or other pursuit. You may employ narrative-descriptive, comparison and contrast, or other techniques. Your essay should convey what your activity is and suggest your attitude toward it.

MICHAEL DORRIS

The educator and author Michael Dorris (1945–1997) wrote *The Broken Cord,* which is about his adopted son, Abel, a victim of fetal alcohol syndrome. In this essay he discusses fetal alcohol syndrome (and other addictions) beginning with reference to Abel, who died soon after publication of this essay. This piece explores a serious social problem through the vehicle of extended definition. Definition essays tackling social problems can be particularly effective by identifying the problem, heightening awareness of it, and sketching out possible solutions. As you read this essay, think about how Dorris uses extended definition to suggest the boundaries of an important problem.

Fetal Alcohol Syndrome:
A National Perspective

At the time I adopted my oldest son, Abel, in 1971, I knew that his birth mother had been a heavy drinker, but even the medical textbooks in those days stated that exposure to alcohol could not damage a developing fetus. I knew that Abel had been born small and premature, had "failed to thrive," and was an initially slow learner, but for ten years as a single parent I convinced myself that nurture, a stimulating environment, and love could open up life to my little boy.

It wasn't true. At the University of Washington and elsewhere, biochemists and psychologists now confirm that for some women even moderate doses of prenatal exposure to alcohol can permanently stunt a human being's potential. According to the U.S. surgeon general, *no* level of ethanol is guaranteed to be "safe."

My grown son has a full range of physical disorders: seizures; curvature of the spine; poor coordination, sight, and hearing. But his most disabling legacy has to do with the impaired ability to reason. Fetal alcohol syndrome (FAS) victims are known for their poor judgment, their impulsiveness, their persistent confusions over handling money, telling time, and in distinguishing right from wrong.

Since the publication of *The Broken Cord* last August, I have received an outpouring of wrenching letters from literally hundreds of readers— rural and urban, religious and agnostic, of all ethnic and economic backgrounds—who share experiences of heartache, grief, and frustration uncannily identical to my wife's and mine. Their sons, daughters, or grandchildren have been repeatedly misdiagnosed with the same amorphous labels: retarded, sociopathic, attention-deficit, unteachable troublemakers.

A majority of full-blown FAS victims are adopted or in state care, but many children who are less drastically impaired (i.e., with fetal alcohol effect [FAE] remain with their natural parents. Depending on the term of pregnancy in which the harmful drinking occurred, these individuals may look perfectly healthy and test in the normal range for intelligence, yet by early adolescence they show unmistakable signs of comprehension problems or uncontrollable rage. It is currently estimated that in the United States some eight thousand babies are born annually with full FAS and another sixty-five thousand with a degree of FAE. Nothing will ever restore them to the people they might otherwise have been.

And it seems that's far less than the half of it. An additional three hundred thousand babies prenatally bombarded with illegal drugs will be born in this country in 1990. Recent studies indicate that crack cocaine, if smoked during pregnancy, causes learning deficits in offspring similar to those caused by alcohol. The "first generation" of children from the 1980s' crack epidemic is about to enter public school, and these children are consistently described as "remorseless," "without a conscience," and passive, apparently lacking that essential empathy, that motivation toward cooperation, upon which a peaceful and harmonious classroom—and society—so depends.

No curriculum or training has so far proven to be completely effective for people with this totally preventable affliction, and a Los Angeles pilot education project costs taxpayers $15,000 a year per pupil. However, the price of doing nothing, of ignoring the issue, is beyond measure.

Nothing like crack—a baby shower gift of choice in certain populations because it is reputed to speed and ease labor—has occurred before. According to one survey, upwards of 11 percent of all U.S. infants in 1988 tested positive for cocaine or alcohol the first time their blood was drawn. A New York City Health Department official estimated that births to drug-abusing mothers had increased there by about 3,000 percent in the past ten years.

Why? Some explanations have to do with a paucity of available services and support. Too many fathers regard their baby's health as solely their partner's concern. Only one residential treatment program specifically for chemically dependent pregnant women exists in New York City, where the State Assembly Committee on Alcoholism and Drug Abuse estimates that "twelve thousand babies will be born addicted . . . in 1989, and the number of children in foster care has doubled in two years from twenty-seven thousand in 1987 to more than fifty thousand today, mainly because of parental drug abuse." The system has broken down. Sixteen percent of all American mothers have had insufficient prenatal medical attention—increasing to 33 percent for unmarried or teenage mothers, 30 percent for Hispanic women, and 27 percent for black women.

At last, thanks to a 1989 act of Congress, liquor bottle labels must include a warning, and signs posted in many bars proclaim the hazards of alcohol to unborn children. But what happens when public education doesn't work as a deterrent, when a pregnant woman herself is a victim of FAS or prenatal crack and therefore cannot understand the long-term disastrous consequences for the life of another resulting from what she drinks or inhales? It isn't that these women don't love the *idea* of their babies. They just can't foresee the cruel realities.

The conflict of competing rights—of protecting immediate civil liberty versus avoiding future civil strife—is incredibly complex, with no unambiguously right or easy answers, but as a nation it's unconscionable to delay the debate. If we close our eyes we condemn children not yet even conceived to existences of sorrow and deprivation governed by prison, victimization, and premature death.

My wife and I think of these tragedies as we wait for our son to have brain surgery that may reduce the intensity of his seizures, though not eliminate them. At twenty-two, despite all of our efforts and his best intentions, he remains forever unable to live independently, to manage a paycheck, or to follow the plot of a TV sitcom, and we worry about the very fabric of society when hundreds of thousands of others with problems similar to his or worse become teenagers, become adults, beyond the year 2000.

DISCUSSION QUESTIONS

1. What two related problems is Dorris defining and discussing? Does his reference to his son's suffering enhance your understanding of FAS? How?

2. Discuss the use of the (somewhat dated) statistics. What purpose do they serve?

3. List the ideas and problems Dorris raises in the ninth paragraph,. Do you think every issue raised is given adequate attention? Why or why not? If not, how would you change the paragraph?

4. FAS and related addictions could be defined in biological terms or in the context of social implications. Which does Dorris choose and why? What other essay technique is most in evidence?

5. Discuss the introductory and concluding paragraphs. Is the author's commentary regarding his son an effective way of introducing and concluding the essay?

6. What is the thesis statement? Can you locate a specific thesis, or paraphrase it?

WRITING PROJECT

Write an extended definition essay exploring the nature of a social issue or problem. You may have an argumentative point to make, and you may employ other essay strategies. Be sure, however, to define the nature and extent of the problem.

Andrew Ward

Andrew Ward is an essayist who has written on a wide variety of social and cultural subjects. In this essay, he defines modern architecture in pejorative terms, as a profession fixated on designing buildings with a bird's eye-view in mind. This piece takes on what he sees as the bad habits of modern architects; his extended definition of architecture zeroes in tightly on architects with their heads in the clouds. In the discussion questions, you will be thinking about how successfully and effectively Ward's definition covers this broad subject.

The Trouble with Architects:
The Bird's-eye Syndrome

A woman I know worked for a time in one of those prestigious sweatshops in which the imposing abodes of America's corporations are designed. A mean woman with an X-acto knife, she was given the job of constructing the little presentation models with which her firm coaxed its clients even further into the frontiers of modern architecture. But she could stand the subsistence pay, the stiff neck, and the enforced veneration for the firm's presiding genius only long enough to complete a single model: a one-inch-to-one-foot cardboard and Mylar prototype of a huge building slated for construction somewhere in downtown Houston.

A few years after she quit the firm she found herself at the Houston airport and decided to kill the two hours she had between planes by taking a cab downtown and finding the building over whose embryo she had labored so long. Though she couldn't remember what company had commissioned it, she figured she had been so intimately acquainted with its design that she could spot it without any trouble.

But after an hour's search up and down the city streets, she could not for the life of her find it, and had to assume, as she boarded her plane, that the design had been changed or the project had been canceled just after she had quit. Then, suddenly, looking down at the retreating city as her plane rose in the sky, she saw her building standing right smack-dab in the middle of Houston. During her search she must have passed it half a dozen times, but only now, with a bird's-eye view of it on a cardboard and Mylar scale, could she recognize it.

I think my friend may have stumbled upon what's wrong with modern architecture: it is best appreciated from a couple of thousand feet off the ground. It is conceived from an aerial point of view, from the Olympian perspective of a god, an angel, a chairman of the board.

I visited a firm a while ago whose work is on such a scale and whose aesthetic is so grandiose that I only wish Albert Speer[14] could have tagged along to give me some guidance. Crammed atop fifty waist-high tables in the center of the main studio were thousands of dollars' worth of presentation models representing millions of dollars' worth of buildings. Some were of structures that are already towering over us; others were of headquarters still rising out of the doomed woodlands of suburban Connecticut; still more were of buildings that shall forever remain a gleam in the architect's eye.

As I wandered through the studio, my natural perspective was from above. During presentations, executives must have had to stoop pretty far down to get some earthbound notion of what the buildings were going to look like, and stooping does not come naturally to your upper-echelon corporate exec. Getting up close to models can wreck the illusion, anyway; you see a flap of Mylar peeling away, a fleck of rubber cement, the little everyday defects that have no place in a meeting where traffic flow patterns, image, and executive toiletry are up for discussion. No, it is far preferable to maintain one's posture and keep one's distance.

What struck me about the models with their breakaway roofs was that they contained some pretty ingenious notions, some intricate and innovative problem-solving, but that none of these could be appreciated by someone trying to walk along a building's barren and wind-whipped façade, or heading for the restroom along one of its dizzying,

[14]Albert Speer was Adolf Hitler's chief architect. He was known for monumental, overwhelming architectural proposals.

sloping corridors, or reading back issues in a brass and glass lobby five stories high.

That we are but grains of sand on the beach of time, droplets in the ocean of life, is a notion worth considering now and then, but it isn't something sane people want to dwell upon, or in. Nature has been doing a fine job of reminding us of our insignificance without a lot of architects seconding the motion. The hitch, of course, is that the men who commission these buildings don't tend to feel as insignificant as the rest of us (maybe because they aren't as insignificant as the rest of us). And it may even be that they don't really mean to make the rest of us feel insignificant. It's just that the same building that makes a visitor feel puny makes its proprietor, whose experience is charged with the thrill of ownership, feel like a giant.

Architecture, especially institutional architecture, may always have been designed and bestowed from above, but since the invention of the airplane the aerial perspective has been given disproportionate validity. Have you ever noticed how exalted our downtown areas appear from the clouds? At some altitudes you could mistake the new convention centers and condo complexes for Utopia. But down on the ground the same places are oppressive, depressing, downright crummy. Part of this effect is a function of distance; from thousands of feet in the air you can't see the litter and the bag ladies. But that can be only part of it, because sometimes the reverse is true.

I lived for a while in Cornwall, Connecticut, conceivably the loveliest town in the nation. Most of the houses were built by country carpenters in the eighteenth and nineteenth centuries, and they coexist in absolute harmony (in marked contrast to their occupants). As one walks along the streets, it seems that everyone's lawn stretches for acres and every grove of trees extends into miles of forest, as if, over time, the town grew organically out of the countryside. But I was once shown some aerial photographs of Cornwall in which the town, stripped of its mystery, looked like a condemned stretch of southern New Jersey. You could see the abandoned cars just beyond the Cotters' back fence, the bald lots gleaned for firewood on the Franklins' hill.

An architect would no more have recreated such a scheme and

proposed it to a developer than he would serve Kool-Aid to Harold Geneen. He would have tidied up those uneven, impracticably distanced houses into evenly staggered modules, pruned the woodlots, landscaped the pastures, gutted the hardware store to make way for a wok outlet and a quiche parlor, unified the churches, consolidated the schools, and tied the whole thing together with pedestrian walkways and bike paths. Only then could his clients, standing over the one-inch-to-ten-feet mock-up like titans 300 feet tall, come to grips with the theme, the continuity, the concept, at a glance.

Maybe the grandiose style is just an outgrowth of the grandiosity of the institutions it services. And perhaps the young turks of modern architecture have already turned their backs on the ostentatious. I don't know. The last young turk I met designed his parents' solar house on the Cape last year; has been reduced to making installation estimates for a carpet warehouse this year; and, if things don't pick up next year, may join his buddy the English major in a cabinetmaking business in Vermont. A look at the major commissions under way just beyond New York's city limits indicates to me that the grandiose is getting grander all the time.

I suppose I won't be satisfied until architects return to Asher Benjamin and the golden mean,[15] but if they have any interest in designing buildings to accommodate people, they should at least design structures in the same way they're built: from the ground up.

[15]Asher Benjamin (1773–1845) was an early American architect and a follower of the more famous Charles Bulfinch. Bulfinch was known for his classical influences and a mastery of proportion. The "golden mean" is a geometric formula for the harmonious proportions advocated by Bulfinch and Benjamin, and missing, according to Ward, from modern architecture.

DISCUSSION QUESTIONS

1. Let's editorially rearrange the first four paragraphs, placing the fourth paragraph first (and deleting the first clause of the sentence). Does this revision improve the opening?

2. What precisely is Ward defining? All architecture, or a certain kind of architecture? Are there any problems with the definition?

3. What evidence does the writer use to amplify and support his thesis?

4. "We are but grains of sand on the beach of time." How does this aphorism relate to the experience of modern architecture, according to Ward?

5. What other types of essay writing are used? Are they effectively employed?

6. Discuss the imagery used in a comparison and contrast mode. How does the author utilize contrasting imagery to enhance his thesis?

WRITING PROJECT

Write an extended definition of something you use or enjoy. The range of possibilities are as wide as your life, from a table saw to a certain kind of rock music. As always, you are encouraged to use other essay types to complement your definition. Remember that your subject should be narrow enough to be successfully explored in a short essay of approximately 500 words.

7

Cause and Effect Essays

The analysis chapter considered the relationship of parts to the whole. This chapter will discuss cause and effect analysis, a type of analysis that asks why something happens (cause) and examines the consequences of that behavior or event (effect). We live our days creating and responding to causes and effects, starting with the six a.m. shriek of the alarm clock, caused by our setting of the clock the night before. Cause and effect thinking influences everything from such simple alarm clock events to extremely complex historical, political, scientific, or other phenomena. Much of your course work will call for essays employing this type of analysis or at least for the application of cause and effect reasoning.

Establishing the cause(s) of something is often complex and sometimes debatable. For instance, let's propose a question: what are the causes of photosynthesis? The causes are somewhat complicated, but the science of biology has given us a definite, clear-cut answer. If we try to determine something like the causes of the Vietnam War, however, we run into problems. Here, too, the causes are complicated but also highly debatable. This would certainly be a intriguing essay topic, but writers of such papers should be prepared to defend their choice of causes against those who propose different causes or give different emphases to the same set of causes. Determining why something happens can be a prickly problem and should be approached with care.

Nailing down the effects of an action or event also runs the gamut from the simple to the complex. We know why the alarm clock rings, and we also know on a more complex but nevertheless definitive level the effects of photosynthesis. However, when arguable cause and effect problems are on the table, many people fall into a common *post hoc* fallacy. This occurs when one event is presumed to have caused another, just because someone sees an emotional or coincidental connection between the two things. For instance, if a rap group sings about burning down City Hall, and City Hall does burn, some people might assume that the group had caused or inspired that event. Jumping from the fire (effect) to the lyrics (presumed cause) ignores a whole range of other possible causes that may be completely unrelated to the supposedly incendiary rap lyrics. Similarly, Alan Dershowitz warns us on page 261 in the combined techniques chapter that the famous illustration of yelling fire in a crowded theater seldom applies to more complicated freedom of speech issues, because of *post hoc* errors assuming shaky or nonexistent connections between controversial speech and its effects.

Many cause and effect essays you will write will pull you toward the challenging territory of explaining an action, a behavior, or an event when the relationship between cause and effect is murky or arguable. The pitfalls of *post hoc* fallacies are best avoided by citing ample evidence and examples supporting your cause and effect analysis. Do not be afraid of debate, but learn how to use it wisely. It would probably be foolhardy to claim that a rap group's lyrics caused a specific crime, but it is plausible to claim a causal connection between violent rock lyrics and an increase in the general level of violence. (It is also possible to claim the opposite, that there is no connection between the two.) The arguments often used in fortifying debatable causes will be more fully explored in the following chapter. This kind of analysis will also frequently call on your definition, description, and other essay writing skills, as the following readings will illustrate.

We have used cause and effect as one term, but there are several possible variations of this essay form. We can focus primarily on causes, or on effects, or on cause and effect together. The option selected depends upon the nature of your topic and how you approach it. Some essays might call for an emphasis on causes, as in Meg Cimino's "Vigilance" on page 182. Cimino portrays a world composed of dangerous "sharp corners"; life in this world is chock-full of hazardous causes, and the effects are largely assumed or left to the imagination. The essay selection by George F. Will, page 178, considers the problems of freedom of expression, and demands serious attention to both cause and effect. There are no definite guidelines telling us as writers what to emphasize, but the readings in this chapter will give you a sense of how other writers handle the problem.

Cause and effect analysis is one of the most challenging forms of essay you will write, but also one of the most rewarding. It is always satisfying to know—or at least persuasively suggest—why something happens as it does, which is the essence of this type of analysis. As we noted in the introductory paragraph, you will use this skill in much of your course work, your work life, in your whole range of thought and action. As you read the selections in this chapter, you will appreciate that this type of analysis can be profitably applied to a wide range of subjects, limited only by the experience, knowledge, and imagination of the writer.

CAROLYN HANIG

Cause and effect analysis sometimes explores life and death actions and consequences. Carolyn Hanig is a flight nurse whose son was killed in a traffic accident. The cause of her son's death is the subject of this essay, and the author uses this tragic personal experience to analyze the cause and effect ramifications of wearing seat belts. The connections between cause and effect are crucially important to this essay; watch for how clearly and effectively Hanig explores those connections.

My Own Son Didn't Listen

As a flight nurse employed by a hospital-based aeromedical helicopter service, I regularly respond to life-and-death situations. For 18 years I have flown to the scenes of some of the most terrible crashes you can imagine. But nothing in my experience or my training prepared me for what happened on this past Mother's Day weekend.

I was on duty when we received a request to respond to a head-on collision approximately 30 miles from Tulsa, Okla. En route to the scene it was reported by our communication center that this was a mass-casualty incident involving several vehicles. As we observed the scene from the air, we could see many victims lying on the highway and by the roadside. We hoped none had been ejected from their vehicles.

When we arrived, our crew was directed to an area where many of the victims were being stabilized. My partner and I were asked to assist with a young man who was in serious trouble. As I stepped into the ambulance I could see that he was already receiving cardio-pulmonary resuscitation. As I moved in to help, I suddenly froze. I recognized the young man's shoes. They belonged to my 17-year-old son, Nik. In seconds my whole world crashed in around me. Nik was so gravely injured, I knew he was not going to survive.

Three of the four teenagers in the vehicle Nik was riding in were not wearing their seat belts. Two of the three unbelted passengers were killed: the driver and my son, who was in the back seat. The other unbelted back-seat-passenger was ejected and seriously injured. The front-seat-passenger, the only one wearing his seat belt, walked away with minor cuts and bruises.

I lost my son on Mother's Day weekend because he was not wearing his seat belt. Our family—and the families of more than 9,000 sons, daughters, mothers and fathers who will die this year because they were unbelted—will never be the same.

It is not just the families who suffer. The community pays a price as well. Those of us who buckle up are paying in higher health-care and insurance costs for those who don't. The hospital costs for treating unbelted crash victims are 50 percent higher than those for belted crash victims. And 85 percent of those inpatient costs are paid by society, not by the individual. Any way you look at it—the loss of human life or the financial strain on society—the results are catastrophic.

Despite the recent focus on the terrible problems of drunken driving or on newly identified problems such as aggressive driving, increasing seat-belt use is still the single most effective thing we can do to save lives on America's roadways. As a flight nurse and an emergency health-care giver, I have witnessed the difference a seat belt makes. The most satisfying part of my job is the opportunity to help save lives. The most difficult part is seeing unbelted children and adults who have been violently ejected from their vehicles or thrown into the windshield and knowing that their terrible injuries or death could have been prevented. The only reason Nik died was that he was not wearing his seat belt.

Based on my firsthand experience, I tried to drill into my four children the importance of wearing seat belts. When Nik was learning to drive, I had him take a driver's ed course sponsored by my auto insurance company. We even made a visit to a young man recovering in an intensive-care unit who is now a quadriplegic because he wasn't wearing his seat belt.

I did everything I could think of to get Nik to buckle up. Unfortunately, the threat of serious injury or even death is not enough to persuade some people—especially young people, who believe they are invincible—to always buckle up.

The only proven way to get people who can't be convinced through public education to use a seat belt is a real threat of a ticket and fine. Belt use is about 15 percent higher in states with "standard" enforcement laws, where police officers treat failure to buckle up like every other traffic offense. In states with weak "secondary" enforcement, officers must first observe a motorist committing a traffic violation before ticketing for failure to use a belt. I feel certain that if Nik had known there was a real chance of getting stopped and given a ticket for not wearing his seat belt, he would still be alive today.

Ironically, in the months before my son's death, I had joined my local Safe Kids Coalition to help increase belt use by working to pass a standard belt law. While the challenge to me seemed great—belt use in Oklahoma was 48 percent—we were encouraged by the experiences of other states. Louisiana, which recently upgraded its belt law to standard enforcement, saw its belt use jump from 50 to 68 percent in just three years.

Through my advocacy work I also learned how weak belt laws leave innocent young children at risk. Adults who don't buckle up are telling children it's all right not to use a seat belt. More than 75 percent of the time, when the driver is unbelted, children and other passengers in that vehicle will be unbelted as well. If every state in the nation adopted a standard-enforcement law, we could save 1,900 lives and prevent more than 49,000 injuries a year.

After my son's funeral, I heard that Oklahoma's proposed belt law was in trouble. So I went to Oklahoma City to meet with the governor and several legislators. I told them my story and pleaded with them to do what they could to pass this bill. It passed, and I now know that it will save lives.

I have since told my story to the Ohio legislature, which is considering a stronger belt law similar to Oklahoma's. I plan to keep telling it because I think it's time we made protecting lives with seat belts as important as other traffic laws.

I know that when I go back to my job, each time I fly to a crash scene I will be reminded of the terrible day when I lost my son. But I also carry a little hope that Nik's life can make a difference. And that by telling his story, it may help to improve our laws and save lives.

DISCUSSION QUESTIONS

1. What is the thesis statement? Where is it located?

2. The most dramatic use of cause and effect here is personal, relating to Hanig's son. Name and discuss three other ways the author employs cause and effect in discussing the general issue of seat belts.

3. Consider the first four paragraphs of the essay. What essay techniques are being employed? How effective are these paragraphs as a lead-in to the thesis and the more general discussion of the last half of the essay?

4. What kinds of evidence does the writer cite demonstrating the beneficial effects of wearing seat belts? Is the evidence convincing?

5. How does Hanig propose increasing the use of seat belts? What is the evidence cited for her assertion that other methods of encouraging such use are ineffective? Is this evidence convincing?

6. Comment on the overall structure of the essay, including the conclusion. How would you describe the structure, and how effective is it?

WRITING PROJECT

Employ cause and effect analysis as a means of understanding a hazardous activity or practice. Why is the activity dangerous, and how can you bring cause and effect analysis to bear to suggest ways to make it less hazardous? Your essay can address actions where the cause of harm is relatively obvious (mountain climbing, smoking) or more debatable (the ill effects of continuously staring at the computer screen). You may need to use argument or other techniques to discuss the danger, but your essay should suggest what the potential danger is and what to do about it.

GEORGE F. WILL

George F. Will is a columnist, a television commentator, and the author of many books of political and social criticism. This essay and the Dershowitz selection (in the chapter on combined techniques) both tackle freedom of speech problems from a cause and effect perspective, but Will approaches the subject from a different angle. He specifically focuses on pornography as one cause of a decline in "civil" life; he applauds efforts in New York City to crack down on pornography as an effective means of combating crime and reversing the decline in civility. This essay demands close attention to the links between cause and effect; Will's analysis depends on hotly debated claims about the effects of pornography. (The New York Supreme Court has upheld the constitutionality of the law discussed in this essay.)

A Course Correction in the Capital of Liberalism

This could get conservatives' dander up. A category of small businesses is being subjected to injurious regulation in New York City. That city, the capital of liberalism and hence of overbearing government, is disrupting the free market by burdening, with the intent to discourage, a form of commerce involving a legal commodity. The government is doing this because it disapproves of the practice of supplying the particular commodity for which there is a demand. Furthermore, the government wants to engage in social engineering, shaping the social climate of neighborhoods by purging this commerce from most of the places where market forces have produced it.

It is enough to make conservatives' blood boil. Or maybe not. The commodity is pornography and other "adult" entertainment. Hence the conservatives' conundrum: Can they square their advocacy of smaller, less intrusive government with a more ambitious moral agenda for government?

New York City's government is acting against the pollution of social atmosphere, and in the name of such conservative causes as neighborhood preservation and family values. So the city's new censoriousness provides an interesting coda to this political season. Many conservatives have been bewildered almost to the point of vertigo by the rapid reversal of their fortunes. Two years ago their blanket castigations of government seemed to be resonating with a national majority. Today the national mood about government's uses seems more ambivalent, conflicted, nuanced. Conservatives seeking a small confrontation with their own ideological tangles can take a stroll down West 39th Street in Manhattan, to Richard Kunis's store.

Large lettering on his front window announces YOUR NEIGHBOR-HOOD VIDEO STORE SINCE 1985. In the 1970s he sold office furniture. His inventory is all . . . what? "Erotic" is not the word. Watching an "adult" movie is an experience about as erotic as reading "Gray's Anatomy." Suffice it to say that Kunis's movies are energetically pornographic. Customers can rent them, buy them or view them in booths in the store. He is building a "handicapped-accessible" booth.

Kunis thinks his transactions with consenting adults are private enterprise without any consequences that are the proper concern of public authorities. The city says: Just as smoking in confined public places is not a purely private matter because second-hand smoke is offensive to, and perhaps injurious to, other people, so, too, the activities of Kunis and the operators of about 180 other "adult" businesses, in the dense living conditions of a city, have injurious secondary effects against which government can act.

The city says those effects include decreased property values, retarded economic development, damage to neighborhood character and to children. And when such businesses are clustered, there is increased illegal sexual activities and other crime, as well as loitering and littering and other nuisances. The new zoning law will disperse such businesses to designated manufacturing and commercial areas and will require buffer zones between them and places, such as residential areas, schools and churches, that are particularly vulnerable to the secondary effects.

The pornographers say that precisely proving the various secondary effects is problematic. However, precision should not be necessary. One does not need a moral micrometer to gauge the fact that the sex industry turned Times Square into a slum. And arcane arguments are not needed to establish the principle that residential neighborhoods merit some protection from forms of commerce that abrade the spirits of the residents.

Pornography merchants argue that the new law will put most of them out of business and relegate the remainder to inaccessible locales, thereby unconstitutionally burdening the exercise of a fundamental right, freedom of expression. They say the law patently discriminates against their form of expression because of its content, and therefore violates the constitutional requirement of content-neutrality. The city replies that pornography will still be available, and many laws regulate the "time, place and manner" of expression (e.g., no loudspeakers near hospitals).

But the larger significance of the law is this: A course correction is underway in the capital of liberalism, where for decades the tension between individual rights and community values has been resolved too often in favor of the former. In liberal social analysis, the individual is the only reality, and the community is an abstraction without claims. No more. Panhandling is no longer invested with constitutional grandeur as (in the words of a liberal judge) "informative and persuasive speech." Instead, it is seen as a form of disorder. Graffiti is no longer regarded as a "statement" by the voiceless and downtrodden, but as ominous evidence of an uncontrolled environment.

A substantial amount of the recent decline in the nation's crime occurred in this city, which has not increased the number of police. What has increased is intolerance, which can be a virtue. The mayor understands that there simply is no such thing as a "minor crime" because all crime breeds disorder, which is an infectious social disease. It atomizes communities, increases anxiety, wariness, avoidance and truculence and dissolves the sense of mutual regard and obligations of civility. Note that word.

Selling pornography is not a crime, but by catering to, and inflaming, vulgarians' sensibilities, it contributes to the coarsening of the culture, which erodes civility. In its original meaning, "civility" denoted the virtues requisite for civic life—the life of citizenship in a city. For too long now, the word "civil" has appeared in American discourse almost exclusively as an adjective modifying the noun "right." New York's decision to get judgmental, to stigmatize pornography by pushing it to the fringe of city life, rests on this recognition; the words "civil," "civic," citizen" and "city" have a common root and are related in complex ways.

DISCUSSION QUESTIONS

1. The crux of Will's analysis supporting new zoning laws is his approval of the analogy equating the effects of secondhand cigarette smoke with the "secondary effects" of pornography in residential areas. Is this a convincing analogy? Why or why not?

2. Will includes pornography with minor crimes as causes in a decline of "civility." How does he define this term? How does he define pornography? Are these terms adequately defined? Why or why not?

3. Make a list of causes and effects cited by the writer. In each case, is cause, effect, or both more heavily stressed?

4. Could the author be accused of any *post hoc* errors in establishing his connections between cause and effect? If so, what are they?

5. How does the introductory paragraph in this selection resemble the introduction to "My Girl," on page 5?

6. Consider the concluding sentence of this essay. Is Will's assertion of an interrelationship between these words supported and amplified in the essay? What is the nature of the connection between these terms, according to Will?

WRITING PROJECT

Write a cause and effect analysis of some problem plaguing your school or community. Make sure your thesis is narrow enough to allow sufficient treatment in a short essay. Your problem could range from the relatively simple, say the lack of a stoplight at a dangerous intersection, to more complex or debatable problems.

MEG CIMINO

Meg Cimino is a writer and an attorney. This is a cause and effect essay, but it will remind you of the childhood reminiscences of Jane Smiley and Joyce Carol Oates in the narrative and descriptive chapter. The piece has a strong descriptive flavor—as personal memoir often does—but it describes a cause and effect world of danger, actual and potential. This is a radical change of pace from the Will essay, but it should enable you to appreciate the variety possible in this type of essay. As you read the Cimino essay, be especially aware of the looming importance of cause in her family-oriented view of the world.

Vigilance

"He'll trip, and that spoon will go right into his throat." My father and I were watching a videotape of my two-year-old nephew, Cameron—one of those that his mother, my sister Laura, regularly sends. As Cameron ran into view with a spoon sticking out of his mouth, I knew exactly what Dad was going to say; I practically mouthed the words along with him. He spoke again as Cameron raced around the coffee table in the next scene: "He's going to split his head open on that table. They should pad the corners."

"I know," I replied. "I can't believe that they would even have any furniture. And they should teach him at home to avoid the desk corners and all the other germy kids at nursery school."

Dad smiled, as accustomed to my mocking his cautions as I am to hearing his warnings about ubiquitous and mundane hazards. If my father could, he would have all the sharp corners in the world rounded off and padded.

Like most parents, he has always tried to protect his children—me and my six siblings—from all the risks out there. And as a doctor who specializes in public-health and preventive-medicine issues, he is especially conscious of the harm that can result from the seemingly innocuous as well as the obvious dangers surrounding us.

I remember the surprise I felt as a child making cookies at a friend's house that nobody said a word about the possibility of salmonella poisoning when I stuffed raw cookie dough into my mouth. Gum, candy, any food or beverage posed a danger of choking, particularly if you moved or talked while chewing. "Are you choking?" was uttered as often around our house as "Did you wash your hands?" The Heimlich maneuver was a highly valued skill.

Restaurants, Dad warned, presented additional risks, such as careless waiters who might drop hot food or coffee on your head and employees who neither covered their faces while sneezing nor washed their hands regularly. If we scoffed, he could cite examples, from his days as the New York City commissioner of health, of roach-infested kitchens that had been shut down.

Fashion, too, could be dangerous. One could break an ankle in high heels, trip over too-long pants and skirts, or catch flowing clothes in windows, doors, or trash compactors. Not so long ago Dad took away my fuzzy bunny slippers to keep me from sliding downstairs. Pocketbooks, he advised us, should be worn not across your chest but only over your shoulder. Better that a thief get away with your bag than that he drag you along.

A few years ago Dad confiscated a coat of mine because I hadn't hemmed it sufficiently. It's a long rust-colored wool coat, and it still hangs in my parents' coat closet. Sometimes I'll ask about it, as I might about an eccentric family member banished to live in the attic. Dad will put the coat on to demonstrate how serious a problem it is. The coat's neck, shoulders, and sleeves will bunch and strain, and its wide circle of a hemline swirl around him like a cape.

"Look—it's too long even on me. And this material is so heavy, it would pull you down."

I have never heard of anyone injured by too heavy a coat."

"Do you want to be the first? Just cut it off here," he'll say, drawing his hand across his knee, "and maybe it should be tapered also."

In clothing Dad values warmth, impermeability, and traction over style. He has a penchant for leather pants ("You'll never feel the wind through these") and any garment made of space-age microfibers. It is always obvious which gifts under the Christmas tree he is responsible for: woolen balaclavas and mittens, battery-heated socks, slippers with treads, and sharp metal cleats to slip over your boots in the snow, which might be indispensable while ice fishing in Alaska but create an embarrassing clatter on the sidewalks of Manhattan, where I live.

The weather was only one of the many natural menaces from which we were to guard ourselves. To this day, when I walk within a few yards of the branches of a tree, I blink as I hear his voice: "Watch your eyes!" Dad lectured us about Rocky Mountain spotted fever from the ticks that lurked in the grass and on neighborhood dogs, deer, and squirrels; about the rabies carried by raccoons, bats, and dogs. "Don't touch— it'll bite!" was his automatic reaction when one of us reached out to an animal. Our own pets—dogs, rabbit, gerbils, snake, and fish—always seemed nervous around my father, aware, I thought, that he regarded them with suspicion.

Of course, as children, we did not always listen to Dad. We had our broken bones, cuts, near chokings, electric shocks, car accidents, and illnesses, some of which might have been avoided (though he never said so) if we had heeded his advice and not jumped from the top of slides, thrown rocks at one another, run around while eating, yanked the plug while the vacuum cleaner was on, driven too fast, and kissed the dogs. My parents for the most part calmly accepted these traumas as a natural part of growing up, perhaps because my father had predicted every one of them.

But there have also been unanticipated calamities: my bother John's meningitis, my disabling head injury, Dad's prostate cancer. He accepted all patiently, protecting us from our fear. He never revealed his own, though he knew well the painful repercussions: special education and a lifetime of medication for my brother, years of physical therapy for me, surgery and radiation for him. We survived, and these confrontations with our vulnerability left us with some understanding of Dad's desire to control the little that he can.

When my brothers and sisters and I are reminiscing these days, we recall Dad's telling us not to jump on the trampoline in gym class, because of the possibility of spinal injury, and the driving directions he devised so as to minimize the number of left turns. Now we find ourselves uttering similar admonitions. We phone my brother to tell him that we read about someone's dying from the same allergy he has, my sister to tell her about the high lead content of certain mini-blinds or to say that we couldn't sleep last night worrying about that electrical cord we noticed in her house which her kinds could reach.

Now Dad has a new generation to guide. His grandchildren have caught on quickly, knowing to wag their fingers and say "That's dangerous!" at the sight of cleaning fluid, and owning helmets before they could skate or bike. At the holiday dinner table three-year-old Margaret tells her two-year-old cousin, "That's too big a bite—you'll choke," while Dad, inspecting the baby's perfect hands, asks, "Does Vincent have a cut on his finger?" As everyone is leaving, we all laugh when my niece bids Dad good-bye: "Be careful, Poppa!"

After a weekend visit to my parents I have my father drop me off at the quiet suburban train station for my trip back to Manhattan. As I wait, I can see his car in the parking lot; I know that he is watching to see that I board safely, without falling into the space between the platform and the train. He waits no matter what the time of day, no matter how many other passengers are waiting with me. Sometimes he parks the car, steps out, and walks up the stairs to the opposite platform. We wave at each other across the tracks. He stands there until the train comes and he sees me board safely and find a seat.

I watch him walk to his car, wanting, as I do more and more often now, to protect him from the world's sharp edges, the way he has always tried to protect us. I wish I could give him the reassurance his worrying and caring gave me. As the train pulls away, I whisper, "Be careful, Dad."

DISCUSSION QUESTIONS

1. What is most emphasized in this essay—causes, effects, or both? Why?

2. What is the tone? Does the tone shift anywhere in the essay? What effect does a tonal shift have on the mood of the essay?

3. Compare this essay to Jane Smiley's "Confess, Early and Often" (page 10). What are the differences in tone and point of view in the two selections, and how do you account for them?

4. What would you consider the thesis of this essay? Is there any sentence in the piece that could serve as a thesis statement?

5. Other essay techniques employed in this selection may include comparison and contrast, example, and analysis. Which, if any, of these techniques are used in the Cimino essay?

6. This essay shifts back and forth between past and present tense. What impact do these shifts have?

7. "He'll trip, and that spoon will go right into his throat." This opening sentence seems like a simple cause and effect sequence. Is it? How do the experiences described in the essay change our understanding of what at first seems to be a paranoid, overprotective view of life?

WRITING PROJECT

Write a cause and effect essay based on a personal experience where the effect of an action or event was different from what you had anticipated. Your analysis should explain the reasons for the different outcome and the consequences of the altered outcome. For instance, if you as a batter were expecting a fastball and struck out on a curveball, what consequences did that have on your performance and that of the team? Why were you expecting a fastball? (This is only one example; feel free to choose any experience that seems interesting to you.)

NORMAN MACLEAN

Norman Maclean is the author of *A River Runs through It and Other Stories* and *Young Men and Fire,* from which this selection is excerpted. Although this selection is taken from a nonfiction account of a disastrous forest fire in 1949, it can stand alone as a cause and effect account of certain kinds of fires. Notice the swift, deadly interplay of cause and consequence Maclean lays out as he considers the dynamics of forest fires.

from *Young Men and Fire*

Of the two main kinds of forest fires distinguished by their causes, man and nature itself, the Mann Gulch fire was a lightning fire, as 75 percent of the forest fires in the West are. Lightning fires usually start where lightning gets its first chance to strike—high up near the top of a ridge but slightly down its side where the first clump of dead trees stands, and the start of the Mann Gulch fire fits this description. The fire in the dead snag may drop live ashes for several days before starting a fire on the ground, for the ground near a mountaintop is likely to be mostly rocks with at best only a light covering of dead leaves, needles, or grass. But the lightning storm that started the Mann Gulch fire passed over the gulch on August 4, and by the end of the next afternoon on the hottest day ever recorded in nearby Helena thirteen Smokejumpers were dead.

Once started on the ground the lightning fire became simply a "ground fire," a term that includes most fires, and so ground fires are of many sizes, shapes, and intensities, and practically all man-made fires such as campfires and fires set to burn slash or brush but allowed to get away at least start as ground fires. A ground fire may become dangerous, even murderous, but most often it is just a lot of hard work to get under control. Until an hour before the end, that is what the Smokejumpers expected the Mann Gulch fire to be—hard work all night but easing up by morning.

The job of controlling most ground fires starts with the job of scraping a "fire trench" or fire-line around it or its flanks so as to force it onto rocks or open meadows. A fire trench or fire-line is some two to three feet wide, is made with a Pulaski and shovel, and is nothing more than the surface of the ground scraped down to mineral soil. Nothing flammable, such as fallen trees or hanging branches, can be left across it.

The chief danger from a ground fire is that it will become a "crown fire," that is, get into the branches or "crowns" of trees especially where the trees are close together and the branches interlace. So a crew has to be careful that a ground fire doesn't burn into a jack-pine thicket where the branches are close to the ground and can be set afire by low flames. But there is still a very different way for an ordinary-looking fire to explode. A fire doesn't always need flames to advance. A fire may seem under control, burning harmlessly under tall trees with branches too high to be touched by ground flames, but the fire is burning with such intensity that most of the oxygen has been burned out of the air near it, which is heated above the point of ignition. If the wind suddenly changes and fresh air is blown in loaded with oxygen, then the three elements necessary for a fire are suddenly present in the lower branches— flammable material, temperature above the point of ignition, and oxygen. An old-timer knows that, when a ground fire explodes into a crown fire with nothing he can see to cause it, he had not witnessed spontaneous combustion but the outer appearance of the invisible pressure of a "fire triangle" suddenly in proper proportions for an explosion.

The crown fire is the one that sounds like a train coming too fast around a curve and may get so high-keyed the crew cannot understand what their foreman is trying to do to save them. Sometimes, when the timber thins out, it sounds as if the train were clicking across a bridge, sometimes it hits an open clearing and becomes hushed as if going through a tunnel, but when the burning cones swirl through the air and fall on the other side of the clearing, starting spot fires there, the new fire sounds as if it were the train coming out of the tunnel, belching black unburned smoke. The unburned smoke boils up until it reaches oxygen, then bursts into gigantic flames on top of its cloud of smoke in the sky. The new firefighter, seeing black smoke rise from the ground and then at the top of the sky turn into flames, thinks that natural law has been reversed. The flames should come first and the smoke from them. The new firefighter doesn't know how his fire got way up there. He is frightened and should be.

A fire-line, unless a river or a wide right-of-way on a trail is being used as a line, is not much good when a crown fire is off and running. It usually takes a "backfire" to stop a big crown fire, and the conditions are seldom right for the foreman to start one. He has to build piles of fast-burning twigs, shavings, or dried bunch grass in front of the main fire and, before starting his backfire, must wait until the wind blows back toward the main fire, and often it never does. When you fool with a backfire, you are really fooling with fire—you are counting on the wind to continue to blow your backfire toward the main fire. If the wind changes again and blows toward you, your backfire may only have given the main fire a fatal jump on you.

It's perhaps even more unpredictable if there isn't much of a wind to begin with, because a big crown fire can make its own wind. The hot, lighter air rises, the cold, heavier air rushes down to replace it in what is called a "convection effect," and soon a great "fire whirl" is started and fills the air with burning cones and branches which drop in advance of the main fire like the Fourth of July and start spot fires. The separate spot fires soon burn together, and life is trapped between the main fire coming from behind and the new line of fire now burning back toward it.

Then something terrible can happen. The space between the converged spot fires as they burn close to the main fire can become hotter than the point of ignition. If the convection effect or a change in the wind blows fresh oxygen between the two fires, suddenly replenishing the burned-out air, there can be a "blowup," although a blowup can be caused in still other ways. Not many have seen a blowup, even fewer have seen one and lived, and fewer still have tried afterwards to recover and record out of their seared memories exactly what happened. Later on in Mann Gulch we shall try to recreate a blowup seen by almost no one who lived to record it, and it might help as preparation if we turn briefly to the great pioneer in the science of fire behavior, Harry T.

Gisborne, who was one of the first to observe and describe a blowup accurately.

In 1929 Gisborne was on what was up to then Montana's largest man-caused fire, the ninety-thousand-acre Half Moon fire in Glacier National Park (640 acres being a section or a square mile). As he says, measured "runs" show that even a big crown fire advances not much faster than a half-mile to a mile an hour. The blowup that Gisborne witnessed demolished over two square miles in possibly two minutes, although probably in a minute flat.

Returning two days later, he found the perfectly balanced body of a young grouse, neck and head "still alertly erect in fear and wonder," the beak, feathers, and feet seared away. Within a few yards was a squirrel, stretched out at full length. "The burned-off stubs of his little hands were reaching out as far ahead as possible, the back legs were extended to the full in one final, hopeless push, trying, like any human, to crawl just one painful inch further to escape this unnecessary death."

Although young men died like squirrels in Mann Gulch, the Mann Gulch fire should not end there, smoke drifting away and leaving terror without consolation of explanation, and controversy without lasting settlement. Probably most catastrophes end this way without an ending, the dead not even knowing how they died but "still alertly erect in fear and wonder," those who loved them forever questioning "this unnecessary death," and the rest of us tiring of this inconsolable catastrophe and turning to the next one. This is a catastrophe that we hope will not end where it began; it might go on and become a story. It will not have to be made up—that is all-important to us—but we do have to know in what odd places to look for missing parts of a story about a wildfire and of course have to know a story and a wildfire when we see one. So this story is a test of its own belief—that in this cockeyed world there are shapes and designs, if only we have some curiosity, training, and compassion and take care not to lie or be sentimental. It would be a start to a story if this catastrophe were found to have circled around out there somewhere until it could return to itself with explanations of its own mysteries and with the grief it left behind, not removed, because grief has its own place at or near the end of things, but altered somewhat by the addition of something like wonder—wonder, for example, because now we can say that the fire whirl which destroyed was caused by three winds on a river. If we could say something like this and be speaking both accurately and somewhat like Shelley when he spoke of clouds and winds, then what we would be talking about would start to change from catastrophe without a filled-in story to what could be called the story of a tragedy, but tragedy would be only part of it, as it is of life.

DISCUSSION QUESTIONS

1. Definitions are important to the understanding of this selection. Briefly define the following terms: *ground fire, crown fire, backfire, fire whirl,* and *blowup.*

2. In the introduction to this chapter, we suggested there is a simple, direct connection between cause and effect in some events, that is, the setting and ringing of an alarm clock. Is there such a simple connection between cause and effect in the types of fire described here? Why or why not?

3. Discuss the structure of this selection. How do the events described build toward the "blowup?" Does the structure help your understanding of how the cause and effect patterns are working?

4. "Old-timers" know that with some fires effects seemingly come first, not causes. What is meant by this statement?

5. What is the tone of this selection? How does the writer mix objective analysis of cause and effect with descriptive similes to create tone and mood?

6. How would you assess the relative importance of cause and effect to the phenomena described here?

7. Imagine yourself as a "new firefighter" witnessing the apparent chaos of a "blowup." Now consider Maclean's assertion "that in this cockeyed world there are shapes and designs, if only we have some curiosity,

training, and compassion." Keeping in mind the structure of this selection, what do you think he means by this?

WRITING PROJECT

Write a cause and effect analysis of a physical process. The description and results from a lab experiment in a science class would certainly make one good possibility, but there will be many other possibilities to be drawn from your daily experiences. Try to choose an event or a phenomenon featuring a complex or challenging connection between cause(s) and effect(s).

ANNE C. LEWIS

Anne C. Lewis is a national education policy writer. This essay asks
some basic questions of our education system: who is succeeding or failing, how are we paying for it, and what do we do about the failures?
Cause and effect analysis is employed to explore the relationship between investment in education and achievement, particularly in poorer
school districts. In this essay, consider how the cause and effect links
are established and their relation to the recommendations ending the
selection.

The Price of Poverty

Those bundled up against blizzards in the Plains states often console
themselves with the belief that the positive things in their states compensate for the cold. Suburban families go through a similar rational-
ization when they accept the isolation in exchange for the security and
expansive lawns. Such choices are to some degree deceptive, however,
because no matter where one lives, high prices must be paid for ignoring those who don't enjoy the privileges of small-town or suburban
living.

It might come as a surprise to those in the Dakotas to realize, for example, that between 1993 and 1995 their policy makers slashed funding for higher education by 3% to 5%, while they increased funding for
corrections from 35% to more than 42%. Or it might give those living
in the suburbs pause when they realize that 17% of the children in their
midst are living in poverty—and that a large and growing number of
them are white.

These data come from two national reports: one specifically deals
with children in poverty; the other, with the links between state investments in education and the educational attainment and income of the
neediest members of society. Together they are wake-up calls not for
the poor, but for the rest of us.

In this, the richest nation on Earth, one out of every four children lives in poverty. That amounts to some six million children under age 6 (not counting the estimated 1.1 million children who will be added to the list when the new welfare reform takes effect a few months from now). Before we start conjuring images of welfare moms when we hear these figures, we should remember that two-thirds of these children live in working families that are not on the welfare dole. In addition, according to *One in Four,* the report of the National Center for Children in Poverty of the Columbia University School of Public Health, between 1989 and 1994 the poverty rate for white children grew twice as fast as that for black children. In fact, the report says, the poverty rate among white children in this nation "is substantially higher than that for children in other Western democracies."

The second report—*Education Watch: The 1996 Education Trust State and National Data Book*—is an incredible collection of data compiled by the Education Trust, which is based in Washington, D.C. Four pages of statistical data, in chart form, describe each state's annual personal income by level of education and race/ethnicity, as well as each state's investments in education, percentage of students taking challenging academic courses, qualifications of teachers, student academic achievement, college completion rates, and so on. The data show what each state is accomplishing with its minority populations, including even such fine-grained comparisons as the differences between freshman enrollment in college and degrees awarded. It is sobering news for educators and policy makers everywhere.

True, more students than ever before are earning high school diplomas, and more of them are going on to higher education. But, says the Education Trust report, "The diplomas and degrees we award mean little." Schools are failing to educate most Americans to high levels. Furthermore, minority/poor students "are consigned to an academic diet of low expectations and the most rudimentary skills."

The Trust, which is working with communities around the country to create a seamless system of education running from kindergarten through college graduation, goes further than any report so far in showing exactly where the money goes and exactly what results our investments buy. One year at the main campus of the University of Kansas, for example, costs less than $5,500 in tuition. One year in a Kansas state prison costs the public more than $20,500. In 1990 a black person in California who had completed a bachelor's degree was making an average of more than $50,000 in annual personal income; a black high school graduate in that state was making less than half that amount; a dropout, less still. It might also surprise all Californians to learn that, without regard to the poverty level of the school, one-fourth of the state's classes in 1990-91 were being taught by teachers who lacked even a minor in the field they were teaching.

In Connecticut, the income gap between the college-educated and high school dropouts, no matter what their race, is even greater than in California. So is the investment gap. The difference in that state allocations between the highest-spending and the lowest-spending districts in Connecticut is more than $3,200.

In almost every state, minority students (other than Asians) score well below white students on college entrance tests, a fact that is reflected in college enrollment rates. Although most states are pursuing standards-based reforms—and such states as Kentucky and Maryland are doing so vigorously—the gaps between whites and nonwhites continue to grow. The Education Trust asks, "Why?" Because "standards-based reform is too often rolled out generically, as if all systems were operating on a level playing field to begin with." Until the reformers acknowledge and deal with inequities, even more students will be left behind, the report says.

The Trust report recommends that each community take four actions to reduce inequities:

• Set high standards for what all students should know and be able to do. Everyone—teachers, parents, and students—should know what good work is.

• Ensure that all students receive a challenging curriculum. The curriculum should be aligned with the standards, and schools must eliminate watered-down courses.

• Make sure that all children have expert teachers. Because of the long neglect of teacher quality, this will require large investments in professional development.

• Keep its own education watch. Kati Haycock, who heads the Education Trust, is a data-driven reformer who believes that, when people have accurate information, they cannot be excused from acting on that information. (The Trust has prepared a manual for communities on how to collect and analyze data on educational achievement and investments.)

The Education Trust report acknowledges that some people will resist the idea of high standards for all out of concern that tougher expectations will force poor and/or minority children out of school. However, simply giving those students more mentoring and counseling will not compensate for holding them to lower expectations.

At the Trust's recent annual conference, a panel of young people thanked the teachers honored by the Trust who had helped the students overcome barriers and head for or enroll in college. One student, a teenage mother now working on a degree in psychology, pleaded with the audience: "Push us. We need you desperately." That's a strong message that should echo in every state, community, and school.

DISCUSSION QUESTIONS

1. Lewis's analysis is based on "two national reports." What is the relevance of one report to the other?

2. What are the general causes of poor educational performance, according to the writer? What evidence does she present supporting these causes?

3. How successfully does the statistical discussion establish cause and effect connections in the seventh and eighth paragraphs of the essay?

4. Write a thesis statement for this selection, and indicate where it should be placed in the essay. Has the addition of a thesis statement changed or improved the essay in any way?

5. With the addition of a thesis statement, would you retain the introductory paragraph or change it? Why?

6. Is the concluding list of recommendations sufficiently supported by the cause and effect analysis? Why or why not?

WRITING PROJECT

Consider the general issue of social inequities: social, economic, educational, disablement, and so forth. Be sure to narrow your thesis, dealing with a problem in your community, and write a cause and effect analysis of the impact of your chosen problem.

ROBERT WRIGHT

Robert Wright is a columnist for *Time* magazine. This magazine essay appeared soon after the announcement that Scottish scientists had successfully cloned a sheep, setting off widespread debate about the possibility and advisability of cloning humans. Wright approaches the prospect of cloning ourselves from a cause and effect angle: cloning is the cause, and the effects of this process are the human "copies" of ourselves. The author considers what sort of effects will arise from this cause—how would our clones resemble or differ from us? This essay illustrates how one writer deals with uncertain or speculative cause and effect relationships.

Can Souls Be Xeroxed?

The world has had a week to conjure up nightmare scenarios, yet no one has articulated the most frightening peril posed by human cloning: rampant self-satisfaction. Just consider. If cloning becomes an option, what kind of people will use it? Exactly—people who think the world could use more of them; people so chipper that they have no qualms about bestowing their inner life on a dozen members of the next generation; people, in short, with high self-esteem. The rest of us will sit there racked with doubt, worried about inflicting our tortured psyches on the innocent unborn, while all around us shiny, happy people proliferate like rabbits. Or sheep, or whatever.

Of course, this assumes that psyches get copied along with genes. That seems to be the prevailing assumption. People nod politely to the obligatory reminder about the power of environment in shaping character. But many then proceed to talk excitedly about cloning as if it amounts to Xeroxing your soul.

What makes the belief in genetic identity so stubborn? In part a natural confusion over headlines. There are zillions of them about how genes shape behavior, but the underlying stories spring from two different sciences. The first, behavioral genetics, studies genetic differences among people. (Do you have the thrill-seeking gene? You do? Mind if I drive?) Behavioral genetics has demonstrated that genes matter. But does that mean that genes are destiny, that your clone is you?

Enter the second science, evolutionary psychology. It dwells less on genetic difference than on commonality. In this view, the world is already chock-full of virtual clones. My next-door neighbor—or the average male anywhere on the globe—is a 99.9%-accurate genetic copy of me. And paradoxically, many of the genes we share empower the environment to shape behavior and thus make us different from one another. Natural selection has preserved these "malleability genes" because they adroitly tailor character to circumstance.

Thus, though some men are more genetically prone to seek thrills than others, men in general take fewer risks if married with children than if unattached. Though some people may be genetically prone to high self-esteem, everyone's self-esteem depends heavily on social feedback. Genes even mold personality to our place in the family environment, according to Frank Sulloway, author of *Born to Rebel,* the much discussed book on birth order. Parents who clone their obedient oldest child may be dismayed to find that the resulting twin, now lower in the family hierarchy, grows up to be Che Guevara.

This malleability could, in a roundabout way, produce clones who are indeed soul mates. Your clone would, after all, look like you. And certain kinds of faces and physiques lead to certain kinds of experiences that exert certain effects on the mind. Early in this century, a fledgling effort at behavioral genetics divided people into such classes as mesomorphs—physically robust, psychologically assertive—and ectomorphs—skinny, nervous, shy. But even if these generalizations hold some water, it needn't mean that ectomorphs have genes for shyness. It may just mean that skinny people get pushed around on the junior-high playground and their personality adapts. (This is one problem with those identical twins-reared-apart studies by behavioral geneticists: Do the twins' characters correlate because of "character genes" or sometimes just because appearance shapes experience which shapes character?)

People who assume that genes are us seem to think that if you reared your clone, you would experience a kind of mind meld—not quite a fusion of souls, maybe, but an uncanny empathy with your budding carbon copy. And certainly empathy would at times be intense. You might know exactly how nervous your frail, gawky clone felt before the high school prom or exactly how eager your attractive, athletic clone felt.

On the other hand, if you really tried, you could similarly empathize with people who weren't your clone. We've all felt an adolescent's nervousness, and we've all felt youthfully eager, because these feelings are part of the generic human mind, grounded in the genes that define our species. It's just that we don't effortlessly transmute this common experience into empathy except in special cases—with offspring or siblings or close friends. And presumably with clones.

But the cause of this clonal empathy wouldn't be that your inner life was exactly like your clone's (it wouldn't be). The catalyst, rather, would be seeing that familiar face—the one in your high school yearbook, except with a better haircut. It would remind you that you and your clone were *essentially* the same, driven by the same hopes and fears. You might even feel you shared the same soul. And in a sense, this would be true. Then again, in a sense, you share the same soul with everyone.

DISCUSSION QUESTIONS

1. Definitions are important to appreciating Wright's reasoning. Define the following terms: *behavioral genetics, evolutionary psychology,* and *malleability gene.*

2. Discuss, in terms of cause and effect, the "roundabout way" in which the malleability gene can produce "soul mates."

3. What does Wright mean by his concluding statement that "in a sense, you share the same soul with everyone."

4. Write a thesis statement answering the title question. Does your thesis provide a yes or no answer?

5. What other essay writing techniques are employed by Wright? How do they help develop his speculations about the effects of cloning?

6. What determines human personality? In the genetic versus environmental debate, Wright says yes to both sides. How is this so?

7. Many people have rejected the idea of cloning humans as an unacceptable threat to human identity. Does Wright view cloning as a threat? Why or why not?

WRITING PROJECT

Write a cause and effect essay in which the relationship between cause and effect is variable or uncertain. You may use cloning as your subject, or some other process or event of your choice. Watch out for *post hoc* fallacies. It might be helpful to select a controversial subject about which you have strong opinions or knowledge.

8

Argumentative Essays

Argumentative essays are a peaceful form of verbal warfare; we marshall ideas and send them into battle. Children on playgrounds or nations at war may argue their point with physical force, with more or less serious consequences. In a verbal argument between friends, however, or in an argumentative essay, persuasion rules. In an essay of this type we convince readers of the virtue of our ideas by advancing a proposition, or thesis, and supporting it with a series of reasons backed by evidence. Writers do not invade and conquer by force; they sway others through the application of reason and evidence to argument.

A casual argument does not follow any established rules. The give and take of two or more people arguing an issue ordinarily has an impromptu, spontaneous nature as reason and emotion, subjectivity and objectivity are whipped together in a rich conversational stew. An argumentative essay is more challenging—to be convincing we must observe general rules of logic and evidence that are somewhat bendable, but not breakable. There are some rules that are common to all forms of essay writing; all essays should include a thesis and end with a conclusion, and most require some form of evidence or illustration. For instance, in her comparison and contrast essay "Once I Was a Hoosier; Now I Am a Texan," Latricia Dennis illustrates the sharp contrast between life in rural Indiana and urban Texas with examples ranging from the weather to the necessity of locking doors: no in Indiana, yes in Galveston.

An argumentative essay, however, follows certain rules of logic and evidence that do not necessarily apply to other forms of essay writing. Let's take the rules of logic first. Argument in essay form generally follows either inductive or deductive methods of argument. Inductive reasoning moves from the particular to the general and deductive from the general back to the particular. Inductive reasoning begins with a series of specific or isolated events that point to a general thesis. For example, we may establish that Whoopi Goldberg is solely a comic actor after considering the long list of her comic roles—we have moved from the specific list of her starring comic roles to the general premise that she is solely a comic actor.

Deduction uses syllogism to move from a general thesis to a specific application of that thesis. A syllogism is an impressive sounding term for a logical operation that we all use: progressing from a major premise to a minor premise to a conclusion. When parents teach their children about the danger of burning their fingers on the stove they are expecting their four-year-olds to appreciate a syllogism. Children begin to learn logic (and safety) by following the syllogism:

> Major premise: Heated burners cause burned fingers.
>
> Minor premise: You are reaching for a heated burner.
>
> Conclusion: If you touch it, you will burn your fingers.

Induction and deduction can be and often are used in tandem, moving full circle from an inductive observation, to a general thesis, back to an application of that thesis to particular instances. Applying our inductive reasoning about Whoopi Goldberg films to a deductive syllogism, we conclude the following:

> Major premise: Whoopi Goldberg is a comic actor.
>
> Minor premise: Whoopi Goldberg starred in *Sister Act*.
>
> Conclusion: Whoopi Goldberg played a comic role in
>
> *Sister Act*.

As we can see, through the application of inductive and deductive reasoning we have tied up our thesis about the range of Whoopi Goldberg's acting roles in a neat little package.

Argumentative essays are not merely exercises in logic, however: they need to be supported by evidence. Considering our thesis about Whoopi Goldberg, avid moviegoers may attack the premise with inconvenient questions such as, What about her starring dramatic role in *The Color Purple* or her smaller role in *The Ghosts of Mississippi?* Supplying evidence and examples in our essays gives our readers reasons for appreciating the force of our arguments. Evidence may include factual data, historical information, personal observation, or anything that readers will find persuasive when considering our side in a controversial subject. We should also recognize that emotional commitment, while not sufficient in itself in a formal essay, can help shape and drive the force of our arguments. For example, Christine Gregoire's concluding sentence in "It's Not about Money, It's about Smoke," is an emotional plea, but a plea capping a long, carefully reasoned and supported essay about the tobacco settlement. Edward Abbey's "Walking," on the other hand, ignores reason and evidence to make a deliberately idiosyncratic declaration of personal preference. (As we will see, Abbey's essay is an offbeat variation of the argumentative form.)

Argument is by nature controversial; recognition of the controversy means that we both believe in our argument and acknowledge that no one person has a definitive answer. Acknowledging the other side can actually strengthen our own argument. A commonly used argumentative strategy is to discuss other viewpoints as a means of asserting your own. There are several ways of doing this. For example, in "Curfews Are for Parents to Set," Geoffrey Canada begins his essay acknowledging that curfews are widely embraced as a tool against teenage crime and cites the apparently positive experience of Dallas with curfews. At the other end of the spectrum, some writers will introduce an opposing point of view only to reduce it to smoking ash; this strategy admits to no merit in conflicting ideas. The reading selections will show us several variations of dealing with opposing arguments. What every good argumentative essay has in common, however, is to honestly acknowledge and discuss conflicting points of view.

The following selections will illustrate a variety of approaches to the argumentative essay form. There will be dramatic differences in tone and in the credence granted to conflicting ideas. There will also be echoes of other essay writing forms, including narrative-descriptive and critical analysis. In some essays a passionate moral commitment to the thesis will play a large role, in others it will not. The discussion questions will address these differences and also ask that you consider the common elements that help define these variable pieces as argumentative essays.

MICAH C. LASHER

As a high school student in New York City, Micah Lasher wrote this argumentative essay, in which he argues against the growing popularity of requiring uniforms for high school students. In this reading, watch for how Lasher approaches the arguments against his position and how his own arguments develop.

School Uniforms, the $80 Million Boondoggle

Last week, William C. Thompson Jr., the president of the New York City Board of Education, proposed "a mandatory uniform policy" for all public elementary schools in New York City. Later in the week, Schools Chancellor Rudy Crew and Mayor Rudolph Giuliani also jumped on the uniform bandwagon. But if enacted in New York, as proposed, by the fall of 1999, the program could be a financial disaster.

While some claim that uniforms would reduce students' clothing expenses, each uniform would cost $100 to $200. The city would probably have to buy uniforms for families that can't afford them. About 75 percent of the 550,000 students in New York's elementary schools now qualify for the Federal free-lunch program. That's more than 400,000 students. The cost of outfitting them in uniforms could exceed $80 million. That's a hefty price to pay when school buildings are crumbling from disrepair and teachers remain badly underpaid.

Advocates of uniforms say that uniforms have been successful in other school districts. But most of the evidence is anecdotal and unreliable.

Consider Long Beach, Calif. That school system has one of the oldest uniform programs, which has been praised by President Clinton for bringing about a dramatic drop in disciplinary problems. But at the same time school uniforms were introduced, other, more traditional disciplinary measures, like having more teachers patrol hallways, also went into effect.

More positive initiatives like these will better promote discipline and academic success. More after-school programs, for example, may reduce youth violence. Internships in workplaces can bolster academic achievement. And the millions of dollars that Mr. Thompson wants to pump into uniforms could be used to repair school buildings, hire more teachers and reduce class size.

Clothing remains an important means of self-expression for students—especially in a place as diverse as New York. School uniforms would infringe on that freedom. But more important, they would cost the city millions of dollars at a time when schools are still being heated with coal furnaces.

DISCUSSION QUESTIONS

1. What con arguments does Lasher cite? Review the introduction to the chapter on cause and effect. What part of that introduction pertains to Lasher's critique of the con arguments? How?

2. At one point in his essay, Lasher uses a paragraph transition to turn a con argument back into a pro argument supporting his position. Where and how does he do this?

3. How does Lasher employ budgetary and demographic statistics in support of his argument?

4. The writer claims that advocates of school uniforms focus on discipline, but Lasher has a broader agenda. What is it? How does Lasher's agenda develop from uniform and discipline concerns?

5. Does Lasher's thesis statement encompass the arguments in his essay? If not, how would you rewrite the thesis?

6. In his conclusion, the writer introduces a new idea: student self-expression. Does this idea receive enough attention? Has Lasher omitted any con arguments that could be applied to this notion?

WRITING PROJECT

Write an argumentative essay for or against a specific school policy or educational proposal. You may tackle a policy in your own school if you wish or do some research and go further afield. Here are a few ideas:

1. In the nineteenth and early twentieth centuries, many American Indian tribal reservation schools required their students to wear uniforms and speak only English. Were these good ideas? Write an argumentative essay for or against these policies.

2. Should schools have the right to randomly search student lockers for drugs and other contraband? Write an argumentative essay for or against this practice.

3. "School-to-work programs are the best way to prepare students for the demands of the twenty-first century." Write an argumentative essay for or against the trend of tailoring curricula and teaching to meet the needs of the business world.

SAMUEL JOHNSON

Samuel Johnson (1709–1784) was an established literary figure in eighteenth-century England. He was best known as the author of *Johnson's Dictionary* and as the subject of *The Life of Samuel Johnson*, a biography by his friend Boswell. In this argumentative essay, written in the form of a letter, Johnson argues against the practice in the England of his time of imprisoning debtors at the request of their creditors. (Criminal penalties were generally severe at that time: capital punishment was commonly invoked for a wide variety of offenses, including petty theft.) As you read this essay, watch for how structure and tone enable Johnson to shift the focus of blame.

Debtor's Prisons
To The Idler [16]

Sir,

As I was passing lately under one of the gates of this city, I was struck with horror by a rueful cry, which summoned me 'to remember the poor debtors'.

The wisdom and justice of the English laws are, by Englishmen at least, loudly celebrated; but scarcely the most zealous admirers of our institutions can think that law wise which, when men are capable of work, obliges them to beg; or just which exposes the liberty of one to the passions of another.

The prosperity of a people is proportionate to the number of hands and minds usefully employed. To the community sedition is a fever, corruption is a gangrene, and idleness an atrophy. Whatever body, and whatever society, wastes more than it acquires must gradually decay; and every being that continues to be fed, and ceases to labor, takes away something from the public stock.

The confinement, therefore, of any man in the sloth and darkness of

---

[16] *The Idler* was a series of papers contributed by Johnson to the *Universal Chronicle*, or *Weekly Gazette*, from 1758 to 1760.

a prison is a loss to the nation, and no gain to the creditor. For of the multitudes who are pining in those cells of misery, a very small part is suspected of any fraudulent act by which they retain what belongs to others. The rest are imprisoned by the wantonness of pride, the malignity of revenge, or the acrimony of disappointed expectation.

If those who thus rigorously exercise the power which the law has put into their hands be asked why they continue to imprison those whom they know to be unable to pay them, one will answer that his debtor once lived better than himself; another, that his wife looked above her neighbors, and his children went in silk clothes to the dancing school; and another, that he pretended to be a joker and a wit. Some will reply that if they were in debt they should meet with the same treatment; some, that they owe no more than they can pay, and need therefore give no account of their actions. Some will confess their resolution that their debtors shall rot in jail; and some will discover that they hope, by cruelty, to wring the payment from their friends.

The end of all civil regulations is to secure private happiness from private malignity; to keep individuals from the power of one another; but this end is apparently neglected when a man, irritated with loss, is allowed to be the judge of his own cause, and to assign the punishment of his own pain; when the distinction between guilt and unhappiness, between casualty and design, is entrusted to eyes blind with interest, to understandings depraved by resentment.

Since poverty is punished among us as a crime, it ought at least to be treated with the same lenity as other crimes; the offender out not to languish at the will of him whom he has offended, but to be allowed some appeal to the justice of his country. There can be no reason why any debtor should be imprisoned, but that he may be compelled to payment; and a term should therefore be fixed in which the creditor should exhibit his accusation of concealed property. If such property can be discovered, let it be given to the creditor; if the charge is not offered, or cannot be proved, let the prisoner be dismissed.

Those who made the laws have apparently supposed that every deficiency of payment is the crime of the debtor. But the truth is that the creditor always shares the act, and often more than shares the guilt of improper trust. It seldom happens that any man imprisons another but for debts which he suffered to be contracted in hope of advantage to himself, and for bargains in which he proportioned his profit to his own opinion of the hazard; and there is no reason why one should punish the other for a contract in which both concurred.

Many of the inhabitants of prisons may justly complain of harder treatment. He that once owes more than he can pay is often obliged to bribe his creditor to patience, by increasing his debt. Worse and worse commodities, at a higher and higher price, are forced upon him; he is impoverished by compulsive traffic, and at last overwhelmed, in the common receptacles of misery, by debts which, without his own consent, were accumulated on his head. To the relief of this distress, no other objection can be made but that by an easy dissolution of debts, fraud will be left without punishment, and imprudence without awe,[17] and that when insolvency shall be no longer punishable, credit will cease.

The motive to credit is the hope of advantage. Commerce can never be at a stop while one man wants what another can supply; and credit will never be denied while it is likely to be repaid with profit. He that trusts one whom he designs to sue is criminal by the act of trust; the cessation of such insidious traffic is to be desired, and no reason can be given why a change of the law should impair any other.

We see nation trade with nation, where no payment can be compelled. Mutual convenience produces mutual confidence, and the merchants continue to satisfy the demands of each other, though they have nothing to dread but the loss of trade.

It is vain to continue an institution which experience shows to be ineffectual. We have now imprisoned one generation of debtors after another, but we do not find that their numbers lessen. We have now learned that rashness and imprudence will not be deterred from taking credit; let us try whether fraud and avarice may be more easily restrained from giving it.

I am, Sir, etc.

1758

[17]In Samuel Johnson's time, the term *awe* suggested the power to inspire fear of authority.

DISCUSSION QUESTIONS

1. What is the thesis statement? Does the thesis statement accurately summarize Johnson's arguments?

2. What opposing arguments does Johnson cite in favor of debtor's prisons? Summarize the arguments Johnson uses favoring a change in the laws governing such prisons. Does he specifically refute every opposing argument?

3. Are Johnson's pro arguments primarily inductive or deductive? Briefly discuss ways in which the prevailing mode of argument could have been differently presented.

4. What is Johnson's attitude toward creditors? How does his attitude affect his argument?

5. By the conclusion of the essay, Johnson has placed blame squarely on the creditors. How has he accomplished this? Cite two passages showing his evolving attitude toward creditors.

6. Consider your answer to question 4, and discuss the tone of this essay. How does the writer use the opening paragraph to establish the shape of his argument?

WRITING PROJECT

Credit cards are a blessing or a curse, depending on point of view. What is your point of view? Write an argument for or against the use of credit cards. You may use personal experience, national trends, or a combination of the two.

GEOFFREY CANADA

In this essay, writer Geoffrey Canada, author of *Fist, Stick, Knife, Gun* and *Reaching Up for Manhood,* mixes personal anecdote and experience with more general arguments to build a case against the increasing use of teenage curfews imposed by American cities and towns. Canada mixes the personal and the general and also inductive and deductive methods to construct his argument. The discussion questions will consider how the author integrates these contrasting modes and methods into an effective argumentative essay.

Curfews Are for Parents to Set

One reason I was able to grow up in the South Bronx of the 1950's and 1960's without getting into major trouble was that I lived under a curfew. The penalty for violating the curfew was swift and severe. Although I got to plead my case—a watch that didn't work, the train was running late—the judge was seasoned and cynical (she had heard it all before). The usual verdict: guilty. The sentence: confinement to the apartment, when I wasn't at school, for a whole week.

This curfew was set, of course, by my mother, who raised four sons by herself. Like my mother, I am a strong believer in curfews. But I don't believe cities or states should impose them.

The calls for teen-age curfews by President Clinton and Bob Dole and, earlier this month, by Thomas V. Ognibene, a New York City Councilman, are part of a disturbing trend. Though New York doesn't have a curfew, most big cities now do. Increasingly, politicians are viewing the problems of youth solely through the prism of crime and punishment.

Indeed, while violent adult crime is falling in many big cities, youth crime and violence are generally on the rise. At the same time, the population of children in the 5- to 8-year-old range has risen by more than 20 percent over the past decade. So, by the year 2005, the thinking goes, we may have an explosion of violence led by young people— including children who are being called "superpredators." The result: almost all proposals for young people involve "getting tough"—prosecuting juveniles as adults, for example.

So what is wrong with official curfews? Many of the biggest American cities have them on the books. Dallas has reported that a curfew has helped reduce crime significantly. (No accurate data exist on the effectiveness of curfews nationwide.) But there are plenty of problems with curfews.

• *The wrong people impose them.* At a time when many people are clamoring for less government, why pass curfew laws that usurp the rights of parents to raise their children as they see fit? Families are a better context for kids to learn that freedoms come with responsibilities. Each year, I had to renegotiate my curfew with my mother; the older I got, the later the curfew. If there was a dance or a party, I got special permission from her, not the police, to say out late. As a high school senior, I worked in a factory after classes and didn't get home until 11 P.M. My mother was skeptical about my ability to juggle work and school. But she gave me permission to try, with the proviso that if my grades dipped or I didn't get up on time, the job was over. My freedom to stay out late, for fun or work, depended on my maturity and on meeting the expectation of my mother and my teachers.

• *Curfews create a new category of criminal behavior.* These are tough times for young people. Guns claim thousands of their lives; schools are failing (some are even falling down). Jobs are hard to find in minority communities. Yet programs have been cut: summer employment, health and mental health services and after-school centers—even though children are more likely to get into trouble between 3 P.M. and 6 P.M. than at any other time, according to a report issued last year by the National Center for Juvenile Justice. The last thing kids need is a new way to be negatively classified—as delinquent curfew-breakers.

• *Curfews may worsen community problems with police and racism.* If you are a person of color and male, you invariably have a story to tell about police harassment or worse. I have my own stories. Will curfews be enforced uniformly? Many in the African-American and Latino communities doubt this. In New York City, police abuse in their neighborhoods includes the use of excessive force and the death of suspects in custody, according to an Amnesty International report issued last month.

A curfew won't work if adults do not support it because they think the police act unfairly. Besides, it puts police in a tough situation. Can *you* tell the difference between a 19-year-old (who may be exempt from a curfew) and a 17-year-old (who may not be)? A law that gives the police the right—indeed, requires them—to stop people on the basis of their perceived age is an invitation to trouble.

I know that some parents need help with their children. I also know that when help is offered, parents respond. If political leaders really want to help, they should stop cutting resources for youth. Until then, if you want to know about curfews, before you talk to the President or a city councilman, talk to my mother.

DISCUSSION QUESTIONS

1. What is the thesis statement? How well does it summarize Canada's argument?

2. Consider the con arguments that appear toward the beginning of the essay. Does the author specifically refute these arguments? If not, is his argument weakened as a result?

3. How does Canada use personal experience to move inductively from the specific to the general? In the sixth paragraph, the author supports a general argument with personal anecdotal evidence. Is this argumentative strategy successful? Why or why not?

4. Analyze the seventh through tenth paragraphs. Are they primarily inductive or deductive? Is there a shift in argumentative strategy? If so, does it effectively complement the first part of the essay?

5. How does Canada use nationwide trends and evidence—pro and con—in his essay? Is there adequate consideration of national evidence and examples?

6. Where is analysis employed? What effect does the use of analysis have?

7. Does the conclusion successfully summarize and reflect Canada's evidence and arguments?

WRITING PROJECT

Write an argumentative essay about some local, state, or national law or policy that affects you personally. (Possible topics are curfews, school and workplace policies, drug laws, or discrimination laws.) You may cite personal experience, but make sure it is relevant to and strengthens your argument.

COLLABORATIVE ACTIVITY

Divide into two groups, with one group producing an argument in support of curfews, and the other against. Which is the more effective? Why?

TED SIZER

Ted Sizer, an education professor at Brown University, is chairman of the Coalition for Essential Schools and director of the Annenburg Institute for School Reform.

Virtually all of us, from elementary school on, have been classified, tracked, and granted or denied admission based on standardized tests we have sat through with a number two pencil clutched firmly in hand. In this essay, Sizer argues that standardized tests pose only very limited uses, which do not include predicting the long-term abilities and capabilities of individuals. The discussion questions will consider the nature of the evidence Sizer employs against a broad application of standardized testing, as well as the importance of inductive reasoning to Sizer's argument.

What's Wrong with Standardized Tests?

Over the years I have listened to many parents talk about their children and their children's schools. Thoughtful parents want us teachers to know and respect their youngsters and their specialness: the talents and weaknesses, the volatility, the vulnerability, the poignant hope. They want their kids to be cared for, understood, and thereby judged, as *individuals*—and as individuals of promise and potential.

At the same time there *are* patterns to growth and development, patterns that transcend the individual, which teachers (and parents too) should ponder and understand. But the patterns are just that—tendencies, generalized expectations, useful guideposts.

An intensely painful reality for American educators is that we have turned these well-intentioned testing guideposts into hitching posts, into benevolent "systems" through which children can predictably move. Students are judged by norms based on chronological age. They are taught with a common pedagogy, at a common pace within their assigned groupings.

One of American educators' greatest conceits is the belief that people can be pigeonholed, in effect sorted by some scientific mechanism, usually the standardized test.

The results of even the most carefully and sensitively crafted tests cannot be used fairly for high-stakes purposes for individuals: the belief that they can persists stubbornly in the educational community, in spite of an avalanche of research that challenges the tests' precision—and in spite of parents' common sense.

All of us who have taught for a while know "low testers" who became wonderfully resourceful and imaginative adults and "high testers" who as adults are, sadly, brittle and shallow people. We cringe as we remember how we so unfairly characterized them.

Danny Algrant's writing and directing of the 1994 film, "Naked in New York," certainly was not completely evident when I taught him. Danny was an ebullient itch, even as a high school senior, a trial—but a worthy one—for his teacher. All that ebullient itchiness I gather now has been focused in successful film making. And so on: the awkward adolescent who now juggles the myriad demands of an inner-city school as principal, or the "low-tester" who is now a successful writer.

As a high-school principal, I sadly experienced a conversation with a highly placed education official who spun out for me both colorful descriptions of his own *very* special, *very* talented and *very* particular children and in the same breath admiring testimony about his state's narrowly standardized testing program and the student assignments that would arise from it. This elaborate system, of course, was for other people's children. His children needed the special attention of a private school. To this day, the irony eludes him.

There is tremendous public reluctance to question the usage and values of such tests. Being against conventional "testing" makes one appear to be against "standards." Test scores both give those in charge a device to move large numbers of students around and provide a fig leaf to justify labeling and tracking them in one way or another. How can we, they say, accept each little person as complicated, changeable, special? Impossible. It would take too much time. (Then privately, But not for *my* child. Let me tell you about her.)

It would be silly, however, to dismiss all standardized testing. If carefully crafted and interpreted, these tests can reveal certain broad trends, even if they tell us only a bit about individual children. Such testing is helpful at the margins: it can signal the possibility of a troubled or especially gifted or otherwise "special" youngster. It can signal competence at immediate and comparable work if the classroom task to be completed (effective close reading of a text) is similar to the test (made up of prose passages and related questions) and if the task is attempted shortly after taking the test.

But none of the major tests used in American elementary and secondary education correlates well with long-term success or failure. S.A.T. scores, for examples, suggest likely grades in the freshman year at college; they do not predict much thereafter.

On the contrary, conventional tests can distort and thereby corrupt schooling. Most do not measure long-term intellectual habits. Indeed, many undermine the value of such by excessively emphasizing immediate, particular facts and skills considered out of context.

Those characteristics that we most value fail to be "tested": the qualities of mind and heart upon which we count for a healthy culture.

And a competitive work force. Send me, says the business leader, young employees who know something about using important knowledge, who learn readily and independently, who think for themselves and are dependable in the deepest sense. The college teacher says much the same, perhaps describing the qualities somewhat differently. Unfortunately, when classifying students, schools still peg kids by brief paper records and scores. "If the combined S.A.T. scores are below 1100, we will not consider the student," the admissions staff says, knowing full well that some high scorers are less worthy potential students than some low scorers.

Assessment and accountability are worthy goals. The task is to create a system that usefully and fairly assesses what we care about and that does not distort the process of learning. Such a system cannot be done on the cheap. There is no shortcut to a fair and full understanding of a human being.

An accountable system should depend largely on students' real work rather than on data emerging from test booklets duly recorded on a transcript. It should not only "look at" this work—an essay or an evolved mathematical proof—but ask the student to defend it. If defense of a conclusion were a part of the expected assessment, students would work hard to go deeper than the mere recollection of particular answers.

For each student, a variety of assessments should be in constant development, with no fixed assignment of merit. Schools should accept the reality that young people change and that assessments of them at one point may not be relevant later. The practical effect of this is the elimination of rigid tracking, the institutional form of stereotyping.

The parents' plea to me-the-principal that my school not pigeonhole their child, that I should see instead the complex and forming person before me, cut deep. I myself had once been pigeonholed, as "not really college material." Only by the vociferous advocacy of my father did I get a fair shot. What of the youngster who has no such advocate, whom the school system, with all its well-intentioned "science," has written off?

DISCUSSION QUESTIONS

1. Inductive reasoning is central to Sizer's argument against standardized tests as commonly used. Discuss.

2. Does Sizer's use of personal experiences and observations strengthen his argument? In what way?

3. The essay does assign a limited usefulness to standardized tests. What effect does this have upon Sizer's thesis? Does the admission of a limited legitimacy enhance his argument?

4. Consider this statement of Sizer's: "Those characteristics that we most value fail to be 'tested': the qualities of mind and heart upon which we count for a healthy culture." What does the author mean by this? Is this statement supported and explained anywhere in the essay?

5. Summarize the arguments Sizer uses against standardized tests. Does he effectively employ specific evidence and examples supporting his assertions?

6. After reviewing the final four paragraphs of the essay, review the thesis statement. What changes would be necessary to write a divided thesis, and what changes might a divided thesis make to the structure of the selection?

WRITING PROJECT

Write an argumentative essay about specific tests results that you feel did not fairly reflect your abilities. For the purposes of this assignment, you must use a regional or national test, not a particular classroom test assigned by one of your instructors. Drawing on your personal experience, build an argument for or against standardized tests or some kinds of standardized tests. If your experience of such tests has always been positive, you may argue in support of testing.

EDWARD ABBEY

The following essay by the essayist and novelist Edward Abbey takes a good deal of creative license with the argumentative form. The tone is chatty and descriptive, and the apparent thesis statement at the beginning leads us down a false trail. Abbey's essay strolls through likes and dislikes, feeling and anecdote; the demands of reasoned argument and the evidence to support it are on vacation here. As a student, you may never write an argumentative essay quite like this one, but you can still appreciate Abbey's offbeat "argument." The discussion questions will focus on how this piece works as an argumentative essay.

Walking

Whenever possible, I avoid the practice myself. If God had meant us to walk, he would have kept us down on all fours, with well-padded paws. He would have constructed our planet on the model of the simple cube, so that the notion of circularity and consequently the wheel might never have arisen. He surely would not have made mountains.

There is something unnatural about walking. Especially walking uphill, which always seems to me not only unnatural but so *unnecessary.* That iron tug of gravitation should be all the reminder we need that in walking uphill we are violating a basic law of nature. Yet we persist in doing it. No one can explain why. George H. Leigh-Mallory's asinine rationale for climbing a mountain—"because it's there"—could easily be refuted with a few well-placed hydrogen bombs. But our common sense continues to lag far behind the available technology.

My own first Group Outing was with the United States Infantry. The experience made a bad impression on my psyche—a blister on my soul that has never healed completely. Of course, we were outfitted with the very best hiking equipment the army could provide: heavy-gauge steel helmet; gas mask; knee-length wool overcoat; fully loaded ammunition belt around the waist, resting on the kidneys; full field pack including a shovel ("entrenching tool"), a rugged canvas tarpaulin ("shelter half") and a pair of wool blankets for bivouac; steel canteen filled with briny water (our group leader insisted on dumping salt tablets into each member's canteen at the beginning of the hike); and such obvious essentials as combat boots, bayonet, and the M-1 rifle. Since resigning from the infantry, some time ago, I have not participated in any group outings.

However, some of us do walk best under duress. Or only under duress. Certainly my own most memorable hikes can be classified as Shortcuts that Backfired. For example, showing my wife the easy way to drive down from Deadhorse Point to Moab, via Pucker Pass, I took a wrong turn in the twilight, got lost in a maze of jeep trails, ran out of gas. We walked about twenty miles that night, through the rain, she in tennis shoes and me in cowboy boots. Better than waiting for the heat of the day. Or take the time I tried to force a Hertz rented car up Elephant Hill on the Needles Jeep trail—another long, impromptu walk. Or one night on the eastern outskirts of Albuquerque, New Mexico, when a bunch of student drunks decided to climb the Sandia Mountains by moonlight. About twelve started; two of us made it, arriving at the crest sixteen hours later, famished, disillusioned, lacerated, and exhausted. But it sure cured the hangover.

There are some good things to say about walking. Not many, but some. Walking takes longer, for example, than any other known form of locomotion except crawling. Thus it stretches time and prolongs life. Life is already too short to waste on speed. I have a friend who's always in a hurry; he never gets anywhere. Walking makes the world much bigger and therefore more interesting. You have time to observe the details. The utopian technologies foresee a future for us in which distance is annihilated and anyone can transport himself anywhere, instantly. Big deal, Buckminster.[18] To be everywhere at once is to be nowhere forever, if you ask me. That's God's job, not ours; that's what we pay Him for. Her for.

The longest journey begins with a single step, not with a turn of the

---

[18] a reference to Buckminster Fuller (1895–1983), an inventor and a designer who believed that futuristic technologies could solve most human problems

ignition key. That's the best thing about walking, the journey itself. It doesn't much matter whether you get where you're going or not. You'll get there anyway. Every good hike brings you eventually back home. Right where you started.

Which reminds me of circles. Which reminds of wheels. Which reminds me my old truck needs another front-end job. Any good mechanics out there wandering through the smog?

DISCUSSION QUESTIONS

1. What is the tone of the opening paragraph? How does the tone of the opening paragraph convey the impression that Abbey is not really serious about his objections to walking?

2. Where is the thesis statement in the essay? The thesis seems to be a grudging admission that there may be some advantages to walking, after all. Does the sudden, offhand introduction of the thesis make it more or less effective? How?

3. Consider the examples employed for and against Abbey's argument. Are the evidence and examples used for and against walking different in nature?

4. Let's say an editor added this statement to Abbey's essay: "Walking is always valuable, but often unpleasant, painful, or silly." What would Abbey say to this addition, and why?

5. Imagine you were considering moving this selection to a different chapter in this text. Where would you put it, and why? Now consider yourself the instructor grading the essay. What grade would "Walking" receive?

WRITING PROJECT

Write an argumentative essay supporting or opposing an activity you enjoy. For instance, if you are addicted to computer games, you could try to develop an argument demonstrating that this activity is beneficial to your physical and mental health. Be controversial, and remember that you must support your argument with evidence and examples.

Christine Gregoire is the attorney general for the state of Washington. In her argumentative essay she defends the agreement reached in the summer of 1997 between attorneys general of various states (including Washington) and the tobacco industry to regulate the sale of cigarettes. Following the Gregoire selection, Eugene J. Craig, a Seattle attorney and author of legal and public service articles, attacks the tobacco settlement, criticizing it for not going far enough to combat the deadly effects of smoking. Taken together, these two essays illustrate how a complex subject—the tobacco settlement—can be evaluated from radically different and conflicting perspectives. Your task in reading these selections will not be determining who is right or wrong in this debate, but examining how the writers construct their arguments. The information imparted supporting these arguments is intricate and densely packed; the discussion questions will ask that you pay close attention to content as well as structure. (The tobacco bill died in the 1998 congressional session; Gregoire has since joined five other attorneys general in a new round of negotiations with the tobacco companies.)

CHRISTINE GREGOIRE

It's Not about Money, It's about Smoke

It has been 30 days since a comprehensive tobacco plan was presented to the American people by the attorneys general. In those 30 days, 90,000 kids have started smoking and 30,000 of them will die prematurely because of their decision to smoke.

In those same 30 days, approximately 36,000 Americans have died from a tobacco-related illness.

Those grim statistics about tobacco's toll of addiction and death underscore why four other attorneys general and I spent three grueling months convincing the industry to agree to a settlement plan that would save millions of lives by dramatically changing tobacco policy in America.

As public discussion of the settlement plan has begun, some have said it doesn't go far enough. We find that criticism disheartening in light of the fact that for the past 40 years, Congress has maintained the status quo on tobacco policy. Lawsuits brought neither relief to consumers nor changed conduct by the industry. Neither Congress nor our state legislatures took steps to reduce the death, disease and financial ruin from tobacco.

This agreement is not about whether enough money is extracted from tobacco companies, whether the Food and Drug Administration's jurisdiction is broad enough, whether we have punished the industry enough or whether any action is enough short of putting the industry out of business.

The agreement is about saving our kids from addiction, preventing Americans from dying and changing the unlawful tactics of a multibillion dollar industry which targets kids as its next generation of addicted customers. It will end the status quo which has existed for nearly half a century and left tobacco, which is an addictive, deadly product, legal and unregulated.

A Well-Stocked Tool Box

The agreement provides this nation with a well-stocked tool box to address the wide-ranging issues associated with a product which kills more than 400,000 people a year.

It provides strong smoking-prevention and cessation programs, tough new enforcement efforts, clear FDA authority to regulate nicotine as a drug, a change in corporate culture, full disclosure of industry research, protections from environmental tobacco smoke and, based on the industry's deplorable record, the largest financial settlement in the history of the world.

I would like to open the doors of the negotiations a bit for you and give you some insights about some of the key issues we discussed.

Ever since news of our talks broke in mid-April (about two weeks into the negotiations), many people have focused on how much Big

Tobacco would have to pay. In reality, we spent relatively little time, until the final days of the talks, discussing money.

From day one of negotiations, when Geoffrey Bible, chief executive officer of Philip Morris Cos., and Steve Goldstone, chief executive of RJR Nabisco, asked us to consider a settlement, the other attorneys general and I told the industry that this settlement isn't about money. It is about kids and public health.

It has been hard, however, to escape the focus on money. Perhaps it is because for some, we can only provide justice with dollars. Bet let's face it, there isn't enough money to repay Americans for the loved ones who have lost their lives, for the pain and suffering, and for the dollars to care for the sick and dying.

A Settlement That Lasts Forever

But is this a reasonable financial settlement of the 40 lawsuits filed by attorneys general? Yes. It is a settlement that lasts forever. Tobacco companies will make payments in perpetuity. Over the next 25 years alone they will pay $368.5 billion (at least $530 billion with inflation).

For perspective, the settlement far exceeds the combined payout by Union Carbide for the deadly gas leak in Bhopal, India, Exxon for the Valdez oil spill and the hundreds of asbestos cases from around the country.

While distribution of the dollars still must be worked out, I estimate Washington could recover about $100 million a year—forever—from the settlement.

The issue of regulatory authority for the FDA received far less public attention than the money payout, but I can tell you it was far more contentious and time consuming and will have a far greater return in improving public health. Tobacco companies, wielding their tremendous legal and lobbying power, until now have successfully fought off regulation, even though their products are addictive and can kill you.

As the lead AG for youth and public health issues, I was pressing to give the FDA authority to regulate nicotine and all unhealthy components of tobacco products. We need to be concerned about both the addictiveness and health impacts from tobacco. If we want any hope of stopping the addiction of 3,000 kids a day, we need to look at regulating nicotine.

But people aren't dying from nicotine. They die from tar and other components of tobacco products.

Tobacco negotiators dug their heels in and resisted regulation. When both sides refused to budge, the talks nearly broke down. But in the final four days of nearly round-the-clock talks, the tobacco companies finally agreed—for the first time, by federal statute—to give FDA regulatory authority over not only nicotine, but tar and other deadly components.

The agreement includes criteria for the FDA to reduce nicotine, tar and other harmful components. Since the agreement was announced, some have speculated the criteria limit the FDA's authority. That is simply not true. The criteria will provide the FDA full authority, funding and a mandated timeline to regulate tobacco and demand the companies produce a less-addictive, less-deadly product for consumers.

Anti-smoking advocates want the FDA to be able to reduce and ban nicotine. I agree, but we found the solution was not as simple. It became clear during our research and talks that scientists do not agree to what level nicotine can be reduced before it presents additional public-health risks.

Reducing nicotine not that simple

The fear is that by reducing nicotine, addicted smokers would smoke more to maintain the same level of nicotine they are used to. So we could turn a one-pack-a-day smoker into a two-pack-a-day smoker, thereby doubling the health risk by exposing them to twice the level of tar and other deadly components.

To address this concern we included a provision that the FDA must determine a reduction of nicotine will promote public health.

The FDA also must determine that reduction in nicotine would not result in a significant demand for contraband. If nicotine is reduced too fast and too much, consumers may turn to an illegal product which is a much greater health risk because of higher levels of tar, other harmful components and nicotine.

This country has 50 million smokers and 6 million smokeless tobacco users. A contraband market could result in a huge health and law enforcement crisis. FDA itself warned about contraband this past fall and we left authority to determine what is a significant demand for contraband with the FDA.

Another of the more difficult issues we wrestled constantly with was the proper level of punishment for an industry which has lied and deceived the public and preyed on our children.

We spent hours arguing over penalty levels for not only past actions, but appropriate penalty levels for future misdeeds by the companies.

Penalty Will Benefit Health of All

Under the agreement the industry will pay $60 billion in punitive damages for its past misconduct. To date, no one has ever collected punitive damages from tobacco companies and in some states, such as Washington, the law doesn't allow punitive damages. The penalty is unprecedented in our legal history (it is four times the amount paid by Exxon for the Valdez oil spill) and the money will be used to benefit the health of all Americans.

For future regulatory violations, the agreement imposes fines in some cases which are 10 times greater than those for any other industry.

Despite weeks of opposition from the industry, we also added a completely new idea which would impose fines for failing to achieve youth smoking reduction goals, which call for a 67 percent reduction in youth smoking from current levels within ten years. The fines amount to about $80 million for every percentage point short of the goal, with a cap of $2 billion. The fine would strip the industry of all profit it would make over the lifetime of a teen who starts smoking. The amount of the fines is unprecedented.

The other difficult question we had to struggle with was one we hear primarily from the long-time tobacco warriors. Have you done enough if the industry is still allowed to operate?

It is not the role of attorneys general to put an industry out of business. That was never the intent of our lawsuits. Our role is to ensure the industry abides by our laws as they manufacture and sell what is a legal product in this country.

If Congress approves the settlement, there is nothing in the agreement which would prevent people from seeking more aggressive tobacco policies.

When I filed Washington's lawsuit a little over a year ago, I believed we had a good case against the industry, but never in my wildest dreams would I have believed we could have achieved the kind of settlement we agreed to late last month.

Promised to Get Rid of Joe Camel

As we got involved in the settlement talks, the other attorneys general and I realized our lawsuits had provided us with the leverage to do what no one else has done in half a century in this country to develop a legally binding comprehensive plan for addressing the leading, preventable cause of death in America.

For the past three months I have taken so many red-eye flights to Washington, D.C., that the flight attendants started recognizing me and welcoming me back. I have talked tobacco Mondays through Fridays and usually twice again during Saturday and Sunday conference calls at my home.

In the end, we produced an agreement which could change forever the tobacco industry in America.

We are already beginning to see small changes. When RJR announced last week that it would put the cigarette advertising icon Joe Camel out to pasture, it was the culmination of a promise Bible and Goldstone made to us in the opening days of the negotiations. They pledged to us that April morning in Washington, D.C. that they would get rid of Joe and the Marlboro Man as a sign that they were intent in changing the way the companies do business.

Joe Camel has been a particular irritant to me since he has been the poster boy of the industry's advertising to kids. Since 1988 when RJR started using Joe in advertising and marketing campaigns, Camel's share of the children's market has rocketed from 0.05 percent to about

33 percent. And when I asked an RJR executive once why they advertised to kids who can't legally smoke, he replied, "If they choose to smoke, we have a right to go after that market."

Is the comprehensive plan perfect? No. Is the comprehensive tobacco settlement enough? It exceeds the goals and any potential outcome of the attorneys general in their lawsuits. It goes well beyond anything individual states could do legislatively. And, it does what no Congress has been willing to do.

The settlement offers this nation a chance to help our kids avoid a lifetime of addiction and save our loved ones from a premature death. We can't afford another child lost or another life taken from us.

DISCUSSION QUESTIONS

1. After reading the thesis statement and then the paragraph immediately preceding it, do you see any potential problems with Gregoire's thesis?

2. Identify and discuss two other essay techniques employed by Gregoire in her essay. What purpose do these techniques serve in her argument?

3. Because this essay is a defense of the settlement, it must have critics. What are the opposing arguments cited? Are they discussed in enough detail?

4. Gregoire claims the agreement gives the nation "a well-stocked tool box" to fight the effects of smoking. Briefly summarize the evidence she marshals supporting this assertion. Is her evidence persuasive? Why or why not?

5. What achievements does Gregoire claim for the settlement but not explain or discuss in the essay? Are they significant omissions?

6. Consider the conclusion and particularly the concluding sentence. Do the claims the writer makes for the settlement support the wish expressed in this statement?

EUGENE J. CRAIG

The Deal's Too Good for Big Tobacco;
What about the Public?

May I suggest the task of government and its officials in the matter of the tobacco litigation is to protect the health of the public and to reduce or eliminate the 450,000 deaths to Americans caused yearly by tobacco products. May I also suggest that the proposed resolution of the litigation should include the following:

1. The declaration that tobacco and tobacco products are addictive.

2. The FDA should have jurisdiction over tobacco and tobacco products that is unrestricted and unconditional and designed to limit the use of such products by both children and adults.

3. The FDA jurisdiction should include, but not be limited to, regulation over all forms of tobacco manufacturing, merchandising and advertising.

4. Smoking of tobacco and tobacco products should be banned from all facilities and areas where the people gather. (Vented rooms for smoking are not sufficient.)

On the first point, there is strong and compelling medical evidence that tobacco is addictive. That should be acknowledged by the industry.

On the second point, the trend of the cases and government policy points to greater authority and jurisdiction of the FDA over tobacco without the settlement. The current settlement proposal limits the future authority and jurisdiction of the FDA. It handicaps the FDA from protecting the health of the public. *The proposed settlement makes the FDA largely ineffective.* The FDA is probably the only viable government agency that could be in the position of protecting the public health now and in the future. It should not now be limited by the proposed settlement for what it may be able to accomplish in the future without the proposed settlement.

The seriousness of adverse and death-threatening effects of tobacco and tobacco products are evident. It means that my mother-in-law who has been addicted to tobacco for 40 years requires oxygen on a 24 hours a day basis . . . a requirement for the past two years and a continuing requirement for the remainder of her life. Everywhere she goes, she carries an oxygen tank. On plane trips, special arrangements need be made for oxygen pick-up at the departure airport, oxygen delivery aboard the aircraft and oxygen delivery at the arriving airport. Her life-expectancy has been materially shortened.

It further means that a client in her mid-40's, a teacher by profession and an intelligent individual, is not able to break the nicotine habit acquired in high school.

It means watching a logger, healthy and burly in all regards except for emphysema, slowly perish from decades of smoking. There are hundreds of thousands of these situations. How can a settlement be proposed where these health hazards will continue?

On the third point, *the FDA should be empowered to limit, and even ban, merchandising and advertising in the future.* The banning of Joe Camel, the Marlboro Man and sports sponsorship is fine for the present time but the tobacco industry and its advertising agencies are sure to develop other means of merchandising and advertising which are just as effective.

We are seeing increasing advertising through movies with scenes of Hollywood celebrities smoking cigarettes and cigars. These scenes which are viewed by *all* ages including children leave the suggestion that it is the appropriate thing to do socially or under stressful situations. We are seeing an increase in cigar advertising in magazines, the promotion of the "cigar rooms" in restaurants and the placing of cigar displays in pro shops of golf courses. The ingenuity of the tobacco industry and its advertising agencies in alternate forms of advertising and merchandising should never be underestimated.

On the fourth point, the *non-smoking public should be free of the adverse health effects and nuisance of secondhand smoke.* Last month I stayed in a first-class hotel where the previous occupant, or maybe occupants, smoked. The odor was not only an annoyance but the air-conditioning system circulated the odor into my clothes.

We need to appreciate the voluntary efforts of hotels, car-rental agencies and restaurants which specify smoke-free environments. We need to require that our public officials extend this effort to all places where people gather.

The proposed settlement includes no real and meaningful way to regulate the industry in the future. The limitations of the proposal placed on the FDA make it a bulldog with a muzzle. *Jurisdiction needs to vest in the FDA over manufacturing, merchandising and advertising.* This is probably not as great a threat to the industry as it may appear since the industry already enjoys enormous clout over governmental policies and agencies, but at least it is the best of available alternatives.

While it is important to put in place those regulations that will discourage children from smoking, it is also important to protect the health of adults. The argument that adults can fend for themselves, or that they should be free to choose, is fallacious, because many adults are addicted and do not have the will power to overcome the addiction.

The government's tobacco subsidies should be abolished. It is difficult to reconcile the payment to the tobacco growers of a crop that is death threatening and death-causing to the public. Why haven't the litigators included the termination of subsidies to the growers?

The payment of lump-sum damages is not a major issue to me. Why? First, the damages in last analysis will not come from the industry but will come from the smoking public who will pay more for tobacco and tobacco products. It may be ironic that those who are addicted by the industry will end up paying the amount of damages.

It may very well be in the best interest of the public to continue the litigation in the event that the above goals are not part of the proposed settlement. The justice system can resolve the matter of damages. The FDA has been pursuing jurisdiction over future health concerns. It has made considerable strides and is likely to expand its jurisdiction and involvement in the future without the proposed settlement.

The settlement, as proposed, miserably fails to satisfy major future health issues. It abdicates the public interest to the tobacco-products industry. The best interest of the public, both present and future, is to separate damages from health protection and pursue each separately until the public health interest is fully protected.

DISCUSSION QUESTIONS

1. Craig uses a four part divided thesis. Identify and discuss how effectively he uses other essay techniques in support of his argument.

2. What general roles and importance does Craig assign to monetary damages and regulation?

3. Discuss the tone of this essay. Does the use of such statements as "miserably fails" have any effect on his argument?

4. Gregoire and Craig focus on somewhat different issues. Discuss the contrasts between what each considers important features of a settlement.

5. Imagine you have Gregoire and Craig in a room together, with an opportunity to question them both. What questions would you ask of each, with the purpose of amplifying and illuminating their arguments?

WRITING PROJECT

Here are several writing project options:

1. Write an argumentative essay for or against this position: The tobacco settlement should be rejected because it is another "big government solution" to a social problem.

2. Write an argumentative essay for or against this position: Increasing the price of cigarettes by $1.50 per pack over several years will not be enough to curb teen smoking.

3. Write an argumentative essay for or against this position: Nicotine should be strictly regulated by the FDA as an addictive drug.

4. The "tobacco wars" are a fast-moving field of social and political contention. By the time you have read the Gregoire and Craig selections, other legislation may have been proposed or enacted. Research this issue and write an argumentative essay pro or con on any subsequent proposals or legislation pertaining to tobacco.

LISE FUNDERBURG

In this argumentative essay, writer Lise Funderburg addresses the proposed "multiracial" designation on census (and other) forms. This proposal, intended to reflect more accurately the racial identity of the increasing number of Americans of mixed heritage, is stirring much controversy. In this short essay, Funderburg rejects the inclusion of a multiracial option in favor of a different alternative. Watch for the author's use of inductive reasoning in a special way, based on personal history. The discussion questions will consider the kind of argument offered and the author's handling of pro and con arguments. (The Census Bureau recently ruled in favor of the "check any" boxes that apply option favored by Funderburg.)

Boxed In

People say I can't have it both ways. Yes, I'm part black and part white, but every day I am forced to choose one or the other. On mortgage applications, school forms and on the decennial United States census, I've been asked to pick from four exclusive categories: black, white, American Indian and Asian and Pacific Islander.

Pressure is mounting to include a multiracial option for the census in the year 2000. But for me, this revision would hardly reflect my racial identity.

Changing categories is nothing new for the census. Since the first survey was taken in 1790, when it segmented the population into "slaves, free whites and other free persons," the categories have been overhauled repeatedly—1920 was the last year to offer "mulatto," for instance, and in 1940 "Hindu" was a choice.

Proponents of the multiracial box argue that this is a way of mainstreaming a still marginalized group and an opportunity to expose the fallacy of race in America, where for decades the notorious "one drop" rule reigned: anyone who had one drop of black blood was defined as black and therefore considered inferior. It's true that there are medical reasons (bone-marrow matching, for example) for improving the current categories. And the multiracial box, advocates claim, is a step toward recognizing how more and more Americans see themselves.

But I fear that this proposal simply creates another category which multiracial people must force themselves into. I don't think of myself as multiracial; I think of myself as black and white.

A multiracial identity should not be exclusive, but inclusive. People of mixed heritage (which includes up to 75 percent of African-Americans) should be able to check any boxes that apply. Let all Americans speak truthfully about who they are.

Recent experiments by the Census Bureau suggest that neither the multiracial box nor my proposal would significantly change the balance in any one category. These results should ease the concerns of some that the enforcement of civil rights laws—covering everything from affirmative action to redistricting—would be undermined.

Yes, my proposal makes demographic tabulation more complicated. But increasingly, the United States is made up of a complicated population.

When I tell people about my idea, they usually throw up their hands. "You can't have it both ways," they say. "You have to choose." But that's just the point. I can have it both ways. In fact, I do.

DISCUSSION QUESTIONS

1. Identify Funderburg's thesis. How does the author support a thesis based on personal preference with more universal reasons?

2. Funderburg includes some historical information about the census and about the idea of race generally. Is this relevant to her argument? Does the background information bolster her thesis?

3. Are the con arguments for the multiracial option fairly stated? How does Funderburg use a con argument to support her own proposal?

4. Funderburg uses inductive and deductive methods in a mutually reinforcing way. How does she do this?

5. The author's conclusion is an eloquent statement of personal preference. How does it affect her argument?

WRITING PROJECT

Think of a public issue (for example, minimum wage, health care) that has affected you personally. Write an argumentative essay that discusses your personal experiences and also connects your experiences to more general reasons and evidence for or against your issue.

9

Combined Techniques Essays

Each chapter in this book explores a different writing mode, demonstrating how writers build essays using narrative techniques, cause and effect, argument, and so forth. It is also true, however, that writers organizing their essays around any one technique use other ways to enhance and fortify their writing. Virtually every reading selection in this book employs other techniques in a supporting role: an argumentative essay may include paragraphs of comparison and contrast; a critical analysis essay may use definition and argument. This chapter shows how some essays—typically of greater length and/or complexity—give equal weight to a combination of techniques. Combining techniques gives us the flexibility of attacking difficult subjects from a variety of angles and can help make essays more persuasive and intriguing.

Academic essays are usually built around a basic structure of a thesis statement, with paragraphs developed from topic sentences, and the essay as a whole organized primarily around argument, analysis, or some other technique. This is the basic recipe for coherence and clarity of expression, but writers tackling more challenging topics may sometimes improvise within the basic essay structure. With this more complex style of essay, we as writers try to deepen our understanding of more difficult subjects by combining and blending several techniques within the basic essay form. Let's say you are assigned an essay on some hot-button issue or controversial idea, like same-sex marriage or welfare reform. It is certainly feasible to view these subjects through the lens of a single technique, arguing pro or con on same-sex marriage or analyzing welfare reform. Sometimes, though, our understanding of such issues and ideas is enhanced by combining techniques. For instance, in Barbara Ehrenreich's "Oh, Those Family Values," the writer attacks this emotionally charged term from several perspectives: definition, analysis, and argument are all employed as she considers the meaning and implications of family values.

The more complex essays featuring a combination of techniques are also often good examples of writing that takes a more flexible approach to such essay writing conventions as thesis statements, introductions, and conclusions. A well-written essay can still be clearly and effectively developed when the writer plays variations on the fundamental rules, much as a jazz musician will create variations on a basic theme. In Saul Bellow's "Chicago: The City That Was, The City That Is" for example, Bellow's portrait of Chicago not only employs several techniques but also plays variations on the formula of thesis statements, introductions, and conclusions that most academic essays adhere to. As readers, we appreciate that Bellow's intensely personal, first-person point of view is clearly and compellingly written but nevertheless strays somewhat from essay conventions. Journalistic writing also often differs from academic writing conventions, as Esther Schrader's "Of Time and the River" in the chapter on comparison and contrast illustrates. A personal meditation such as Bellow's or a newspaper feature story can work as an effective essay despite the fact that the thesis may not appear until, say, the fourth paragraph, or the concluding paragraph may not fully summarize the points developed in the essay. Good readers can digest the meaning of such writing and also appreciate how well the more improvisational structure of such essays does or does not work.

The first eight chapters of this book have prepared you for the generally more complex and variable readings in this chapter. Many of the selections in previous chapters have included isolated, limited use of multiple techniques, and much of the professional writing has shown at least some variation on the basic essay structure. This concluding chapter will point you toward a better understanding of how experienced writers can shape the essay form to create stimulating, sharp expressions of their ideas. The introduction to combining techniques in this chapter should hone your critical powers as readers and open the door to developing greater flexibility, eloquence, and expressiveness as writers.

Emma Scanlan

Emma Scanlan attended Indiana University. This essay blends several techniques as she examines her response to a civil rights lecture on an unexpected topic, stirring surprising emotions in her "liberal" mind. As you read the essay, consider how Scanlan uses different essay techniques to gain perspective on her complex reactions to an important social issue.

Which Side Am I On? Discrimination and Self-Discovery

On September 10, 1996, the civil rights trial of the decade began in Honolulu, Hawaii. *Baehr v. Miike* is a case involving same-sex couples who feel that it is their right to have a marriage that is given all the economic and legal recognition that heterosexual unions receive. This case will directly challenge the "Defense of Marriage Act," which gives states the legal means to deny recognition of same-sex marriages enacted in another state. The on-going court battle in Hawaii will demand that the American people think about the meaning of the words equality, rights, marriage, and federalism. Are we willing to say that we have second-class citizens that are treated as such solely because of their sexual orientation?

The senior attorney in *Baehr v. Miike* is Evan Wolfson, a member of the Lambda Legal Defense and Education Fund, Inc. He was invited to speak at Indiana University by Steve Sanders, a member of IU's gay, lesbian, and bisexual advisory board. Last Wednesday on my way to class I picked up a copy of the Indiana Daily Student and the front page headline read, "GLB civil rights expert to speak at IU." I immediately assumed that the lecture would have something to do with ethnic minority groups and discrimination or affirmative action. Instead, I was surprised to find that he was lecturing on gays and lesbians rights to marry. Still considering law school and finding the issue quite interesting, I decided to attend. After all, I considered myself to be quite liberal and definitely in favor of any civil rights battle that hoped to rectify the problems of inequality in the United States.

Upon entering Whittenberger Auditorium I was surprised to find myself feeling very uncomfortable and for the first time wondering if I was dressed femininely or not. I had expected the lecture hall to be full of gay rights activists and law students; instead I found all the people to look rather obviously gay, if such a thing can be said, and I felt quite out of place. I was about five minutes late as usual; Mr. Wolfson had already begun speaking and I had no more time to worry about the appearance of my sexual orientation. As I began to listen I felt ashamed of my initial reactions, as Dolly Parton said, "Even if I was gay, would it matter?" Wolfson made jokes about the political climate and the Christian Coalition's hypocrisy in supporting family values and screaming if people wanted to make a lifelong monogamous commitment to each other. This eased my anxiety and reminded me that I was in a room full of people who shared many of my beliefs, opinions, and ambitions.

Everything was going fine and I was absorbed in an argument being made about the reality of federalism in this country when I looked to my left and saw a guy who is in my modern dance class. Averting my eyes very quickly, I prayed that he had not seen me. Why did I do that? He caught me in my attempt to not notice noticing him and I felt myself turn red with shame. What was I thinking? I highly doubt that he was on the verge of standing up and announcing my presence to the entire auditorium. Swallowing any pride I had left I turned and waved at him, he acknowledged the greeting and smiled. Contrary to my emotional devastation he did not give any hint that he had noticed my rudeness. At the time I did not even want to try to understand what had come over me. The thought that I was prejudiced was not something I felt comfortable dealing with during what had turned out to be a very startling lecture.

Wolfson explained quite effectively why it was necessary for the heterosexual community to become involved in the fight for same-sex marriage. He said that without the support of all civil rights organizations and gay rights sympathizers their mission did not stand a chance. This is what finally made me get hold of myself. If I was going to try to explain to people the necessity of equality for all citizens under civil law I needed to be comfortable with sitting in a room of people whose only difference from me was who they chose to have intimate relationships with.

The main focus of this event was community involvement and grass-roots organizations. Wolfson believed the struggle to enlighten voters' minds was at least as important as legal battles. Gay rights has already made significant headway; fifty years ago that kind of open forum would never have happened at Indiana University. But, to me things did not seem all that different. When the question period was over and Steve Sanders announced that refreshments would be served in the room across the hall, I got up and walked through the double doors. Much to my surprise, there were two policemen standing on either side of the main doors as we exited. They seemed nervous and uncomfortable, one of them caught my eye and then proceeded to tie a shoe that already seemed to have the perfect knot. The sponsors of the night's event had a card table set up with flyers and information booklets on it, I grabbed a few that looked interesting and hesitated. Did I want to go to the reception? After two minutes of dillydallying hesitation, I turned and walked away. The policemen's presence and the general atmosphere created by people passing by had made me self-conscious again. As I walked down the stairs I turned my flyers so that their headlines faced my leg and hurried to my car.

When I got home I immediately called my mom and told her everything that had happened and how I had reacted to it. She was surprised by my feelings but reassured me that it was not unjustifiable that I had felt threatened in a state that was probably going to be carried by the Dole/Kemp platform. After all Senator Bob Dole, before his resignation, had been one of the key supporters of the Defense of Marriage Act. That made me feel a little bit better but I was still appalled by my unwillingness to even be associated with the gay community. I had always assumed it did not matter if people thought me a lesbian. I was not. So what if they guessed I was?.

Looking back, I am still shocked by my conduct and fear. I've even begun to question whether or not I would have supported the black freedom movement if I had been born a generation earlier. The fight for rights has always been led and supported by people who were not afraid to go against the status quo. For the first time in my life I have begun to question whether or not I am really one of those people. Upon speaking to my Urban Policy professor about this I got an additional warning that really drove home all my uncertainties. She told me about this girl who had applied for a research assistant program at IU and had the best incoming scores and transcripts. The girl had not been chosen first, in fact, she had been the last person to be chosen as an assistant. I asked why this obvious deviation from the university's firm policy of meritocracy had occurred. She told me, much to my horror, that the girl had listed involvement and active participation in many gay rights organizations on the activities section of the application. She was not a lesbian but was very sympathetic to the cause of gay rights. I laughed and assured her that I would not be attending graduate school at Indiana University and had no worries about the possibility of being denied grants and participation based on the organizations that I participated in. As I left the classroom I began to feel a lot more anxiety and outrage. Why should it matter if I support gay rights or not? If I was gay, what would it have to do with my academic and intellectual abilities? These were questions that if I inserted the word black where gay was would have been valid just thirty years ago in this same institution.

For the last couple of days I have been thinking about this a lot and finally mailed the form indicating that I wanted to get involved. I figure if I am going to talk the talk I better be able to walk the walk. Never in my life has such a seemingly harmless event shaken the foundations of my beliefs about myself with such force. If someone had asked me two weeks ago if I would feel uncomfortable attending a lecture on same-sex marriages I would have laughed, of course not. Now I would probably hesitate before giving such a bold admonition.

For once in my heterosexual, Euro-American, upper-middle-class life I have gotten some hint of what it must feel like to be discriminated against: it was not pleasant. But on the whole I do not regret it. If I want to be active in the civil rights area I need to learn what it feels like when people look at you and all they see is your sexual orientation. In fact, this would be a valuable experience for anyone who is a member of the dominant culture. We walk around all day not fearing the look that pick-up driver on the highway might give us, not fearing the Christian Coalition or its very real supporters. I am going to get involved and try to help, but I now know that I will feel a little bit squeamish the next time I walk into a gay rights meeting.

DISCUSSION QUESTIONS

1. After reading the introduction, what type of essay do you think will follow this opening paragraph?

2. Name three essay techniques employed in the essay and discuss how each is used.

3. What technique shapes the organization of this essay? Is this technique effectively used as a means of organizing the writing?

4. The sentence ending the introductory paragraph appears to be a thesis statement. Is it? If not, can you find a sentence or sentences that better reflect the theme(s) of the essay?

5. How would you characterize the tone? How does the collision between Scanlan's general beliefs and principles and her response to a particular unfamiliar situation affect the shifts in tone?

6. What happens in the conclusion? Does it bear any relation to the introduction? If not, what is the purpose of the conclusion?

WRITING PROJECT

Write a combined techniques essay about a lecture, speech, debate, or other event that had some personal significance for you and that took a position on a subject you agreed or disagreed with, or were excited or disturbed by. Your essay should integrate several techniques to explore your beliefs and opinions on the subject.

SAUL BELLOW

Saul Bellow is a Nobel and Pulitzer Prize–winning American novelist who has spent much of his life in Chicago, where the bulk of his fiction is set. This essay was written in 1983; Bellow surveys the city and his place in it from that point in time. Bellow's essay blends several techniques; the discussion questions will ask that you identify and consider how these techniques work in this selection. As you read the essay, consider how Bellow uses a combination of techniques to shape his experience and insights into the city of Chicago.

Chicago: The City That Was, The City That Is

To be concise about Chicago is harder than you might think. The city stands for something in American life, but what that something is has never been altogether clear. Not everybody likes the place. A Chicagoan since 1924, I have come to understand that you have to develop a taste for it, and you can't do that without living here for decades. Even after decades you can't easily formulate the reasons for your attachment, because the city is always transforming itself, and the scale of the transformations is tremendous.

Chicago builds itself up, knocks itself down again, scrapes away the rubble, and starts over. European cities destroyed in war were painstakingly restored. Chicago does not restore; it makes something wildly different. To count on stability here is madness. A Parisian can always see the Paris that was, as it has been for centuries. A Venetian, as long as Venice is not swallowed up in mud, has before him the things his ancestors saw. But a Chicagoan as he wanders about the city feels like a man who has lost many teeth. His tongue explores the gaps—let's see now: Here the Fifty-fifth Street car turned into Harper Avenue at the end of the trolley line; then the conductor hurried through the car, reversing the cane seats. Then he reset the trolley on the power line. On this corner stood Kootich Castle, a bohemian rooming house and hangout for graduate students, photographers, would-be painters, philosophical radicals, and lab technicians (one young woman kept white mice as pets). Harper Avenue wasn't exactly the banks of the Seine; none of the buildings resembled Sainte-Chapelle. They were downright ugly, but they were familiar, they were ours, and the survival of what is ours gives life its continuity. It is not our destiny here to get comfort from old familiar places. We can't, we Chicagoans, settle back sentimentally among our souvenirs.

From the west, your view of the new skyscrapers is unobstructed. The greatest of them all, the Sears Tower, shimmers among its companions, all of them armored like Eisenstein's Teutonic knights staring over the ice of no-man's-land at Alexander Nevsky. The plan is to advance again westward from the center of the city and fill up the vacant streets, the waste places, with apartment buildings and shopping malls. Nobody at present can say whether this is feasible, whether the great corporations and banks will have sufficient confidence in the future of a city whose old industries are stalled, whose legendary railyards are empty. Ours is the broadest band of rust in all the Rust Belt.

A fiction writer by trade, I see myself also as something of a historian. More than thirty years ago, I published *The Adventures of Augie March,* a novel that is in part a record of Chicago in the twenties and thirties. I see by the college catalogues that my book is studied in a considerable number of schools. It is read in Yugoslavia, too, and in Turkey and China, so that throughout the world people are forming a picture of Chicago, the setting of Augie's adventures. But that Chicago no longer exists. It is to be found only in memory and in fiction. Like the Cicero of Al Capone, like Jack London's Klondike, like Fenimore Cooper's forests, like Gauguin's Pacific paradise, like Upton Sinclair's Jungle, it is now an imaginary place only. The thirties have been wiped out: houses in decay, vacant lots, the local characters—grocers, butchers, dentists, neighbors—gone to their reward, the survivors hidden away in nursing homes, doddering in Florida, dying of Alzheimer's disease in Venice, California. A lively new Latin population occupies my old ward, the Twenty-sixth. Its old houses have collapsed or been burned. The school dropout rate is one of the city's highest, the dope pushers do their deals openly. Revisiting Division Street on a winter day, examining the Spanish graffiti, the dark faces, reading strange inscriptions on shop windows, one feels as Rip Van Winkle might have felt if after his long sleep he had found, not his native village, but a barrio of San Juan, Puerto Rico. This crude, brazen city of European immigrants is now, in large part, a city of blacks and Hispanics.

The speed of the cycles of prosperity and desolation is an extraordinary challenge to historians and prophets. Chicago was founded in 1833, so it hasn't been here long enough to attract archaelogists, as Rome and Jerusalem do. Still, longtime residents may feel that they have their own monuments and ruins and that accelerated development has compacted the decades, making them comparable to centuries, has put Chicagoans through a crash program in aging. If you've been here long enough, you've seen the movement of history with your own eyes and have had a good taste of history, of eternity, perhaps.

So many risings and fallings, so much death, rebirth, metamorphosis, so many tribal migrations. To young Midwesterners at the beginning of the century, this was the electrifying regional capital. Here students from Ohio or Wisconsin studied their trades, becoming doctors, engineers, journalists, architects, singers. Here they made contact with civilization and culture. Here Armour, Insull, and Yerkes accumulated huge fortunes in pork, gas, electricity, or transit. Their immigrant employees, hundreds of thousands of them, lived in industrial villages— Back of the Yards, out by the steel mills, the Irish on "Archie Road," the Greeks, Italians, and Jews on Halsted Street, the Poles and Ukrainians along Milwaukee Avenue.

It wasn't so long ago in calendar years that Carl Sandburg was celebrating Chicago the youthful giant, the hog butcher of the world, the player with railroads. But the farm boys, seduced under streetlamps by prostitutes, have vanished (as have the farms from which they came). The stockyards long ago moved to Kansas and Missouri, the railyards are filling up with new "Young Executive" housing. And even Sandburg's language is dated. It is the language of the advertising agencies of the twenties and in part recalls the slogans that came from City Hall when Big Bill Thompson was mayor. "Boost, don't knock," he told us. "Lay down your hammer. Get a horn."

What would we have been boosting? Real power in the city belongs to the Insulls and other magnates, to La Salle Street, to the venal politicians. From his headquarters in Cicero and on Twenty-second Street, the anarch Al Capone and his mob of comical killers sold beer and booze, ran the rackets. They bought cops and officials as one would buy popcorn. Big Bill was one of our fun politicians, like Bathhouse John and Hinky-Dink Kenna, politician-entertainers who kept the public laughing. I was one of hundreds of thousands of kids to whom Big Bill's precinct captains distributed free passes to Riverview Park to ride the Bobs and make faces in fun-house mirrors, to eat cotton candy that tickled you like a beard and disintegrated instantly on your tongue. If you had a nickel to spare, you could try to win a Kewpie doll in the shooting gallery. At the age of twelve, I was one of Big Bill's fans. Schoolchildren loved him.

The mayor liked to show himself in public, and after his retirement, in his declining years, you saw him chauffeured through the Loop in his limousine. He was solitary, glum, silent. One great paw hung through the velvet strap. Part of his youth was spent on the range, so he generally wore a cowboy hat. Under it he looked swollen and corrupted. Rouault might have liked to do a portrait of him, one of those mountainous faces he painted—this one against a background of blazing Chicago boredom.

Big Bill is as remote from us today as Sennacherib or Ashurbanipal.[19] Only antiquarians ever think of him. But Chicago still "boosts." Under Mayor Daley (the first) we were "The City That Works." The developers who have remade the north end of Michigan Boulevard announced that they had created a Magnificent Mile. Nothing less. Here Neiman-Marcus, Lord & Taylor, Marshall Field's, Gucci, and Hammacher Schlemmer have established themselves in all their pride. A thick icing of comfort and luxury has been spread over the northern end of the business district, with its boutiques, bars, health clubs, and nouvelle cuisine

[19]Assyrian kings in the seventh and eighth centuries B.C.

restaurants. The John Hancock Tower and One Magnificent Mile are the most prestigious addresses in town. From their privileged windows you look over Lake Michigan, with its pleasure boats and water pumping stations. To the south you see the refineries of Hammond and Gary, and the steel mills, or what is left of them. Turning westward you see the notorious Cabrini Green public housing blocks, one of the many projects built for a welfare population. Actually, the slums are best seen from the elevation of a ninety-five-story skytop restaurant—a wonderful opportunity for landscape lovers.

You can't be neutral about a place where you have lived so long. You come to recognize at last how much feeling you have invested in it. It's futile, to think like Miniver Cheevy, that you might have done better in another time, in a more civilized city. You were assigned to this one, as were your parents, brothers, cousins, classmates, your friends—most of them in the cemeteries beyond city limits. Where fires, wrecking balls, and falling masonry have done so much demolition, human attachments rise in value. So I seek out my cousin the baker, I go to see an old chum try a case in criminal court. I attend city council meetings and public hearings, I talk with Winston Moore about black politics or lunch at the Bismarck with one of the late Mayor Daley's assistants. City politics are comic opera. Circuit judges are convicted of racketeering. One can only guess how many grand juries are hearing testimony and preparing indictments. On my rounds, feeing like an unofficial, unsalaried inspector, I check out the new apartment houses on the banks of the Chicago River, in my time an industrial wasteland. To call these expeditions sad wouldn't be accurate. I am not heavyhearted. I am uneasy but also terribly curious, deeply intrigued. After all, I am no mere spectator, for I have invested vital substance in these surroundings, we have exchanged influences—in what proportions I can't say.

In moments of weakness you are tempted to take seriously the opinions of those urbanologists who say that the great American cities of the North are nineteenth-century creations belonging to an earlier stage of capitalism and that they have no future. But then a *Chicago Tribune* article announces that two hundred national retailers, developers, and leasing agents have met at the Hilton to plan new stores outside the

Loop. Do they see a dying city dominated by youth gangs who do battle in ruined streets? They do not! Urban shopping strips are "creating vibrant inner-city communities," we are told. Mayor Washington and "city council stalwarts" are "selling Chicago" to dozens of prospective investors.

Like other Chicagoans of my generation, I ask myself how it's all going to come out. In the past, we watched events. We had no control over them, of course. But they were lively, they were good entertainment. The Democratic bosses—Tony Cermak, Kelly-Nash, and Richard Daley—did not take a terribly high view of human nature, nor were they abstractly concerned with justice. They ran a tight oligarchy. Politicians made profitable arrangements but governed with a fair degree of efficiency. The present administration has little interest in efficiency. The growing black and Hispanic population has made a successful bid for power. Irish, Greek, Polish, and Italian voters are vainly resisting. As conflicts widen and lawsuits multiply, property taxes go up and services diminish. Not many people mourn the disintegration of the machine, but what will replace it? Everything seems up for grabs, and everybody asks, "Will we make it?" Middle-class whites, the city's tax base, have moved to the suburbs. For suburbanites the city is a theater. From Schaumburg, Barrington, and Winnetka they watch us on their TV screens.

Will Chicago, that dauntless tightrope walker who has never yet fallen, get a charley horse in the middle of the high wire? Those of us, like myself, who have never abandoned Chicago—the faithful—tell ourselves that he's not going to fall. For we simply can't imagine what America would be without its great cities. What can the boondocks offer us? We, too, would become mere onlookers, and U.S. history would turn into a TV show. To be watched like any other program: the death of the tropical rain forests, or the history of Egypt's pyramids.

Walking on Le Moyne Street, looking for the house the Bellow family lived in half a century ago, I find only a vacant lot. Stepping over the rubble, I picture the rooms overhead. There is only emptiness around, not a sign of the old life. Nothing. But it's just as well, perhaps, that there should be nothing physical to hang on to. It forces you inward, to look for what endures. Give Chicago half a chance, and it will turn you into a philosopher.

DISCUSSION QUESTIONS

1. Identify the essay writing techniques Bellow employs, and locate examples of each in the text.

2. Discuss each technique used in the essay. Why does the writer use these particular techniques? Do they enhance your understanding of what Bellow is saying? In what way?

3. Several techniques are important to this selection. Can you identify any one technique that has an overriding importance to the essay? If so, what would it be, and why?

4. Consider the introduction and conclusion. If you were assigned to write an introduction to this essay, containing a thesis statement, and a summarizing conclusion, would they be different? How?

5. Someone once said that "all history is personal history." Discuss ways in which Bellow's essay illustrates this dictum.

6. If you had to summarize the definition of Chicago in a short paragraph, what would you say?

7. The author calls himself one of the "faithful." What does this self-description imply about the tone and attitude displayed in the essay?

WRITING PROJECT

Consider a place you are familiar with, and write an essay combining several techniques to develop an appreciation of that place. Your essay may start as a narrative and branch into analysis and definition, or you may use comparison and contrast to explore personal and social history. There are many routes open to you; remember that the techniques you select must all be of roughly equal importance and integral to your essay.

Option: In recent years Saul Bellow has moved from Chicago to Vermont. After doing some research, write a combined techniques essay exploring the reasons for this move. Why did Bellow leave Chicago? What does his departure imply about the attitudes and opinions expressed in "Chicago: The City That Was, The City That Is"?

BARBARA EHRENREICH

Barbara Ehrenreich is an essayist who has written for many magazines and published nine books on subjects of social and political concern. In this essay, taken from *The Snarling Citizen,* she examines the dynamics of "family values." Ehrenreich dissects this popular and oftentimes vague term to expose the hope—and the menace—lying within the institution of the family. This subject could obviously be wrapped into a definition essay—what exactly are those family values? Definition is important to this reading, but for Ehrenreich other techniques are equally important instruments to explore her concerns.

Oh, Those Family Values

A disturbing subtext runs through our recent media fixations. Parents abuse sons—allegedly, at least, in the Menendez case—who in turn rise up and kill them. A husband torments a wife, who retaliates, in the best-known case, with a kitchen knife. Love turns into obsession, between the Simpsons anyway, and then perhaps into murderous rage. The family, in other words, as personal hell.

This accounts for at least part of our fascination with the Bobbitts and the Simpsons and the rest of them. We live in a culture that fetishizes the family as the ideal unit of human community, the perfect container for our lusts and loves. Politicians of both parties proudly link "profamily"; even abortion-rights bumper stickers are aggressively "profamily" and "prochoice." Only with the occasional celebrity crime do we allow ourselves to think the nearly unthinkable: that the family may not be the ideal and perfect living arrangement after all—that it can also be a nest of pathology and a cradle of gruesome violence.

It's a scary thought, since the family is at the same time our "haven in a heartless world." Theoretically, and sometimes actually, the family nurtures warm, loving feelings, uncontaminated by greed or power hunger. Within the family, and often only within the family, individuals are loved "for themselves," and whether or not they are infirm, incontinent, infantile, or eccentric. The strong (adults and, especially, males) lie down peaceably with the small and the weak.

But consider the matter of wife battery. We managed to dodge it in the Bobbitt case and downplay it as a force in Tonya Harding's life. Thanks to O.J., though, we're caught up now in a mass consciousness-raising session, grimly absorbing the fact that in some areas domestic violence sends more women to emergency rooms than any other form of illness, injury, or assault.

Still, we shrink from the obvious inference: for a woman, home is, statistically speaking, the most dangerous place to be. Her worst enemies and potential killers are not strangers but lovers, husbands, and those who claimed to love her once. Similarly, for every Polly Klaas who is killed by a deranged criminal on parole, dozens of children are abused and murdered by their own parents, uncles, or stepfathers. Home is all too often where the small and the weak fear to lie down and shut their eyes.

At some deep, queasy Freudian level we all know this. Even in the ostensibly "functional," nonviolent family, where no one is killed or maimed, feelings are routinely bruised and even twisted out of shape. There is the slap or put-down that violates a child's shaky sense of self; the cold, distracted stare that drives a spouse to tears; the little digs and rivalries. At best, the family teaches the finest things human beings can learn from one another—generosity and love. But it is also, all too often, where we learn nasty things like hate and rage and shame.

Americans act out their ambivalence about the family without ever owning up to it. Millions adhere to creeds—religious and political—that are militantly "profamily." But at the same time, millions flock to therapists and self-help groups that offer to heal the "inner child" from damage inflicted by family life. Legions of women band together to revive the self-esteem they lost in supposedly loving relationships and to learn to love a little less. We are all, it is often said, "in recovery." And from what? Our families, in most cases.

There is a long and honorable tradition of what might be called "antifamily" thought. The early-nineteenth-century French philosopher

Charles Fourier taught that the family was a barrier to human progress and encouraged the formation of family-free alternative communities. Early feminists saw a degrading parallel between marriage and prostitution, and challenged the patriarchal authority of the husband/father. In the 1960s, radical psychiatrists denounced the family as a hotbed of neurosis, and the renowned British anthropologist Edmund Leach stated that "far from being the basis of the good society, the family, with its narrow privacy and tawdry secrets, is the source of all our discontents."

But the communes proved harder to sustain than plain old couples, and the conservatism of the 1980s crushed the last vestiges of "lifestyle experimentation." Today, even gays and lesbians are eager to get married and take up family life. Feminists have learned to couch their concerns as "family issues," and public figures would sooner advocate crack-cocaine as a cure for stress than propose the family as a target for reform. Hence our unseemly interest in O.J., Erik, Lyle, and Lorena: they allow us, however gingerly, to break the silence on the hellish side of family life.

But the discussion needs to become a lot more open and forthright. We may be stuck with family—at least until someone invents a sustainable alternative—but the family, with its deep, impacted tensions and longings, can hardly be expected to be the moral foundation of everything else. In fact, many families could use a lot more outside interference in the form of counseling and policing, and some are so dangerously dysfunctional that they ought to be encouraged to disband right away. Even healthy families need outside sources of moral guidance to keep those tensions from imploding—and this means, among other things, a public philosophy of gender equality and concern for child welfare. When, instead, the larger culture aggrandizes wife beaters, degrades women, or nods approvingly at child slappers, the family gets a little more dangerous for everyone, and so, inevitably, does the larger world.

DISCUSSION QUESTIONS

1. What other techniques—besides definition—are employed in this selection. Are they given equal weight?

2. What is the thesis? How does each technique contribute to our understanding of the thesis?

3. The author describes the polar extremes of family values in terms of "warm, loving feelings," and a "nest of pathology." In what terms does she depict the workings of families living between these extremes?

4. How would you characterize family values? How does your characterization compare to Ehrenreich's?

5. This essay includes a brief survey of "alternative communities." What purpose does this serve in the piece?

6. Ehrenreich makes several assertions in her conclusion. Are they all clearly developed from the essay?

WRITING PROJECT

Think of a commonly used word or phrase that has multiple or vague meanings. Write a combined techniques essay, examining the elements of your chosen word phrase with the goal of arriving at a clearer understanding of the term. If you wish, you can expand upon your answer for question 4 above.

ALAN DERSHOWITZ

Alan Dershowitz is best known as a criminal defense attorney representing celebrity defendants in much publicized capital cases, but he is also a noted constitutional scholar. In this essay, he examines freedom of speech versus censorship from the perspective of evaluating the constitutional legitimacy of various types of controversial speech. Dershowitz develops this piece by considering various kinds of analogies. Analogy, sometimes used as an essay technique itself, is a type of comparison revealing similarities between apparently dissimilar things; for example, "shouting fire in a crowded theater is like . . ." Dershowitz employs several essay techniques to explore what shouting fire is or is not like.

Shouting "Fire!"

When the Reverend Jerry Falwell learned that the Supreme Court had reversed his $200,000 judgment against *Hustler* magazine for the emotional distress that he had suffered from an outrageous parody, his response was typical of those who seek to censor speech: "Just as no person may scream 'Fire!' in a crowded theater when there is no fire, and find cover under the First Amendment, likewise, no sleazy merchant like Larry Flynt should be able to use the First Amendment as an excuse for maliciously and dishonestly attacking public figures, as he has so often done."

Justice Oliver Wendell Holmes's classic example of unprotected speech—falsely shouting "Fire!" in a crowded theater—has been invoked so often, by so many people, in such diverse contexts, that it has become part of our national folk language. It has even appeared—most appropriately—in the theater: in Tom Stoppard's play *Rosencrantz and Guildenstern Are Dead* a character shouts at the audience, "Fire!" He then quickly explains: "It's all right—I'm demonstrating the misuse of free speech." Shouting "Fire!" in the theater may well be the only jurisprudential analogy that has assumed the status of a folk argument.

A prominent historian recently characterized it as "the most brilliantly persuasive expression that ever came from Holmes' pen." But in spite of its hallowed position in both the jurisprudence of the First Amendment and the arsenal of political discourse, it is and was an inapt analogy, even in the context in which it was originally offered. It has lately become—despite, perhaps even because of, the frequently and promiscuousness of its invocation—little more than a caricature of logical argumentation.

The case that gave rise to the "Fire!"-in-a-crowded-theater analogy, *Schenck* v. *United States,* involved the prosecution of Charles Schenck, who was the general secretary of the Socialist party in Philadelphia, and Elizabeth Baer, who was its recording secretary. In 1917 a jury found Schenck and Baer guilty of attempting to cause insubordination among soldiers who had been drafted to fight in the First World War. They and other party members had circulated leaflets urging draftees not to "submit to intimidation" in a war being conducted on behalf of "Wall Street's chosen few."

Schenck admitted, and the Court found, that the intent of the pamphlets' "impassioned language" was to "influence" draftees to resist the draft. Interestingly, however, Justice Holmes noted that nothing in the pamphlet suggested that the draftees should use unlawful or violent means to oppose conscription: "In form at least [the pamphlet] confined itself to peaceful measures, such as a petition for the repeal of the act" and an exhortation to exercise "your right to assert your opposition to the draft." Many of its most impassioned words were quoted directly from the Constitution.

Justice Holmes acknowledged that "in many places and in ordinary times the defendants, in saying all that was said in the circular, would have been within their constitutional rights." "But," he added, "the character of every act depends upon the circumstances in which it is done." And to illustrate that truism he went on to say:

> The most stringent protection of free speech would not protect
> a man in falsely shouting fire in a theater, and causing a panic.
> It does not even protect a man from an injunction against
> uttering words that may have all the effect of force.

Justice Holmes then upheld the convictions in the context of a wartime draft, holding that the pamphlet created "a clear and present danger" of hindering the war effort while our soldiers were fighting for their lives and our liberty.

The example of shouting "Fire!" obviously bore little relationship to the facts of the Schenck case. The Schenck pamphlet contained a substantive political message. It urged its draftee readers to *think* about the message and then—if they so chose—to act on it in a lawful and nonviolent way. The man who shouts "Fire!" in a crowded theater is neither sending a political message nor inviting his listener to think about what he has said and decide what to do in a rational, calculated manner. On the contrary, the message is designed to force action *without* contemplation. The message "Fire!" is directed not to the mind and the conscience of the listener but, rather, to his adrenaline and his feet. It is a stimulus to immediate *action*, not thoughtful reflection. It is—as Justice Holmes recognized in his follow-up sentence—the functional equivalent of "uttering words that may have all the effect of force."

Indeed, in that respect the shout of "Fire!" is not even speech, in meaningful sense of that term. It is a *clang* sound, the equivalent of setting off a nonverbal alarm. Had Justice Holmes been more honest about his example, he would have said that freedom of speech does not protect a kid who pulls a fire alarm in the absence of a fire. But that obviously would have been irrelevant to the case at hand. The proposition that pulling an alarm is not protected speech certainly leads to the conclusion that shouting the word "fire" is also not protected. But the core analogy is the nonverbal alarm, and the derivative example is the verbal shout. By cleverly substituting the derivative shout for the core alarm, Holmes made it possible to analogize one set of words to another—as he could not have done if he had begun with the self-evident proposition that setting off an alarm bell is not free speech.

The analogy is thus not only inapt but also insulting. Most Americans do not respond to political rhetoric with the same kind of automatic acceptance expected of schoolchildren responding to a fire drill. Not a single recipient of the Schenck pamphlet is known to have changed his mind after reading it. Indeed, one draftee, who appeared as a prosecution witness, was asked whether reading a pamphlet asserting that the draft law was unjust would make him "immediately decide that you must erase that law." Not surprisingly, he replied, "I do my own thinking." A theatergoer would probably not respond similarly if asked how he would react to a shout of "Fire!"

Another important reason why the analogy is inapt is that Holmes emphasizes the factual falsity of the shout "Fire!" The Schenck pamphlet, however, was not factually false. It contained political opinions and ideas about the causes of the war and about appropriate and lawful responses to the draft. As the Supreme Court recently affirmed (in *Falwell* v. *Hustler*), "The First Amendment recognizes no such thing as a 'false' idea." Nor does it recognize false opinions about the causes of or cures for war.

A close analogy to the facts of the Schenck case might have been provided by a person's standing outside a theater, offering the patrons a leaflet advising them that in his opinion the theater was structurally unsafe, and urging them not to enter but to complain to the building inspectors. That analogy, however, would not have served Holmes's argument for punishing Schenck. Holmes needed an analogy that would appear relevant to Schenck's political speech but that would invite the conclusion that censorship was appropriate.

Unsurprisingly, a war-weary nation—in the throes of a know-nothing hysteria over immigrant anarchists and socialists—welcomed the comparison between what was regarded as a seditious political pamphlet and a malicious shout of "Fire!" Ironically, the "Fire!" analogy is nearly all that survives from the Schenck case: the ruling itself is almost certainly not good law. Pamphlets of the kind that resulted in Schenck's imprisonment have been circulated with impunity during subsequent wars.

Over the past several years I have assembled a collection of instance—cases, speeches, arguments—in which proponents of censorship have maintained that the expression at issue is "just like" or "equivalent to" falsely shouting "Fire!" in a crowded theater and ought to be banned, "just as" shouting "Fire!" out to be banned. The analogy is generally invoked, often with self-satisfaction, as an absolute argument-stopper. It does, after all, claim the high authority of the great Justice Oliver

Wendell Holmes. I have rarely heard it invoked in a convincing, or even particularly relevant, way. But that, too, can claim lineage from the great Holmes.

Not unlike Falwell, with his silly comparison between shouting "Fire!" and publishing an offensive parody, courts and commentators have frequently invoked "Fire!" as an analogy to expression that is not an automatic stimulus to panic. A state supreme court held that "Holmes' aphorism . . . applies with equal force to pornography"—in particular to the exhibition of the movie *Carmen Baby* in a drive-in theater in close proximity to highways and homes. Another court analogized "picketing . . . in support of a secondary boycott" to shouting "Fire!" because in both instances "speech and conduct are brigaded." In the famous Skokie case one of the judges argued that allowing Nazis to march through a city where a large number of Holocaust survivors live "just might fall into the same category as one's 'right' to cry fire in a crowded theater."

Outside court the analogies become even more badly stretched. A spokesperson for the New Jersey Sports and Exposition Authority complained that newspaper reports to the effect that a large number of football players had contracted cancer after playing in the Meadowlands—a stadium atop a landfill—were the "journalistic equivalent of shouting fire in a crowded theater." An insect researcher acknowledged that his prediction that a certain amusement park might become roach-infested "may be tantamount to shouting fire in a crowded theater." The philosopher Sidney Hook, in a letter to the *New York Times* bemoaning a Supreme Court decision that required a plaintiff in a defamation action to prove that the offending statement was actually false, argued that the First Amendment does not give the press carte blanche to accuse innocent persons "any more than the First Amendment protects the right of someone falsely to shout fire in a crowded theater."

Some close analogies to shouting "Fire!" or setting off an alarm are, of course, available: calling in a false bomb threat; dialing 911 and falsely describing an emergency; making a loud, gunlike sound in the presence of the President; setting off a voice-activated sprinkler system by falsely shouting "Fire!" In one case in which the "Fire! analogy was directly to the point, a creative defendant tried to get around it. The case involved a man who calmly advised an airline clerk that he was "only here to hijack the plane." He was charged, in effect, with shouting "Fire!" in a crowded theater, and his rejected defense—as quoted by the court—was as follows: "If we built fire-proof theaters and let people know about this, then the shouting of 'Fire!' would not cause panic."

Here are some more-distant but still related examples: the recent incident of the police slaying in which some members of an onlooking crowd urged a mentally ill vagrant who had taken an officer's gun to shoot the officer; the screaming of racial epithets during a tense confrontation; shouting down a speaker and preventing him from continuing his speech.

Analogies are, by their nature, matters of degree. Some are closer to the core example than others. But any attempt to analogize political ideas in a pamphlet, ugly parody in a magazine, offensive movies in a theater, controversial newspaper articles, or any of the other expressions and actions catalogued above to the very different act of shouting "Fire!" in a crowded theater is either self-deceptive or self-serving.

The government does, of course, have some arguably legitimate bases for suppressing speech which bear no relationship to shouting "Fire!" It may ban the publication of nuclear-weapon codes, of information about troop movements, and of the identity of undercover agents. It may criminalize extortion threats and conspiratorial agreements. These expressions may lead directly to serious harm, but the mechanisms of causation are very different from that at work when an alarm is sounded. One may also argue—less persuasively, in my view—against protecting certain forms of public obscenity and defamatory statements. Here, too, the mechanisms of causation are very different. None of these exceptions to the First Amendment's exhortation that the government "shall make no law . . . abridging the freedom of speech, or of the press" is anything like falsely shouting "Fire!" in a crowded theater; they all must be justified on other grounds.

A comedian once told his audience, during a stand-up routine, about the time he was standing around a fire with a crowd of people and got in trouble for yelling "Theater, theater!" That, I think, is about as clever and productive a use as anyone has ever made of Holmes's flawed analogy.

DISCUSSION QUESTIONS

1. What is the thesis of this essay? What essay technique does the thesis exemplify?

2. Summarize the kinds of speech that, according to the writer, justify censorship, and those that do not. What essay techniques does Dershowitz employ to establish the crucial differences between justified and unjustified censorship?

3. Is there any one technique of preeminent importance in this selection? In considering this question, think about how an analogy comes to be revealed as a "false" analogy, according to Dershowitz?

4. What is the significance of analogy to the most important technique employed in the essay?

5. What is the author's attitude toward what he regards as misleading analogies that would suppress or censor certain kinds of speech? Find words or phrases that reveal this tone or attitude.

6. Read the First Amendment to the U.S. Constitution. Does this essay broaden your understanding of what freedom of speech means under the First Amendment? In what way?

WRITING PROJECT

The following questions may be used as subjects for a combined techniques essay:

1. Reread the George Will essay on page 178. From a First Amendment perspective, should a city have the right to control the location of adult bookstores and other such establishments, as Will claims?

2. In recent years many corporations have brought libel lawsuits against private citizens critical of their activities or products. What are the freedom of speech implications of this practice? Should First Amendment protections be extended in some way to safeguard such speech directed at private organizations?

3. In a recent episode, several students in a Florida high school were suspended for circulating—under a freedom of speech banner—what they claimed was a "satirical" newsletter containing racial slurs and threats against their African-American school principal. Examine this episode, or hate-speech codes generally, and consider this question: when and under what circumstances does hate speech qualify for First Amendment protection, and when does it not?

Index